Henry Wadsworth Longfellow, John Gilbert

The poetical works of Henry Wadsworth Longfellow

Henry Wadsworth Longfellow, John Gilbert

The poetical works of Henry Wadsworth Longfellow

ISBN/EAN: 9783741174131

Manufactured in Europe, USA, Canada, Australia, Japa

Cover: Foto ©Andreas Hilbeck / pixelio.de

Manufactured and distributed by brebook publishing software
(www.brebook.com)

Henry Wadsworth Longfellow, John Gilbert

The poetical works of Henry Wadsworth Longfellow

THE

POETICAL WORKS

OF

HENRY WADSWORTH LONGFELLOW.

A NEW EDITION,
ILLUSTRATED WITH UPWARDS OF ONE HUNDRED DESIGNS,
DRAWN BY JOHN GILBERT,
ENGRAVED BY THE BROTHERS DALZIEL

LONDON:
ROUTLEDGE, WARNE, & ROUTLEDGE,
FARRINGDON STREET
M. DCCC.LXI.

LONDON :
R. CLAY, PRINTER, BREAD STREET HILL.

ADVERTISEMENT.

This Edition contains the whole of LONGFELLOW'S POETICAL WORKS hitherto published, with the exception of THE SPANISH STUDENT, THE GOLDEN LEGEND, and THE SONG OF HIAWATHA. As these Poems from their length would make this Volume too bulky, it is proposed to reserve them for future publication in a collected form, similar in size and style to the present Volume.

Some slight modification has been made in the order of arrangement in this collection, with the view of keeping together Poems of a similar class, as far as is consistent with a due regard to the chronological order of their publication.

CONTENTS.

VOICES OF THE NIGHT.

VOICES OF THE NIGHT.

PLEASANT it was, when woods were green,
　　And winds were soft and low,
To lie amid some sylvan scene,
Where, the long drooping boughs between,
Shadows dark and sunlight sheen
　　Alternate come and go;

Or where the denser grove receives
　　No sunlight from above,
But the dark foliage interweaves
In one unbroken roof of leaves,
Underneath whose sloping eaves
　　The shadows hardly move.

Beneath some patriarchal tree
　　I lay upon the ground;
His hoary arms uplifted he,
And all the broad leaves over me
Clapped their little hands in glee,
　　With one continuous sound;—

A slumberous sound,—a sound that brings
　　The feelings of a dream,—
As of innumerable wings,
As, when a bell no longer swings,
Faint the hollow murmur rings
　　O'er meadow, lake, and stream.

And dreams of that which cannot die,
　　Bright visions, came to me,
As lapped in thought I used to lie,
And gaze into the summer sky,
Where the sailing clouds went by,
　　Like ships upon the sea;

PRELUDE.

Dreams that the soul of youth engage
  Ere Fancy has been quelled;
Old legends of the monkish page,
Traditions of the saint and sage,
Tales that have the rime of age,
  And chronicles of Eld.

And, loving still these quaint old themes,
  Even in the city's throng
I feel the freshness of the streams,
That, crossed by shades and sunny gleams,
Water the green land of dreams,
  The holy land of song.

Therefore, at Pentecost, which brings
  The spring, clothed like a bride,
When nestling buds unfold their wings,
And bishop's-caps have golden rings,
Musing upon many things,
  I sought the woodlands wide.

The green trees whispered low and mild;
  It was a sound of joy!
They were my playmates when a child,
And rocked me in their arms so wild!
Still they looked at me and smiled,
  As if I were a boy;

And ever whispered, mild and low,
  "Come, be a child once more!"
And waved their long arms to and fro,
And beckoned solemnly and slow:
Oh, I could not choose but go
  Into the woodlands hoar;

Into the blithe and breathing air,
  Into the solemn wood,
Solemn and silent everywhere!
Nature with folded hands seemed there,
Kneeling at her evening prayer!
  Like one in prayer I stood.

B 2

VOICES OF THE NIGHT.

Before me rose an avenue
  Of tall and sombrous pines;
Abroad their fan-like branches grew,
And, where the sunshine darted through,
Spread a vapour soft and blue,
  In long and sloping lines.

And, falling on my weary brain,
  Like a fast-falling shower,
The dreams of youth came back again,
Low lispings of the summer rain,
Dropping on the ripened grain,
  As once upon the flower.

Visions of childhood! Stay, oh stay!
  Ye were so sweet and wild!
And distant voices seemed to say,
" It cannot be! They pass away!
Other themes demand thy lay;
  Thou art no more a child!

" The land of Song within thee lies,
  Watered by living springs;
The lids of Fancy's sleepless eyes
Are gates unto that Paradise,
Holy thoughts, like stars, arise,
  Its clouds are angels' wings.

" Learn, that henceforth thy song shall be,
  Not mountains capped with snow,
Nor forests sounding like the sea,
Nor rivers flowing ceaselessly,
Where the woodlands bend to see
  The bending heavens below.

" There is a forest where the din
  Of iron branches sounds!
A mighty river roars between,
And whosoever looks therein,
Sees the heavens all black with sin,—
  Sees not its depths, nor bounds.

PRELUDE

" Athwart the swinging branches cast,
    Soft rays of sunshine pour ;
Then comes the fearful wintry blast ;
Our hopes, like withered leaves, fall fast ;
Pallid lips say, ' It is past !
    We can return no more !'

" Look, then, into thine heart, and write !
    Yea, into Life's deep stream !
All forms of sorrow and delight,
All solemn Voices of the Night,
That can soothe thee, or affright, —
    Be these henceforth thy theme."

VOICES OF THE NIGHT.

Πότνια, πότνια νύξ.
ὑπνοδότειρα τῶν πολυπόνων βροτῶν,
ἐρεβόθεν ἴθι μόλε μόλε κατάπτερος
Ἀγαμεμνόνιον ἐπὶ δόμον·
ὑπὸ γὰρ ἀλγέων, ὑπό τε συμφορᾶς
διοιχόμεθ᾽, οἰχόμεθα.

ΕΥΡΙΠΙΔΗΣ

HYMN TO THE NIGHT.

Ασπασιη, τρικλιστος.

I HEARD the trailing garments of the Night
    Sweep through her marble halls!
I saw her sable skirts all fringed with light
    From the celestial walls!

I felt her presence, by its spell of might,
    Stoop o'er me from above;
The calm, majestic presence of the Night,
    As of the one I love.

I heard the sounds of sorrow and delight,
    The manifold, soft chimes,
That fill the haunted chambers of the Night,
    Like some old poet's rhymes.

From the cool cisterns of the midnight air
    My spirit drank repose;
The fountain of perpetual peace flows there,—
    From those deep cisterns flows.

O holy Night! from thee I learn to bear
    What man has borne before;
Thou layest thy finger on the lips of Care,
    And they complain no more.

Peace! Peace! Orestes-like I breathe this prayer!
    Descend with broad-winged flight,
The welcome, the thrice-prayed for, the most fair,
    The best-beloved Night!

A PSALM OF LIFE.

WHAT THE HEART OF THE YOUNG MAN SAID TO THE PSALMIST.

    TELL me not, in mournful numbers,
      "Life is but an empty dream!"
    For the soul is dead that slumbers,
      And things are not what they seem.

VOICES OF THE NIGHT

Life is real! Life is earnest!
  And the grave is not its goal;
"Dust thou art, to dust returnest,"
  Was not spoken of the soul.

Not enjoyment, and not sorrow,
  Is our destined end or way;
But to act, that each to-morrow
  Find us farther than to-day.

Art is long, and Time is fleeting,
  And our hearts, though stout and brave,
Still, like muffled drums, are beating
  Funeral marches to the grave.

In the world's broad field of battle,
  In the bivouac of Life,
Be not like dumb, driven cattle!
  Be a hero in the strife!

Trust no Future, howe'er pleasant!
  Let the dead Past bury its dead!
Act,—act in the living Present!
  Heart within, and God o'erhead!

Lives of great men all remind us
  We can make our lives sublime,
And, departing, leave behind us
  Footprints on the sands of time;

Footprints, that perhaps another,
  Sailing o'er life's solemn main,
A forlorn and shipwrecked brother,
  Seeing, shall take heart again.

Let us, then, be up and doing,
  With a heart for any fate;
Still achieving, still pursuing,
  Learn to labour and to wait.

THE LIGHT OF STARS.

The night is come, but not too soon;
  And sinking silently,
All silently, the little moon
  Drops down behind the sky.

There is no light in earth or heaven,
  But the cold light of stars;
And the first watch of night is given
  To the red planet Mars.

Is it the tender star of love?
  The star of love and dreams?
O no! from that blue tent above,
  A hero's armour gleams.

And earnest thoughts within me rise,
  When I behold afar,
Suspended in the evening skies,
  The shield of that red star.

O star of strength! I see thee stand
  And smile upon my pain;
Thou beckonest with thy mailèd hand,
  And I am strong again.

Within my breast there is no light,
  But the cold light of stars;
I give the first watch of the night
  To the red planet Mars.

The star of the unconquered will,
  He rises in my breast,

Serene, and resolute, and still,
  And calm, and self-possessed.

And thou, too, whoso'er thou art,
  That readest this brief psalm,
As one by one thy hopes depart,
  Be resolute and calm.

O fear not in a world like this,
  And thou shalt know ere long,
Know how sublime a thing it is
  To suffer and be strong.

THE REAPER AND THE FLOWERS.

There is a Reaper, whose name is Death,
  And, with his sickle keen,
He reaps the bearded grain at a breath,
  And the flowers that grow between.

" Shall I have nought that is fair?" saith he;
  " Have nought but the bearded grain?
Though the breath of these flowers is sweet to me,
  I will give them all back again."

He gazed at the flowers with tearful eyes,
  He kissed their drooping leaves;
It was for the Lord of Paradise
  He bound them in his sheaves.

" My Lord has need of these flowerets gay."
  The reaper said, and smiled;
" Dear tokens of the earth are they,
  Where he was once a child.

" They shall all bloom in fields of light,
  Transplanted by my care,
And saints, upon their garments white,
  These sacred blossoms wear."

And the mother gave, in tears and pain,
  The flowers she most did love;
She knew she should find them all again
  In the fields of light above.

O, not in cruelty, not in wrath,
  The Reaper came that day;
'Twas an angel visited the green earth,
  And took the flowers away.

FOOTSTEPS OF ANGELS.

When the hours of Day are numbered,
   And the voices of the Night
Wake the better soul, that slumbered,
   To a holy, calm delight;

Ere the evening lamps are lighted,
   And, like phantoms grim and tall,
Shadows from the fitful fire-light
   Dance upon the parlour wall;

VOICES OF THE NIGHT.

Then the forms of the departed
    Enter at the open door;
The beloved, the true-hearted,
    Come to visit me once more;

He, the young and strong, who cherished
    Noble longings for the strife,
By the road-side fell and perished,
    Weary with the march of life!

They, the holy ones and weakly,
    Who the cross of suffering bore,
Folded their pale hands so meekly,
    Spake with us on earth no more!

And with them the Being Beauteous,
    Who unto my youth was given,
More than all things else to love me,
    And is now a saint in heaven.

With a slow and noiseless footstep
    Comes that messenger divine,
Takes the vacant chair beside me,
    Lays her gentle hand in mine.

And she sits and gazes at me
    With those deep and tender eyes,
Like the stars, so still and saint-like,
    Looking downward from the skies.

Uttered not, yet comprehended,
    Is the spirit's voiceless prayer,
Soft rebukes, in blessings ended,
    Breathing from her lips of air.

O, though oft depressed and lonely,
    All my fears are laid aside,
If I but remember only
    Such as these have lived and died!

FLOWERS

Speak full well, in language quaint and olden,
One who dwelleth by the castled Rhine,
When he called the flowers, so blue and golden,
Stars, that in earth's firmament do shine.

Stars they are, wherein we read our history,
  As astrologers and seers of old;
Yet not wrapped about with awful mystery,
  Like the burning stars, which they beheld.

Wondrous truths, and manifold as wondrous,
  God hath written in those stars above;
But not less in the bright flowerets under us
  Stands the revelation of his love.

Bright and glorious is that revelation,
  Written all over this great world of ours;
Making evident our own creation,
  In these stars of earth,—these golden flowers.

And the Poet, faithful and far-seeing,
  Sees, alike in stars and flowers, a part
Of the self-same, universal being,
  Which is throbbing in his brain and heart.

Gorgeous flowerets in the sunlight shining,
  Blossoms flaunting in the eye of day,
Tremulous leaves, with soft and silver lining,
  Buds that open only to decay;

Brilliant hopes, all woven in gorgeous tissues,
  Flaunting gayly in the golden light;
Large desires, with most uncertain issues,
  Tender wishes, blossoming at night!

These in flowers and men are more than seeming;
  Workings are they of the self-same powers,
Which the Poet, in no idle dreaming,
  Seeth in himself and in the flowers.

Everywhere about us are they glowing,
  Some like stars, to tell us spring is born;
Others, their blue eyes with tears o'erflowing,
  Stand like Ruth amid the golden corn;

Not alone in Spring's armorial bearing,
  And in Summer's green emblazoned field,
But in arms of brave old Autumn's wearing,
  In the centre of his brazen shield;

FLOWERS.

Not alone in meadows and green alleys,
  On the mountain-top, and by the brink
Of sequestered pools in woodland valleys,
  Where the slaves of nature stoop to drink;

Not alone in her vast dome of glory,
  Not on graves of bird and beast alone,
But in old cathedrals, high and hoary,
  On the tombs of heroes, carved in stone;

In the cottage of the rudest peasant,
  In ancestral homes, whose crumbling towers,
Speaking of the Past unto the Present,
  Tell us of the ancient Games of Flowers;

In all places, then, and in all seasons,
  Flowers expand their light and soul-like wings,
Teaching us, by most persuasive reasons,
  How akin they are to human things.

And with childlike, credulous affection
  We behold their tender buds expand;
Emblems of our own great resurrection,
  Emblems of the bright and better land.

THE BELEAGUERED CITY.

I HAVE read, in some old marvellous tale,
　Some legend strange and vague,
That a midnight host of spectres pale
　Beleaguered the walls of Prague.

Beside the Moldau's rushing stream,
　With the wan moon overhead,
There stood, as in an awful dream,
　The army of the dead.

White as a sea-fog, landward bound,
　The spectral camp was seen,
And, with a sorrowful, deep sound,
　The river flowed between.

No other voice nor sound was there,
　No drum, nor sentry's pace;
The mist-like banners clasped the air
　As clouds with clouds embrace.

But, when the old cathedral bell
　Proclaimed the morning prayer,
The white pavilions rose and fell
　On the alarmèd air.

Down the broad valley fast and far
　The troubled army fled;
Up rose the glorious morning star,
　The ghastly host was dead.

I have read, in the marvellous heart of man,
　That strange and mystic scroll,
That an army of phantoms vast and wan
　Beleaguer the human soul.

Encamped beside Life's rushing stream,
　In Fancy's misty light,
Gigantic shapes and shadows gleam
　Portentous through the night.

Upon its midnight battle-ground
　The spectral camp is seen,
And, with a sorrowful, deep sound,
　Flows the River of Life between.

No other voice, nor sound is there,
　In the army of the grave;
No other challenge breaks the air,
　But the rushing of Life's wave.

And, when the solemn and deep church-bell
　Entreats the soul to pray,
The midnight phantoms feel the spell,
　The shadows sweep away.

Down the broad Vale of Tears afar
　The spectral camp is fled;
Faith shineth as a morning star,
　Our ghostly fears are dead.

MIDNIGHT MASS FOR THE DYING YEAR.

Yes, the Year is growing old,
  And his eye is pale and bleared!
Death, with frosty hand and cold,
  Plucks the old man by the beard,
    Sorely,—sorely!

The leaves are falling, falling,
  Solemnly and slow;
Caw! caw! the rooks are calling,
  It is a sound of woe,
    A sound of woe!

Through woods and mountain passes
  The winds, like anthems, roll;
They are chanting solemn masses,
  Singing; "Pray for this poor soul,
    Pray.—Pray!"

D

And the hooded clouds, like friars,
  Tell their beads in drops of rain,
And patter their doleful prayers ;—
  But their prayers are all in vain,
    All in vain !

There he stands in the foul weather,
  The foolish, fond Old Year,
Crowned with wild flowers and with heather,
  Like weak, despised Lear,
    A king,—a king !

Then comes the summer-like day,
  Bids the old man rejoice !
His joy ! his last ! O, the old man gray
  Loveth that ever-soft voice,
    Gentle and low.

To the crimson woods he saith,—
  To the voice gentle and low
Of the soft air, like a daughter's breath,—
  " Pray do not mock me so !
    Do not laugh at me !"

And now the sweet day is dead ;
  Cold in his arms it lies ;
No stain from its breath is spread
  Over the glassy skies,
    No mist or stain !

Then, too, the Old Year dieth,
  And the forests utter a moan,
Like the voice of one who crieth
  In the wilderness alone,
    " Vex not his ghost !"

  Then comes, with an awful roar,
    Gathering and sounding on,
  The storm-wind from Labrador,
    The wind Euroclydon.
      The storm-wind !

Howl! howl! and from the forest
  Sweep the red leaves away!
Would, the sins that thou abhorrest,
  O Soul! could thus decay,
    And be swept away!

For there shall come a mightier blast,
  There shall be a darker day;
And the stars, from heaven down-cast,
  Like red leaves be swept away!
    Kyrie, eleyson!
    Christe, eleyson!

L'ENVOI.

Ye voices, that arose
After the Evening's close,
And whispered to my restless heart repose!

Go, breathe it in the ear
Of all who doubt and fear,
And say to them, "Be of good cheer!"

Ye sounds, so low and calm,
That in the groves of balm
Seemed to me like an angel's psalm!

Go, mingle yet once more
With the perpetual roar
Of the pine forest, dark and hoar!

Tongues of the dead, not lost,
But speaking from death's frost,
Like fiery tongues at Pentecost!

Glimmer, as funeral lamps,
Amid the chills and damps
Of the vast plain where Death encamps!

EARLIER POEMS.

[WRITTEN FOR THE MOST PART DURING MY COLLEGE LIFE, AND ALL OF THEM
BEFORE THE AGE OF NINETEEN.]

WOODS IN WINTER.

When Winter winds are piercing chill,
  And through the hawthorn blows the gale,
With solemn feet I tread the hill
  That overbrows the lonely vale.

O'er the bare upland, and away
  Through the long reach of desert woods,
The embracing sunbeams chastely play,
  And gladden these deep solitudes.

Where, twisted round the barren oak,
  The summer vine in beauty clung,
And summer winds the stillness broke,
  The crystal icicle is hung.

Where, from their frozen urns, mute springs
  Pour out the river's gradual tide,
Shrilly the skater's iron rings,
  And voices fill the woodland side.

Alas! how changed from the fair scene,
  When birds sang out their mellow lay,
And winds were soft, and woods were green,
  And the song ceased not with the day.

But still wild music is abroad,
  Pale, desert woods! within your crowd;
And gathering winds, in hoarse accord,
  Amid the vocal reeds pipe loud.

Chill airs and wintry winds! my ear
  Has grown familiar with your song;
I hear it in the opening year,—
  I listen, and it cheers me long.

AN APRIL DAY.

When the warm sun, that brings
Seed-time and harvest, has returned again.

'Tis sweet to visit the still wood, where springs
   The first flower of the plain.

I love the season well,
When forest glades are teeming with bright forms,
Nor dark and many-folded clouds foretell
   The coming-on of storms.

From the earth's loosened mould
The sapling draws its sustenance, and thrives ;
Though stricken to the heart with Winter's cold,
   The drooping tree revives.

The softly-warbled song
Comes from the pleasant woods, and coloured wings
Glance quick in the bright sun, that moves along
   The forest openings.

When the bright sunset fills
The silver woods with light, the green slope throws
Its shadows in the hollows of the hills,
   And wide the upland glows.

And, when the eve is born,
In the blue lake the sky, o'er-reaching far,
Is hollowed out, and the moon dips her horn,
   And twinkles many a star.

Inverted in the tide,
Stand the gray rocks, and trembling shadows throw ;
And the fair trees look over, side by side,
   And see themselves below.

Sweet April!—many a thought
Is wedded unto thee, as hearts are wed ;
Nor shall they fail, till, to its autumn brought,
   Life's golden fruit is shed.

AUTUMN.

With what a glory comes and goes the year!
The buds of spring, those beautiful harbingers
Of sunny skies and cloudless times, enjoy
Life's newness, and earth's garniture spread out.
And when the silver habit of the clouds
Comes down upon the autumn sun, and with
A sober gladness the old year takes up
His bright inheritance of golden fruits,
A pomp and pageant fill the splendid scene.

There is a beautiful spirit breathing now
Its mellow richness on the clustered trees,
And, from a beaker full of richest dyes,
Pouring new glory on the autumn woods,
And dipping in warm light the pillared clouds.
Morn on the mountain, like a summer bird,

Lifts up her purple wing, and in the vales
The gentle wind, a sweet and passionate wooer,
Kisses the blushing leaf, and stirs up life
Within the solemn woods of ash deep-crimsoned,
And silver beech, and maple yellow-leaved,
Where Autumn, like a faint old man, sits down
By the wayside a-weary.   Through the trees
The golden robin moves.   The purple finch,
That on wild cherry and red cedar feeds,
A winter bird, comes with its plaintive whistle.
And pecks by the witch-hazel, whilst aloud
From cottage roofs the warbling blue-bird sings,
And merrily, with oft-repeated stroke,
Sounds from the threshing-floor the busy flail.

O what a glory doth this world put on
For him who, with a fervent heart, goes forth
Under the bright and glorious sky, and looks
On duties well performed, and days well spent !
For him the wind, ay, and the yellow leaves,
Shall have a voice, and give him eloquent teachings.
He shall so hear the solemn hymn, that Death
Has lifted up for all, that he shall go
To his long resting-place without a tear.

HYMN OF THE MORAVIAN NUNS OF BETHLEHEM,

AT THE CONSECRATION OF PULASKI'S BANNER.

When the dying flame of day
Through the chancel shot its ray,
Far the glimmering tapers shed
Faint light on the cowléd head ;
And the censer burning swung,
Where, before the altar, hung
The blood-red banner, that with prayer
Had been consecrated there.
And the nun's sweet hymn was heard the while,
Sung low in the dim, mysterious aisle.

" Take thy banner! May it wave
 Proudly o'er the good and brave;
 When the battle's distant wail
 Breaks the sabbath of our vale,
 When the clarion's music thrills
 To the hearts of these lone hills,
 When the spear in conflict shakes,
 And the strong lance shivering breaks.

" Take thy banner! and, beneath
 The battle-cloud's encircling wreath,
 Guard it!—till our homes are free!
 Guard it!—God will prosper thee!
 In the dark and trying hour,
 In the breaking forth of power,
 In the rush of steeds and men,
 His right hand will shield thee then.

" Take thy banner! But, when night
 Closes round the ghastly fight,
 If the vanquished warrior bow,
 Spare him!—by our holy vow,
 By our prayers and many tears,
 By the mercy that endears,
 Spare him!—he our love hath shared!
 Spare him!—as thou wouldst be spared!

" Take thy banner!—and if e'er
 Thou shouldst press the soldier's bier;
 And the muffled drum should beat
 To the tread of mournful feet,
 Then this crimson flag shall be
 Martial cloak and shroud for thee."

The warrior took that banner proud,
And it was his martial cloak and shroud!

SUNRISE ON THE HILLS.

I stood upon the hills, when heaven's wide arch
Was glorious with the sun's returning march,
And woods were brightened, and soft gales
Went forth to kiss the sun-clad vales.
The clouds were far beneath me:—bathed in light,
They gathered mid-way round the wooded height,
And, in their failing glory, shone
Like hosts in battle overthrown,
As many a pinnacle, with shifting glance,
Through the gray mist thrust up its shattered lance,
And rocking on the cliff was left
The dark pine blasted, bare, and cleft.
The veil of cloud was lifted, and below
Glowed the rich valley, and the river's flow
Was darkened by the forest's shade,
Or glistened in the white cascade;
Where upward, in the mellow blush of day,
The misty bittern wheeled his spiral way.

I heard the distant waters dash,
I saw the current whirl and flash,—
And richly, by the blue lake's silver beach,
The woods were bending with a silent reach.
Then o'er the vale, with gentle swell,
The music of the village bell
Came sweetly to the echo-giving hills;
And the wild horn, whose voice the woodland fills,
Was ringing to the merry shout,
That faint and far the glen sent out,
Where, answering to the sudden shot, thin smoke,
Through thick-leaved branches, from the dingle broke.

If thou art worn and hard beset
With sorrows, that thou wouldst forget,
If thou wouldst read a lesson, that will keep
Thy heart from fainting and thy soul from sleep,
Go to the woods and hills!—No tears
Dim the sweet look that Nature wears.

BURIAL OF THE MINNISINK.

On sunny slope and beechen swell,
The shadowed light of evening fell;
And, where the maple's leaf was brown,
With soft and silent lapse came down
The glory, that the wood receives,
At sunset, in its brazen leaves.

Far upward in the mellow light
Rose the blue hills. One cloud of white,
Around a far uplifted cone,
In the warm blush of evening shone;
An image of the silver lakes,
By which the Indian's soul awakes.

But soon a funeral hymn was heard
Where the soft breath of evening stirred
The tall, grey forest; and a band
Of stern in heart, and strong in hand,
Came winding down beside the wave,
To lay the red chief in his grave.

They sang, that by his native bowers
He stood, in the last moon of flowers,
And thirty snows had not yet shed
Their glory on the warrior's head:
But, as the summer fruit decays,
So died he in those naked days.

A dark cloak of the roebuck's skin
Covered the warrior, and within
Its heavy folds the weapons, made
For the hard toils of war, were laid;
The cuirass, woven of plaited reeds,
And the broad belt of shells and beads.

Before, a dark-haired virgin train
Chanted the death dirge of the slain;
Behind, the long procession came
Of hoary men and chiefs of fame,
With heavy hearts, and eyes of grief,
Leading the war-horse of their chief.

Stripped of his proud and martial dress,
Uncurbed, unreined, and riderless,
With darting eye, and nostril spread,
And heavy and impatient tread,
He came; and oft that eye so proud
Asked for his rider in the crowd.

They buried the dark chief—they freed
Beside the grave his battle steed;
And swift an arrow cleaved its way
To his stern heart! One piercing neigh
Arose,—and, on the dead man's plain,
The rider grasps his steed again.

THE SPIRIT OF POETRY.

THERE is a quiet spirit in these woods,
That dwells where'er the gentle south wind blows;
Where, underneath the white-thorn, in the glade,

The wild flowers bloom, or, kissing the soft air,
The leaves above their sunny palms outspread.
With what a tender and impassioned voice
It fills the nice and delicate ear of thought,
When the fast-gathering star of morning comes
O'er-riding the gray hills with golden scarf;
Or when the cowled and dusky-sandaled Eve,
In mourning woods, from out the western gate,
Departs with silent pace? That spirit moves
In the green valley, where the silver brook,
From its full laver, pours the white cascade;
And, babbling low amid the tangled woods,
Slips down through moss-grown stones with endless laughter.
And frequent, on the everlasting hills,
Its feet go forth, when it doth wrap itself
In all the dark embroidery of the storm,
And shouts the stern, strong wind. And here, amid
The silent majesty of these deep woods,
Its presence shall uplift thy thoughts from earth,
As to the sunshine and the pure bright air,
Their tops the green trees lift. Hence gifted bards
Have ever loved the calm and quiet shades.
For them there was an eloquent voice in all
The sylvan pomp of woods, the golden sun,
The flowers, the leaves, the river on its way,
Blue skies, and silver clouds, and gentle winds,—
The swelling upland, where the sidelong sun
Aslant the wooded slope, at evening, goes,—
Groves, through whose broken roof the sky looks in,
Mountain, and shattered cliff, and sunny vale,
The distant lake, fountains,—and mighty trees,
In many a lazy syllable, repeating
Their old poetic legends to the wind.

And this is the sweet spirit, that doth fill
The world; and, in these wayward days of youth,
My busy fancy oft embodies it,
As a bright image of the light and beauty
That dwell in nature,—of the heavenly forms
We worship in our dreams, and the soft hues

That stain the wild bird's wing, and flush the clouds
When the sun sets.   Within her eye
The heaven of April, with its changing light,
And when it wears the blue of May, is hung,
And on her lip the rich, red rose.   Her hair
Is like the summer tresses of the trees,
When twilight makes them brown, and on her cheek
Blushes the richness of an autumn sky,
With ever-shifting beauty.   Then her breath,
It is so like the gentle air of Spring,
As, from the morning's dewy flowers, it comes
Full of their fragrance, that it is a joy
To have it round us,—and her silver voice
Is the rich music of a summer bird,
Heard in the still night, with its passionate cadence.

TRANSLATIONS.

THE GOOD SHEPHERD.

FROM THE SPANISH OF LOPE DE VEGA

SHEPHERD! that with thine amorous, sylvan song
Hast broken the slumber which encompassed me,—
That mad'st thy crook from the accursed tree,
On which thy powerful arms were stretched so long!
Lead me to mercy's ever-flowing fountains;
For thou my shepherd, guard, and guide shalt be;
I will obey thy voice, and wait to see
Thy feet all beautiful upon the mountains.

Hear, Shepherd!—Thou who for thy flock art dying,
O, wash away these scarlet sins, for thou
Rejoicest at the contrite sinner's vow.
O, wait!—to thee my weary soul is crying.—
Wait for me!—Yet why ask it when I see,
With feet nailed to the cross, thou'rt waiting still for me!

TO-MORROW.

FROM THE SPANISH OF LOPE DE VEGA.

Lord, what am I, that, with unceasing care,
Thou didst seek after me,—that thou didst wait,
Wet with unhealthy dews, before my gate,
And pass the gloomy nights of winter there?
O strange delusion!—that I did not greet
Thy blest approach, and O, to Heaven how lost,
If my ingratitude's unkindly frost
Has chilled the bleeding wounds upon thy feet.
How oft my guardian angel gently cried,
" Soul, from thy casement look, and thou shalt see
How he persists to knock and wait for thee!"
And, O! how often to that voice of sorrow,
" To-morrow we will open," I replied,
And when the morrow came I answered still, " To-morrow."

THE NATIVE LAND.

FROM THE SPANISH OF FRANCISCO DE ALDANA

Clear fount of light! my native land on high.
Bright with a glory that shall never fade!
Mansion of truth! without a veil or shade,
Thy holy quiet meets the spirit's eye.

There dwells the soul in its ethereal essence,
Gasping no longer for life's feeble breath ;
But, sentinel'd in heaven, its glorious presence
With pitying eye beholds, yet fears not, death.
Beloved country ! banished from thy shore,
A stranger in this prison-house of clay,
The exiled spirit weeps and sighs for thee !
Heavenward the bright perfections I adore
Direct, and the sure promise cheers the way,
That, whither love aspires, there shall my dwelling be.

THE IMAGE OF GOD.

FROM THE SPANISH OF FRANCISCO DE ALDANA.

O Lord ! that seest, from yon starry height,
Centred in one the future and the past,
Fashioned in thine own image, see how fast
The world obscures in me what once was bright !
Eternal Sun ! the warmth which thou hast given,
To cheer life's flowery April, fast decays ;
Yet, in the hoary winter of my days,
For ever green shall be my trust in Heaven.
Celestial King ! O let thy presence pass
Before my spirit, and an image fair
Shall meet that look of mercy from on high,
As the reflected image in a glass
Doth meet the look of him who seeks it there,
And owes its being to the gazer's eye.

COPLAS DE MANRIQUE.

FROM THE SPANISH.

O LET the soul her slumbers break,
Let thought be quickened, and awake;

TRANSLATIONS.

Awake to see
How soon this life is past and gone,
And death comes softly stealing on,
How silently!

Swiftly our pleasures glide away,
Our hearts recall the distant day
With many sighs;
The moments that are speeding fast
We heed not, but the past,—the past,—
More highly prize.

Onward its course the present keeps,
Onward the constant current sweeps,
Till life is done;
And, did we judge of time aright,
The past and future in their flight
Would be as one.

Let no one fondly dream again,
That Hope and all her shadowy train
Will not decay;
Fleeting as were the dreams of old,
Remembered like a tale that's told,
They pass away.

Our lives are rivers, gliding free
To that unfathomed, boundless sea,
The silent grave!
Thither all earthly pomp and boast
Roll, to be swallowed up and lost
In one dark wave.

Thither the mighty torrents stray,
Thither the brook pursues its way,
And tinkling rill,
There all are equal. Side by side
The poor man and the son of pride
Lie calm and still.

COPLAS DE MANRIQUE.

I will not here invoke the throng
Of orators and sons of song,
The deathless few;
Fiction entices and deceives,
And, sprinkled o'er her fragrant leaves,
Lies poisonous dew.

To One alone my thoughts arise,
The Eternal Truth,—the Good and Wise.
To Him I cry,
Who shared on earth our common lot,
But the world comprehended not
His deity.

This world is but the rugged road
Which leads us to the bright abode
Of peace above;
So let us choose that narrow way,
Which leads no traveller's foot astray
From realms of love.

Our cradle is the starting-place,
In life we run the onward race,
And reach the goal;
When, in the mansions of the blest,
Death leaves to its eternal rest
The weary soul.

Did we but use it as we ought,
This world would school each wandering thought
To its high state,
Faith wings the soul beyond the sky,
Up to that better world on high,
For which we wait.

Yes,—the glad messenger of love,
To guide us to our home above,
The Saviour came;
Born amid mortal cares and fears,
He suffered in this vale of tears
A death of shame.

Behold of what delusive worth
The bubbles we pursue on earth,
    The shapes we chase,
Amid a world of treachery !
They vanish ere death shuts the eye,
    And leave no trace.

Time steals them from us,—chances strange,
Disastrous accidents, and change,
    That come to all ;
Even in the most exalted state,
Relentless sweeps the stroke of fate ;
    The strongest fall.

Tell me,—the charms that lovers seek
In the clear eye and blushing cheek,
    The hues that play
O'er rosy lip and brow of snow,
When hoary age approaches slow,
    Ah, where are they ?

The cunning skill, the curious arts,
The glorious strength that youth imparts
    In life's first stage ;
These shall become a heavy weight,
When Time swings wide his outward gate
    To weary age.

The noble blood of Gothic name,
Heroes emblazoned high to fame,
    In long array ;
How, in the onward course of time,
The landmarks of that race sublime
    Were swept away !

Some, the degraded slaves of lust,
Prostrate and trampled in the dust,
    Shall rise no more ;
Others, by guilt and crime, maintain
The scutcheon, that, without a stain,
    Their fathers bore.

Wealth and the high estate of pride,
With what untimely speed they glide,
How soon depart !
Did not the shadowy phantoms stay,
The vassals of a mistress they,
Of fickle heart.

These gifts in Fortune's hands are found :
Her swift revolving wheel turns round,
And they are gone !
No rest the inconstant goddess knows,
But changing, and without repose,
Still hurries on.

Even could the hand of avarice save
Its gilded baubles, till the grave
Reclaimed its prey,
Let none on such poor hopes rely ;
Life, like an empty dream, flits by,
And where are they ?

Earthly desires and sensual lust
Are passions springing from the dust,—
They fade and die ;
But, in the life beyond the tomb,
They seal the immortal spirit's doom
Eternally !

The pleasures and delights, which mask
In treacherous smiles life's serious task,
What are they, all,
But the fleet coursers of the chase,
And death an ambush in the race,
Wherein we fall ?

No foe, no dangerous pass, we heed,
Brook no delay,—but onward speed
With loosened rein ;
And, when the fatal snare is near,
We strive to check our mad career,
But strive in vain.

Could we new charms to age impart,
And fashion with a cunning art
The human face,
As we can clothe the soul with light,
And make the glorious spirit bright
With heavenly grace,—

How busily each passing hour
Should we exert that magic power!
What ardour show,
To deck the sensual slave of sin,
Yet leave the freeborn soul within,
In weeds of woe!

Monarchs, the powerful and the strong,
Famous in history and in song
Of olden time,
Saw, by the stern decrees of fate,
Their kingdoms lost, and desolate
Their race sublime.

Who is the champion? who the strong?
Pontiff and priest, and sceptred throng?
On these shall fall
As heavily the hand of Death,
As when it stays the shepherd's breath
Beside his stall.

I speak not of the Trojan name,
Neither its glory nor its shame
Has met our eyes;
Nor of Rome's great and glorious dead,
Though we have heard so oft, and read,
Their histories.

Little avails it now to know
Of ages passed so long ago,
Nor how they rolled;
Our theme shall be of yesterday,
Which to oblivion sweeps away,
Like days of old.

Where is the King, Don Juan? Where
Each royal prince and noble heir
Of Aragon?
Where are the courtly gallantries?
The deeds of love and high emprise,
In battle done?

Tourney and joust, that charmed the eye,
And scarf, and gorgeous panoply,
And nodding plume,—
What were they but a pageant scene?
What but the garlands, gay and green,
That deck the tomb?

Where are the high-born dames, and where
Their gay attire, and jewelled hair,
And colors sweet?
Where are the gentle knights, that came
To kneel, and breathe love's ardent flame,
Low at their feet?

Where is the song of Troubadour?
Where are the lute and gay tambour
They loved of yore?
Where is the mazy dance of old,
The flowing robes, inwrought with gold,
The dancers wore?

And he who next the sceptre swayed,
Henry, whose royal court displayed
Such power and pride;
O, in what winning smiles arrayed,
The world its various pleasures laid
His throne beside!

But O! how false and full of guile
That world, which wore so soft a smile
But to betray!
She, that had been his friend before,
Now from the fated monarch tore
Her charms away.

The countless gifts,—the stately walls,
The royal palaces, and halls
All filled with gold ;
Plate with armorial bearings wrought,
Chambers with ample treasures fraught
Of wealth untold ;

The noble steeds, and harness bright,
And gallant lord, and stalwart knight,
In rich array,—
Where shall we seek them now ? Alas !
Like the bright dew-drops on the grass,
They passed away.

His brother, too, whose factious zeal
Usurped the sceptre of Castile,
Unskilled to reign ;
What a gay, brilliant court had he,
When all the flower of chivalry
Was in his train !

But he was mortal ; and the breath,
That flamed from the hot forge of Death,
Blasted his years ;
Judgment of God ! that flame by thee,
When raging fierce and fearfully,
Was quenched in tears !

Spain's haughty Constable,—the true
And gallant Master, whom we know
Most loved of all.
Breathe not a whisper of his pride,—
He on the gloomy scaffold died,
Ignoble fall !

The countless treasures of his care,
His hamlets green, and cities fair,
His mighty power,—
What were they all but grief and shame,
Tears and a broken heart, when came
The parting hour ?

His other brothers, proud and high,
Masters, who, in prosperity,
Might rival kings;
Who made the bravest and the best
The bondsmen of their high behest,
Their underlings;

What was their prosperous estate,
When high exalted and elate
With power and pride?
What, but a transient gleam of light,
A flame, which, glaring at its height,
Grew dim and died?

So many a duke of royal name,
Marquis and count of spotless fame,
And baron brave,
That might the sword of empire wield,
All these, O Death, hast thou concealed
In the dark grave!

Their deeds of mercy and of arms,
In peaceful days, or war's alarms,
When thou dost show,
O Death, thy stern and angry face,
One stroke of thy all-powerful mace
Can overthrow.

Unnumbered hosts, that threaten nigh,
Pennon and standard flaunting high,
And flag displayed;
High battlements intrenched around,
Bastion, and moated wall, and mound,
And palisade,

And covered trench, secure and deep,—
All these cannot one victim keep,
O Death, from thee,
When thou dost battle in thy wrath,
And thy strong shafts pursue their path
Unerringly.

O World! so few the years we live,
Would that the life which thou dost give
Were life indeed!
Alas! thy sorrows fall so fast,
Our happiest hour is when at last
The soul is freed.

Our days are covered o'er with grief,
And sorrows neither few nor brief
Veil all in gloom;
Left desolate of real good,
Within this cheerless solitude
No pleasures bloom.

Thy pilgrimage begins in tears,
And ends in bitter doubts and fears,
Or dark despair;
Midway so many toils appear,
That he who lingers longest here
Knows most of care.

Thy goods are bought with many a groan,
By the hot sweat of toil alone,
And weary hearts;
Fleet-footed is the approach of woe,
But with a lingering step and slow
Its form departs.

And he, the good man's shield and shade,
To whom all hearts their homage paid,
As Virtue's son,—
Roderic Manrique,—he whose name
Is written on the scroll of Fame,
Spain's champion;

His signal deeds and prowess high
Demand no pompous eulogy,—
Ye saw his deeds!
Why should their praise in verse be sung?
The name, that dwells on every tongue,
No minstrel needs.

To friends a friend;—how kind to all
The vassals of this ancient hall
And feudal fief!
To foes how stern a foe was he!
And to the valiant and the free
How brave a chief!

What prudence with the old and wise:
What grace in youthful gaieties;
In all how sage!
Benignant to the serf and slave,
He showed the base and falsely brave
A lion's rage.

His was Octavian's prosperous star,
The rush of Cæsar's conquering car
At battle's call;
His, Scipio's virtue; his, the skill
And the indomitable will
Of Hannibal.

His was a Trajan's goodness,—his
A Titus' noble charities
And righteous laws;
The arm of Hector, and the might
Of Tully, to maintain the right
In truth's just cause:

The clemency of Antonine.
Aurelius' countenance divine,
Firm, gentle, still;
The eloquence of Adrian,
And Theodosius' love to man,
And generous will:

In tented field and bloody fray,
An Alexander's vigorous sway
And stern command;
The faith of Constantine; ay, more.
The fervent love Camillus bore
His native land.

He left no well-filled treasury,
He heaped no pile of riches high,
Nor massive plate;
He fought the Moors,—and, in their fall,
City and tower and castled wall
Were his estate.

Upon the hard-fought battle-ground,
Brave steeds and gallant riders found
A common grave;
And there, the warrior's band did gain
The rents, and the long vassal train,
That conquest gave.

And if, of old, his halls displayed
The honored and exalted grade
His worth had gained,
So, in the dark, disastrous hour,
Brothers and bondsmen of his power
His hand sustained.

After high deeds, not left untold,
In the stern warfare, which of old
'Twas his to share,
Such noble leagues he made, that more
And fairer regions, than before,
His guerdon were.

These are the records, half effaced,
Which, with the hand of youth, he traced
On history's page;
But with fresh victories he drew
Each fading character anew
In his old age.

By his unrivalled skill, by great,
And veteran service to the state,
By worth adored,
He stood, in his high dignity,
The proudest knight of chivalry,
Knight of the Sword.

He found his cities and domains
Beneath a tyrant's galling chains
And cruel power;
But by fierce battle and blockade,
Soon his own banner was displayed
From every tower.

By the tried valor of his hand,
His monarch and his native land
Were nobly served;—
Let Portugal repeat the story,
And proud Castile, who shared the glory
His arms deserved.

And when so oft, for weal or woe,
His life upon the fatal throw
Had been cast down;
When he had served with patriot zeal
Beneath the banner of Castile,
His sovereign's crown;

And done such deeds of valor strong
That neither history nor song
Can count them all;
Then, on Ocaña's castled rock,
Death at his portal came to knock,
With sudden call,—

Saying, "Good Cavalier, prepare
To leave this world of toil and care
With joyful mien;
Let thy strong heart of steel this day
Put on its armour for the fray,—
The closing scene.

"Since thou hast been in battle-strife,
So prodigal of health and life,
For earthly fame,
Let virtue nerve thy heart again;
Loud on the last stern battle-plain
They call thy name.

" Think not the struggle that draws near
Too terrible for man,—nor fear
To meet the foe ;
Nor let thy noble spirit grieve,
Its life of glorious fame to leave
On earth below.

" A life of honor and of worth
Has no eternity on earth,—
'Tis but a name;
And yet its glory far exceeds
That base and sensual life, which leads
To want and shame.

" The eternal life, beyond the sky,
Wealth cannot purchase, nor the high
The proud estate ;
The soul in dalliance laid,—the spirit
Corrupt with sin,—shall not inherit
A joy so great.

" But the good monk, in cloistered cell,
Shall gain it by his book and bell,
His prayers and tears ;
And the brave knight, whose arm endures
Fierce battle, and against the Moors
His standard rears.

" And thou, brave knight, whose hand has poured
The life-blood of the Pagan horde
O'er all the land,
In heaven shalt thou receive, at length,
The guerdon of thine earthly strength
And dauntless band.

" Cheered onward by this promise sure,
Strong in the faith entire and pure
Thou dost profess,
Depart,—thy hope is certainty,—
The third—the better life on high
Shalt thou possess."

"O Death, no more, no more delay;
My spirit longs to flee away,
And be at rest;
The will of Heaven my will shall be,—
I bow to the divine decree,
To God's behest.

"My soul is ready to depart,
No thought rebels, the obedient heart
Breathes forth no sigh;
The wish on earth to linger still
Were vain, when 'tis God's sovereign will
That we shall die.

"O Thou, that for our sins didst take
A human form, and humbly make
Thy home on earth;
Thou, that to thy divinity
A human nature didst ally
By mortal birth,

"And in that form didst suffer here
Torment, and agony, and fear,
So patiently;
By thy redeeming grace alone,
And not for merits of my own,
O, pardon me!"

As thus the dying warrior prayed,
Without one gathering mist or shade
Upon his mind;
Encircled by his family,
Watched by affection's gentle eye
So soft and kind;

His soul to Him, who gave it, rose;
God lead it to its long repose,
Its glorious rest!
And though the warrior's arm has set,
Its light shall linger round us yet,
Bright, radiant, blest.

NOTE.

Don Jorge Manrique, the author of the preceding poem, flourished in the last half of the fifteenth century. He followed the profession of arms; and Mariana, in his History of Spain, makes honorable mention of him, as being present at the siege of Uclès; he speaks of him as "a youth of estimable qualities, who in this war gave brilliant proofs of his valour. He died young—having been mortally wounded in a skirmish near Cenavrette in the year 1479—and was thus cut off from long surviving his great virtues, and exhibiting to the world the light of his genius, which was already known to fame."

The name of Rodrigo Manrique, the father of the poet, Conde de Paredes and Maestre de Santiago, is well known in Spanish history and song. He died in 1476; according to Mariana, in the town of Uclès; but according to the poem of his son, in the town of Ocaña. It was his death that called forth the poem upon which rests the literary reputation of the younger Manrique. In the language of his historian, "Don Jorge Manrique, in an elegant ode, full of poetic beauties, rich embellishments of genius and high moral reflections, mourned the death of his father, as with a funeral hymn." This praise is not exaggerated; the poem is a model in its kind. Its conception is solemn and beautiful, and, in accordance with it, the style moves on—calm, dignified, and majestic. It is a great favourite in Spain; and no less than four poetic Glosses, or running commentaries, upon it have been published.

The following stanzas of the poem were found in the author's pocket, after his death on the field of battle:

"O world! so few the years we live,
Would that the life that thou dost give
Were life indeed!
Alas! thy sorrows fall so fast,
Our happiest hour is when at last
The soul is freed.

"Our days are covered o'er with grief,
And sorrows neither few nor brief
Veil all in gloom;
Left desolate of real good,
Within this cheerless solitude
No pleasures bloom.

"Thy pilgrimage begins in tears,
And ends in bitter doubts and fears,
Or dark despair;
Midway so many toils appear,
That he who lingers longest here
Knows most of care.

"Thy goods are bought with many a groan,
By the hot sweat of toil alone,
And weary hearts;
Fleet-footed is the approach of woe,
But with a lingering step and slow
Its form departs."

THE BROOK.

FROM THE SPANISH

Laugh of the mountain!—lyre of bird and tree !
Pomp of the meadow! mirror of the morn !

The soul of April, unto whom are born
The rose and jessamine, leaps wild in thee !
Although where'er thy devious current strays,
The lap of earth with gold and silver teems,
To me thy clear proceeding brighter seems
Than golden sands, that charm each shepherd's gaze.
How without guile thy bosom, all transparent
As the pure crystal, lets the curious eye
Thy secrets scan, thy smooth, round pebbles count !
How, without malice murmuring, glides thy current !
O sweet simplicity of days gone by !
Thou shun'st the haunts of man, to dwell in limpid fount !

THE CELESTIAL PILOT.

FROM DANTE.   PURGATORIO, II.

AND now, behold ! as at the approach of morning,
Through the gross vapors, Mars grows fiery red
Down in the west upon the ocean floor,

Appeared to me,—may I again behold it !—
A light along the sea, so swiftly coming,
Its motion by no flight of wing is equalled,

And when therefrom I had withdrawn a little
Mine eyes, that I might question my conductor,
Again I saw it brighter grown and larger.

Thereafter, on all sides of it, appeared
I knew not what of white, and underneath,
Little by little, there came forth another.

My master yet had uttered not a word,
While the first brightness into wings unfolded;
But, when he clearly recognised the pilot,

He cried aloud: "Quick, quick, and bow the knee!
Behold the Angel of God! fold up thy hands!
Henceforward shalt thou see such officers!

"See, how he scorns all human arguments,
So that no oar he wants, nor other sail
Than his own wings, between so distant shores!

"See, how he holds them, pointed straight to heaven,
Fanning the air with the eternal pinions,
That do not moult themselves like mortal hair!"

And then, as nearer and more near us came
The Bird of Heaven, more glorious he appeared,
So that the eye could not sustain his presence.

But down I cast it; and he came to shore
With a small vessel, gliding swift and light,
So that the water swallowed nought thereof.

Upon the stern stood the Celestial Pilot!
Beatitude seemed written in his face!
And more than a hundred spirits sat within.

"*In exitu Israel* out of Egypt!"
Thus sang they all together in one voice,
With whatso in that Psalm is after written.

Then made he sign of holy rood upon them,
Whereat all cast themselves upon the shore,
And he departed swiftly as he came.

THE TERRESTRIAL PARADISE.

FROM DANTE   PURGATORIO, XXVIII.

Longing already to search in and round
The heavenly forest, dense and living-green,
Which to the eyes tempered the new-born day,

Withouten more delay I left the bank,
Crossing the level country slowly, slowly,
Over the soil, that everywhere breathed fragrance.

A gently-breathing air, that no mutation
Had in itself, smote me upon the forehead,
No heavier blow, than of a pleasant breeze,

Whereat the tremulous branches readily
Did all of them bow downward towards that side
Where its first shadow casts the Holy Mountain;

Yet not from their upright direction bent
So that the little birds upon their tops
Should cease the practice of their tuneful art;

But, with full-throated joy, the hours of prime
Singing received they in the midst of foliage
That made monotonous burden to their rhymes,

Even as from branch to branch it gathering swells,
Through the pine forests on the shore of Chiassi,
When Æolus unlooses the Sirocco.

Already my slow steps had led me on
Into the ancient wood so far, that I
Could see no more the place where I had entered.

And lo ! my farther course cut off a river,
Which, towards the left hand, with its little waves,
Bent down the grass, that on its margin sprang.

All waters that on earth most limpid are,
Would seem to have within themselves some mixture,
Compared with that, which nothing doth conceal,

Although it moves on with a brown, brown current,
Under the shade perpetual, that never
Ray of the sun lets in, nor of the moon.

BEATRICE.

FROM DANTE. PURGATORIO, XXX. XXXI.

Even as the Blessed, in the new covenant,
Shall rise up quickened, each one from his grave,
Wearing again the garments of the flesh ;

So, upon that celestial chariot,
A hundred rose *ad vocem tanti senis*,
Ministers and messengers of life eternal.

They all were saying :   "*Benedictus qui venis*,"
And scattering flowers above and round about,
" *Manibus o date lilia plenis.*"

I once beheld, at the approach of day,
The orient sky all stained with roseate hues,
And the other heaven with light serene adorned,

And the sun's face uprising, overshadowed,
So that, by temperate influence of vapours,
The eye sustained his aspect for long while ;

Thus in the bosom of a cloud of flowers,
Which from those hands angelic were thrown up,
And down descended inside and without

1

With crown of olive o'er a snow-white veil,
Appeared a lady, under a green mantle,
Vested in colour of the living flame.

  * * * * *

Even as the snow, among the living rafters
Upon the back of Italy, congeals,
Blown on and beaten by Sclavonian winds,

And then, dissolving, filters through itself,
Whene'er the land, that loses shadow, breathes,
Like as a taper melts before a fire,

Even such I was, without a sigh or tear,
Before the song of those who chime for ever
After the chiming of the eternal spheres;

But, when I heard in those sweet melodies
Compassion for me, more than had they said,
" O wherefore, lady, dost thou thus consume him ? "

The ice that was about my heart congealed,
To air and water changed, and, in my anguish,
Through lips and eyes came gushing from my breast.

  * * * * *

Confusion and dismay, together mingled,
Forced such a feeble " Yes ! " out of my mouth.
To understand it one had need of sight.

Even as a cross-bow breaks, when 'tis discharged,
Too tensely drawn the bow-string and the bow,
And with less force the arrow hits the mark;

So I gave way under this heavy burden,
Gushing forth into bitter tears and sighs,
And the voice, fainting, flagged upon its passage.

SPRING.

FROM THE FRENCH OF CHARLES D'ORLEANS.

BY. GENTLEY.

GENTLE Spring!—in sunshine clad,
Well dost thou thy power display!

For Winter maketh the light heart sad,
  And thou,—thou makest the sad heart gay.
He sees thee, and calls to his gloomy train,
The sleet, and the snow, and the wind, and the rain ;
And they shrink away, and they flee in fear,
  When thy merry step draws near.

Winter giveth the fields and the trees, so old,
  Their beards of icicles and snow ;
And the rain, it raineth so fast and cold,
  We must cover over the embers low ;
And, snugly housed from the wind and weather,
Mope like birds that are changing feather.
But the storm retires, and the sky grows clear,
  When thy merry step draws near.

Winter maketh the sun in the gloomy sky
  Wrap him round with a mantle of cloud ;
But, Heaven be praised, thy step is nigh ;
  Thou tearest away the mournful shroud,
And the earth looks bright, and Winter surly,
Who has toiled for nought both late and early,
Is banished afar by the new-born year,
  When thy merry step draws near.

———

THE BIRD AND THE SHIP.

FROM THE GERMAN OF MULLER.

"THE rivers rush into the sea,
  By castle and town they go ;
The winds behind them merrily
  Their noisy trumpets blow.

"The clouds are passing far and high,
  We little birds in them play ;
And everything, that can sing and fly,
  Goes with us, and far away.

" I greet thee, bonny boat! Whither, or whence,
    With thy fluttering golden band?"—
" I greet thee, little bird! To the wide sea
    I haste from the narrow land.

" Full and swollen is every sail;
    I see no longer a hill,
I have trusted all to the sounding gale,
    And it will not let me stand still.

" And wilt thou, little bird, go with us?
    Thou mayest stand on the mainmast tall,
For full to sinking is my house
    With merry companions all."—

" I need not and seek not company,
    Bonny boat, I can sing all alone;
For the mainmast tall too heavy am I,
    Bonny boat, I have wings of my own.

" High over the sails, high over the mast,
    Who shall gainsay these joys?
When thy merry companions are still, at last,
    Thou shalt hear the sound of my voice.

" Who neither may rest, nor listen may,
    God bless them every one!
I dart away, in the bright blue day,
    And the golden fields of the sun.

" Thus do I sing my weary song,
    Wherever the four winds blow;
And this same song, my whole life long,
    Neither Poet nor Printer may know."

THE CHILD ASLEEP.

FROM THE FRENCH.

Sweet babe! true portrait of thy father's face,
    Sleep on the bosom, that thy lips have pressed!
Sleep, little one; and closely, gently place
    Thy drowsy eyelid on thy mother's breast.

Upon that tender eye, my little friend,
    Soft sleep shall come, that cometh not to me!
I watch to see thee, nourish thee, defend;—
    'Tis sweet to watch for thee, alone for thee!

His arms fall down; sleep sits upon his brow;
    His eye is closed; he sleeps, nor dreams of harm.
Were not his cheek the apple's ruddy glow,
    Would you not say he slept on Death's cold arm?

Awake, my boy!—I tremble with affright!
    Awake, and chase this fatal thought!—Unclose
Thine eye but for one moment on the light!
    Even at the price of thine, give me repose!

Sweet error!—he but slept,—I breathe again;
    Come, gentle dreams, the hour of sleep beguile!
O! when shall he, for whom I sigh in vain,
    Beside me watch to see thy waking smile?

THE GRAVE.

FROM THE ANGLO-SAXON.

For thee was a house built
Ere thou wast born,
For thee was a mould meant
Ere thou of mother camest.
But it is not made ready,
Nor its depth measured,
Nor is it seen
How long it shall be.
Now I bring thee
Where thou shalt be;
Now I shall measure thee,
And the mould afterwards.

Thy house is not
Highly timbered,
It is unhigh and low;
When thou art therein,
The heel-ways are low,
The side-ways unhigh.
The roof is built
Thy breast full nigh,
So thou shalt in mould
Dwell full cold,
Dimly and dark.

Doorless is that house,
And dark it is within;
There thou art fast detained,
And Death hath the key.
Loathsome is that earth-house,
And grim within to dwell.
There thou shalt dwell,
And worms shall divide thee.

Thus thou art laid,
And leavest thy friends;
Thou hast no friend,
Who will come to thee,
Who will ever see
How that house pleaseth thee;
Who will ever open
The door for thee
And descend after thee,
For soon thou art loathsome
And hateful to see.

TRANSLATIONS

KING CHRISTIAN.

A NATIONAL SONG OF DENMARK.—FROM THE DANISH OF JOHANNES EVALD.

KING CHRISTIAN stood by the lofty mast
    In mist and smoke;
His sword was hammering so fast,
Through Gothic helm and brain it passed;
Then sank each hostile hulk and mast,
    In mist and smoke.
"Fly!" shouted they, "fly, he who can!
Who braves of Denmark's Christian
    The stroke?"

Nils Juel gave heed to the tempest's roar,
    Now is the hour!
He hoisted his blood-red flag once more,
And smote upon the foe full sore,
And shouted loud, through the tempest's roar,
    "Now is the hour!"
"Fly!" shouted they, "for shelter fly!
Of Denmark's Juel who can defy
    The power?"

North Sea! a glimpse of Wessel rent
    Thy murky sky!
Then champions to thine arms were sent;
Terror and Death glared where he went;
From the waves was heard a wail, that rent
    Thy murky sky!
From Denmark, thunders Tordenskiol',
Let each to Heaven commend his soul,
    And fly!

Path of the Dane to fame and might!
    Dark-rolling wave!
Receive thy friend, who, scorning flight,
Goes to meet danger with despite,
Proudly as thou the tempest's might,
    Dark-rolling wave!
And amid pleasures and alarms,
And war and victory, be thine arms
    My grave!

THE HAPPIEST LAND.

FRAGMENT OF A MODERN BALLAD.

FROM THE GERMAN.

THERE sat one day in quiet,
  By an alehouse on the Rhine,
Four hale and hearty fellows,
  And drank the precious wine.

The landlord's daughter filled their cups,
  Around the rustic board;
Then sat they all so calm and still,
  And spake not one rude word.

But, when the maid departed,
  A Swabian raised his hand,
And cried, all hot and flushed with wine,
  " Long live the Swabian land !

" The greatest kingdom upon earth
  Cannot with that compare ;
With all the stout and hardy men
  And the nut-brown maidens there."

" Ha !" cried a Saxon, laughing.—
  And dashed his beard with wine ;
" I had rather live in Lapland,
  Than that Swabian land of thine !

" The goodliest land on all this earth,
  It is the Saxon land !
There have I as many maidens
  As fingers on this hand !"

" Hold your tongues ! both Swabian and Saxon !"
  A bold Bohemian cries ;
" If there's a heaven upon this earth,
  In Bohemia it lies.

" There the tailor blows the flute,
  And the cobbler blows the horn,
And the miner blows the bugle,
  Over mountain gorge and bourn."
    *   *   *   *   *

And then the landlord's daughter
  Up to heaven raised her hand,
And said, " Ye may no more contend.—
  There lies the happiest land !"

THE WAVE.

FROM THE GERMAN OF TIEDGE.

" Whither, thou turbid wave?
Whither, with so much haste,
As if a thief wert thou?"

" I am the Wave of Life,
Stained with my margin's dust;
From the struggle and the strife
Of the narrow stream I fly
To the Sea's immensity,
To wash from me the slime
Of the muddy banks of Time."

THE DEAD.

FROM THE GERMAN OF KLOPSTOCK

How they so softly rest,
All, all the holy dead,   .
Unto whose dwelling-place
Now doth my soul draw near!
How they so softly rest,
All in their silent graves,
Deep to corruption
Slowly down-sinking!

And they no longer weep,
Here, where complaint is still!
And they no longer feel,
Here, where all gladness flies!
And by the cypresses
Softly o'ershadowed,
Until the Angel
Calls them, they slumber!

WHITHER?

FROM THE GERMAN OF MÜLLER.

I HEARD a brooklet gushing
  From its rocky fountain near,
Down into the valley rushing,
  So fresh and wondrous clear.

I know not what came o'er me,
  Nor who the counsel gave;
But I must hasten downward,
  All with my pilgrim-stave;

Downward, and ever further,
  And ever the brook beside;
And ever fresher murmured,
  And ever clearer, the tide.

Is this the way I was going?
  Whither, O brooklet, say!
Thou hast, with thy soft murmur,
  Murmured my senses away.

What do I say of a murmur?
  That can no murmur be;
'Tis the water-nymphs that are singing
  Their roundelays under me.

Let them sing, my friend, let them murmur,
  And wander merrily near;
The wheels of a mill are going
  In every brooklet clear.

BEWARE!

FROM THE GERMAN

I know a maiden fair to see,
Take care!

She can both false and friendly be,
   Beware! Beware!
   Trust her not,
She is fooling thee!

She has two eyes, so soft and brown,
   Take care!
She gives a side-glance and looks down,
   Beware! Beware!
   Trust her not,
She is fooling thee!

And she has hair of a golden hue,
   Take care!
And what she says, it is not true,
   Beware! Beware!
   Trust her not,
She is fooling thee!

She has a bosom as white as snow,
   Take care!
She knows how much it is best to show,
   Beware! Beware!
   Trust her not,
She is fooling thee!

She gives thee a garland woven fair,
   Take care!
It is a fool's-cap for thee to wear,
   Beware! Beware!
   Trust her not,
She is fooling thee!

SONG OF THE BELL.

FROM THE GERMAN.

Bell! thou soundest merrily,
When the bridal party
  To the church doth hie!
Bell! thou soundest solemnly,
When, on Sabbath morning,
  Fields deserted lie!

Bell! thou soundest merrily;
Tellest thou at evening,
  Bed-time draweth nigh!
Bell! thou soundest mournfully;
Tellest thou the bitter
  Parting hath gone by!

Say! how canst thou mourn?
How canst thou rejoice?
  Thou art but metal dull!
And yet all our sorrowings,
And all our rejoicings,
  Thou dost feel them all!

God hath wonders many,
Which we cannot fathom,
  Placed within thy form!
When the heart is sinking,
Thou alone canst raise it,
  Trembling in the storm!

THE CASTLE BY THE SEA

FROM THE GERMAN OF UHLAND.

" Hast thou seen that lordly castle,
  That Castle by the Sea?
Golden and red above it
  The clouds float gorgeously.

L

" And fain it would stoop downward
   To the mirrored wave below ;
And fain it would soar upward
   In the evening's crimson glow."

" Well have I seen that castle,
   That Castle by the sea,
And the moon above it standing,
   And the mist rise solemnly."

" The winds and the waves of ocean,
   Had they a merry chime ?
Didst thou hear, from those lofty chambers,
   The harp and the minstrel's rhyme ?"

" The winds and the waves of ocean,
   They rested quietly ;
But I heard on the gale a sound of wail,
   And tears came to mine eye."

" And sawest thou on the turrets
   The King and his royal bride ?
And the wave of their crimson mantles ?
   And the golden crown of pride ?

" Led they not forth, in rapture,
   A beauteous maiden there ?
Resplendent as the morning sun,
   Beaming with golden hair ?"

" Well saw I the ancient parents ;
   Without the crown of pride ;
They were moving slow, in weeds of woe,
   No maiden was by their side !"

THE BLACK KNIGHT.

FROM THE GERMAN OF UHLAND.

'Twas Pentecost, the Feast of Gladness,
When woods and fields put off all sadness.
  Thus began the King and spake;

"So from the halls
Of ancient Hofburg's walls,
 A luxuriant Spring shall break."

Drums and trumpets echo loudly,
Wave the crimson banners proudly.
 From balcony the King looked on;
In the play of spears,
Fell all the cavaliers,
 Before the monarch's stalwart son.

To the barrier of the fight
Rode at last a sable Knight.
 "Sir Knight! your name and scutcheon, say!"
"Should I speak it here,
Ye would stand aghast with fear;
 I am a Prince of mighty sway!"

When he rode into the lists,
The arch of heaven grew black with mists,
 And the castle 'gan to rock.
At the first blow,
Fell the youth from saddle-bow,
 Hardly rises from the shock.

Pipe and viol call the dances,
Torch-light through the high hall glances;
 Waves a mighty shadow in;
With manner bland
Doth ask the maiden's hand,
 Doth with her the dance begin;

Danced in sable iron sark,
Danced a measure weird and dark,
 Coldly clasped her limbs around.
From breast and hair
Down fall from her the fair
 Flowerets, faded, to the ground.

THE BLACK KNIGHT.

To the sumptuous banquet came
Every Knight and every Dame.
  'Twixt son and daughter all distraught.
With mournful mind
The ancient King reclined,
  Gazed at them in silent thought.

Pale the children both did look,
But the guest a beaker took;
  "Golden wine will make you whole!"
The children drank,
Gave many a courteous thank;
  "Oh, that draught was very cool!"

Each the father's breast embraces,
Son and daughter; and their faces
  Colourless grow utterly.
Whichever way
Looks the fear-struck father gray,
  He beholds his children die.

"Woe! the blessed children both
Takest thou in the joy of youth;
  Take me, too, the joyless father!"
Spake the grim Guest,
From his hollow, cavernous breast,
  "Roses in the spring I gather!"

SONG OF THE SILENT LAND.

FROM THE GERMAN OF SALIS.

Into the Silent Land!
Ah! who shall lead us thither?
Clouds in the evening sky more darkly gather,
And shattered wrecks lie thicker on the strand.
Who leads us with a gentle hand
Thither, O thither,
Into the Silent Land?

Into the Silent Land!
To you, ye boundless regions
Of all perfection! Tender morning-visions
Of beauteous souls! The Future's pledge and band!
Who in Life's battle firm doth stand,
Shall bear Hope's tender blossoms
Into the Silent Land!

O Land! O Land!
For all the broken-hearted
The mildest herald by our fate allotted,
Beckons, and with inverted torch doth stand
To lead us with a gentle hand
Into the land of the great Departed,
Into the Silent land!

THE CHILDREN OF THE LORD'S SUPPER.

FROM THE SWEDISH.

PREFATORY REMARKS.

This Idyl, from the original of Bishop Tegnér, descriptive of scenes of village life in Sweden, enjoys a well-merited reputation in the North of Europe, from its beauty and simplicity as well as from the pure and elevated tone of the writer.

There is something patriarchal still lingering about rural life in Sweden, combined with an almost primeval simplicity, an almost primeval solitude, which renders it a fit theme for song. You pass out from the gate of the city, and, as if by magic, the scene changes to a wild, woodland landscape. Around you are forests of fir, with their long, fan-like branches; while under foot is spread a carpet of yellow leaves. On a wooden bridge you cross a little silver stream; and anon come forth into a pleasant land of farms. Wooden fences divide the adjoining fields. The gates are opened by troops of children, and the peasants take off their hats as you pass. The houses in the villages and smaller towns are built of hewn timber, and are generally painted red. The floors of the taverns are strewn with the fragrant tips of fir-boughs. In many villages there are no taverns, and the peasants take turns in receiving travellers. The thrifty housewife shows you into the best chamber, the walls of which are hung round with rude pictures from the Bible; and she brings you curdled milk from the pan, with oaten cakes baked some months before. Meanwhile, the sturdy husband has brought his horses from the plough, and harnessed them to your carriage. Solitary travellers come and go in uncouth one-horse chaises. Most of them are smoking pipes, and have hanging around their necks in front, a leather wallet, in which they carry tobacco, and the great bank-notes of the country. You meet, also, groups of barefooted Dalekarlian peasant women, travelling in pursuit of work, carrying in their hands their shoes, which have high heels under the hollow of the foot, and soles of birch bark.

Frequent, too, are the village churches, standing by the road-side. In the church-yard are a few flowers, and much green grass. The grave-stones are flat, large, low, and perhaps sunken, like the roofs of old houses; the tenants all sleeping with their heads to the westward. Each held a lighted taper in his hand when he died; and in his coffin were placed his little heart-treasures, and a piece of money for his last journey. Babes that came lifeless into the world were carried in the arms of gray-haired old men to the only cradle they ever slept in; and in the shroud of the dead mother were laid the little garments of the child, that lived and died in her bosom. Near the church-yard gate stands a poor-box, with a sloping roof over it, fastened to a post by iron bands, and secured by a padlock. If it be Sunday, the peasants sit on the church steps and con their psalm-books. Others are coming down the road, listening to their beloved pastor. He is their patriarch, and, like Melchisedek, both priest and king, though he has no other throne than the church pulpit. The women carry psalm-books in their hands, wrapped in silk handkerchiefs, and listen devoutly to the good man's words. But the young men, like Gallio, care for none of these things. They are busy counting the plaits in the kirtles of the peasant girls, their number being an indication of the wearer's wealth.

I will endeavour to describe a village wedding in Sweden. It shall be in summer time, that the early song of the lark and of chanticleer may be heard mingling in the clear morning air, just after sunrise. In the yard there is a sound of voices and trampling of hoofs. The steed is led forth that is to bear the bridegroom, with a bunch of flowers upon his forehead, and a garland of corn-flowers around his neck. Friends from the neighbouring farms come riding in, and the happy bridegroom, with a whip in his hand, and a monstrous nosegay in the breast of his black jacket, comes forth from his chamber; and then to horse and away, towards the village where the bride is demurely waiting.

Foremost rides the Spokesman, followed by some village musicians. Next comes the happy swain between his two groomsmen, and then "heaps of friends," half of them perhaps with firearms in their hands. A wagon laden with food and drink brings up the rear. At the entrance of every village stands a triumphal arch, adorned with flowers and ribands; and as they pass beneath it the wedding guests fire a salute, and the whole procession stops. And straight from many a pocket flies a black-jack, filled with punch or brandy. It is passed from hand to hand among the crowd; provisions are brought from the wagon, and after eating and drinking and hurrahing, the procession moves forward again, and at length draws near the house of the bride. Four heralds ride forward to announce that a knight and his attendants are in the neighbouring forest, and pray for hospitality. "How many are you?" asks the bride's father. "At least three hundred," is the answer; and to this the host replies, "Were you seven times as many, you should all be welcome; and in token thereof receive this cup." Whereupon each herald receives a can of ale; and soon after the whole jovial company pours into the farmer's yard, and, riding round the May-pole in the centre, alights amid a grand flourish of music.

In the hall sits the bride, with a crown upon her head and a tear in her eye; she is dressed in a red bodice and kirtle, with loose linen sleeves. There is a gilded belt around her waist; and around her neck strings of golden beads, and a golden chain. On the crown rests a wreath of wild roses, and below it another of cypress. Loosely over her shoulders falls her flaxen hair; and her blue innocent eyes are fixed upon the ground. But with all this display, she is poor in worldly wealth. Her very ornaments have been hired for this great day. Yet is she rich in health, rich in hope, rich in her first young love. The blessing of heaven be upon thee! So thinks the parish priest, as he joins together the hands of bride and bridegroom, saying in deep, solemn tones,—"I give thee in marriage this damsel, to be thy wedded wife in all honor, and to share the half of thy bed,

thy lock and key, and every third penny which you two may possess, or may inherit,
and all the rights which Upland's laws provide, and the lady king Erik gave."

The dinner is now served, and the bride sits between the bridegroom and the
priest. The Spokesman delivers an oration after the ancient custom, interlarded
with quotations from the Bible; and invites the Saviour to be present at this
marriage feast, as he was at the marriage feast in Cana of Galilee. The table is
not sparingly set forth, and the feast goes cheerly on. Punch and brandy pass
round between the courses, and here and there a pipe is smoked, while waiting
for the next dish. They sit long at table; and then the dance begins. It is led
off by the bride and the priest, who perform a solemn minuet together. Not till
after midnight comes the Last Dance. The girls form a ring around the bride, to
keep her from the hands of the married women, who endeavour to break through
the magic circle, and seize their new sister. After long struggling they succeed; and
the crown is taken from her head and the jewels from her neck, and her bodice
is unlaced and her kirtle taken off; then like a vestal virgin clad all in white
she goes, but it is to her marriage chamber, not to her grave; and the wedding
guests follow her with lighted candles in their hands. And this is a village
bridal.

But I must not forget to speak of the suddenly changing seasons of the Northern
clime. There is no long spring, gradually unfolding leaf and blossom;—no lingering
autumn, pompous with many-colored leaves. But winter and summer are wonderful,
and pass into each other. The quail has hardly ceased piping in the corn, when
winter from the folds of trailing clouds sows broad-cast over the land snow, icicles,
and rattling hail. The days wane apace. Ere long the sun hardly rises above the
horizon, or does not rise at all. The moon and the stars shine through the day;
only, at noon, they are pale and wan, and in the southern sky a red, fiery glow, as of
sunset, burns along the horizon, and then goes out. And pleasantly under the silver
moon, and twinkling stars, ring the steel shoes of the skaters on the frozen sea, and
voices, and the sound of bells.

And now the Northern Lights begin to burn, faintly at first, like sunbeams playing
in the waters of the blue sea. Then a soft crimson glow tinges the heavens. There
is a blush on the cheek of night. The colors come and go; and change from crimson
to gold, from gold to crimson. The snow is stained with rosy light. Twofold from
the zenith, east and west, flames a fiery sword; and a broad land passes athwart the
heavens, like a summer sunset. Soft purple clouds come sailing over the sky, and
through their vapory folds the winking stars shine white as silver. With such pomp
as this is Merry Christmas ushered in, though only a single star heralded the first
Christmas. And in memory of that day the Swedish peasants dance on straw; and
the peasant girls throw straws at the timbered roof of the hall, and for every one
that sticks in a crack shall a groomsman come to their wedding. Merry indeed is
Christmas-time for Swedish peasants: brandy and nut-brown ale in wooden bowls;
and the great Yulecake crowned with a cheese, and garlanded with apples, and
upholding a three-armed candlestick over the Christmas feast.

And now leafy mid-summer, full of blossoms and the song of nightingales, is come!
In every village there is a May-pole fifty feet high, with wreaths and roses and ribands
streaming in the wind, and a noisy weathercock on top. The sun does not set

till ten o'clock at night; and the children are at play in the streets an hour later. The windows and doors are all open, and you may sit and read till midnight without a candle. O how beautiful is the summer night, which is not night, but a sunless yet unclouded day, descending upon earth with dews, and shadows, and refreshing coolness! How beautiful the long, mild twilight, which unites to-day with yesterday! How beautiful the silent hour, when Morning and Evening thus sit together, hand in hand, beneath the starless sky of midnight! From the church-tower in the public square the bell tolls the hour, with a soft, musical chime; and the watchman, whose watch-tower is the belfry, blows a blast in his horn, for each stroke of the hammer and four times, to the four corners of the heavens, in a sonorous voice he chaunts,—

> "Ho! watchman, ho!
> Twelve is the clock!
> God keep our town
> From fire and brand,
> And hostile hand!
> Twelve is the clock!"

From his swallow's nest in the belfry he can see the sun all night long; and farther north the priest stands at his door in the warm midnight, and lights his pipe with a common burning glass.

I trust that these remarks will not be deemed irrelevant to the poem, but will lead to a clearer understanding of it. The translation is literal, perhaps to a fault. In no instance have I done the author a wrong, by introducing into his work any supposed improvements or embellishments of my own. I have preserved even the measure; in which, it must be confessed, the motions of the English Muse are not unlike those of a prisoner dancing to the music of his chains; and perhaps, as Dr. Johnson said of the dancing dog, "the wonder is not that she should do it so well, but that she should do it at all."

Esaias Tegnér, the author of this poem, was born in the parish of By in Wärmland, in the year 1782. In 1799 he entered the University of Lund, as a student; and in 1812 was appointed Professor of Greek in that Institution. In 1824 he became Bishop of Wexiö, which office he still holds. He is the glory and boast of Sweden, and stands first among all her poets living or dead. His principal work is Frithiofs Saga; one of the most remarkable poems of the age. Bishop Tegnér is a prophet, honored in his own country, adding one more to the list of great names that adorn her history.

FROM THE WELDING OF BISHOP TEGNÉR

PENTECOST, day of rejoicing, had come. The church of the village
Gleaming stood in the morning's sheen. On the spire of the belfry,
Tipped with a vane of metal, the friendly flames of the Spring-sun
Glanced like the tongues of fire, beheld by Apostles aforetime.
Clear was the heaven and blue, and May, with her cap crowned with roses,

Stood in her holiday dress in the fields, and the wind and the brooklet
Murmured gladness and peace, God's-peace! with lips rosy-tinted
Whispered the race of the flowers, and merry on balancing branches
Birds were singing their carol, a jubilant hymn to the Highest.
Swept and clean was the churchyard.   Adorned like a leaf-woven arbour
Stood its old-fashioned gate ; and within upon each cross of iron
Hung was a fragrant garland, new twined by the hands of affection.
Even the dial, that stood on a hillock among the departed,
(There full a hundred years had it stood,) was embellished with blossoms.
Like to the patriarch hoary, the sage of his kith and the hamlet,
Who on his birth-day is crowned by children and children's children,
So stood the ancient prophet, and mute with his pencil of iron
Marked on the tablet of stone, and measured the time and its changes,
While all around at his feet, an eternity slumbered in quiet.
Also the church within was adorned, for this was the season
When the young, their parent's hope, and the loved-ones of heaven,
Should at the foot of the altar renew the vows of their baptism.
Therefore each nook and corner was swept and cleansed, and the dust was
Blown from the walls and ceiling, and from the oil-painted benches.
There stood the church like a garden ; the Feast of the Leafy Pavilions *
Saw we in living presentment.   From noble arms on the church wall
Grew forth a cluster of leaves, and the preacher's pulpit of oak-wood
Budded once more anew, as aforetime the rod before Aaron.
Wreathed thereon was the Bible with leaves, and the dove, washed with silver,
Under its canopy fastened, had on it a necklace of wild-flowers.
But in front of the choir, round the altar-piece painted by Hörberg,†
Crept a garland gigantic ; and bright-curling tresses of angels
Peeped, like the sun from a cloud, from out of the shadowy leaf-work.
Likewise the lustre of brass, new-polished, blinked from the ceiling.
And for lights there were lilies of Pentecost set in the sockets.

Loud rang the bells already ; the thronging crowd was assembled
Far from valleys and hills, to list to the holy preaching.
Hark! then roll forth at once the mighty tones from the organ,
Hover like voices from God, aloft like invisible spirits.
Like as Elias in heaven, when he cast off from him his mantle,
Even so cast off the soul its garments of earth ; and with one voice

---

* The Feast of the Tabernacles ; in Swedish, Lösthyddohögtiden, the Leaf-huts'-high-tide.
† The peasant-painter of Sweden.   He is known chiefly by his altar-pieces in the village churches.

Chimed in the congregation, and sang an anthem immortal
Of the sublime Wallin,* of David's harp in the North-land
Tuned to the choral of Luther; the song on its powerful pinions
Took every living soul, and lifted it gently to heaven,
And every face did shine like the Holy One's face upon Tabor.
Lo! there entered then into the church the Reverend Teacher.
Father he hight and he was in the parish; a christianly plainness
Clothed from his head to his feet the old man of seventy winters.
Friendly was he to behold, and glad as the heralding angel
Walked he among the crowds, but still a contemplative grandeur

---

* A distinguished pulpit-orator and poet. He is particularly remarkable for the beauty and sublimity of his psalms.

Lay on his forehead as clear, as on moss-covered grave-stone a sunbeam.
As in his inspiration (an evening twilight that faintly
Gleams in the human soul, even now, from the day of creation)
Th' Artist, the friend of heaven, imagines Saint John when in Patmos,
Gray, with his eyes uplifted to heaven, so seemed then the old man ;
Such was the glance of his eye, and such were his tresses of silver.
All the congregation arose in the pews that were numbered.
But with a cordial look, to the right and the left hand, the old man
Nodding all hail and peace, disappeared in the innermost chancel.

Simply and solemnly now proceeded the Christian service,
Singing and prayer, and at last an ardent discourse from the old man.
Many a moving word and warning, that out of the heart came,
Fell like the dew of the morning, like manna on those in the desert.
Afterwards, when all was finished, the Teacher reëntered the chancel,
Followed therein by the young.   On the right hand the boys had their places,
Delicate figures, with close-curling hair and cheeks rosy-blooming.
But on the left-hand of these, there stood the tremulous lilies,
Tinged with the blushing light of the morning, the diffident maidens,—
Folding their hands in prayer, and their eyes cast down on the pavement.
Now came, with question and answer, the Catechism.   In the beginning,
Answered the children with troubled and faltering voice, but the old man's
Glances of kindness encouraged them soon, and the doctrines eternal
Flowed, like the waters of fountains, so clear from lips unpolluted.
Whene'er the answer was closed, and as oft as they named the Redeemer,
Lowly louted the boys, and lowly the maidens all courtesied.
Friendly the Teacher stood, like an angel of light there among them,
And to the children explained he the holy, the highest in few words,
Thorough, yet simple and clear, for sublimity always is simple,
Both in sermon and song, a child can seize on its meaning.
Even as the green-growing bud is unfolded when Spring-tide approaches,
Leaf by leaf is developed, and, warmed by the radiant sunshine,
Blushes with purple and gold, till at last the perfected blossom
Opens its odorous chalice, and rocks with its crown in the breezes,
So was unfolded here the Christian lore of salvation,
Line by line from the soul of childhood.   The fathers and mothers
Stood behind them in tears, and were glad at each well-worded answer.

Now went the old man up to the altar ;—and straightway transfigured
(So did it seem unto me) was then the affectionate Teacher.
Like the Lord's Prophet sublime, and awful as Death and as Judgment
Stood he, the God-commissioned, the soul-searcher. earthward descending.
Glances, sharp as a sword, into hearts, that to him were transparent,
Shot he ; his voice was deep, was low like the thunder afar off.
So on a sudden transfigured he stood there, he spake and he questioned.

" This is the faith of the Fathers, the faith the Apostles delivered,
This is moreover the faith whereunto I baptized you, while still ye
Lay on your mother's breasts, and nearer the portals of heaven.
Slumbering received you then the Holy Church in its bosom ;
Wakened from sleep are ye now, and the light in its radiant splendor
Rains from the heaven downward ;—to-day on the threshold of childhood
Kindly she frees you again, to examine and make your election,
For she knows nought of compulsion, and only conviction desireth.
This is the hour of your trial, the turning-point of existence,
Seed for the coming days ; without reveration departeth
Now from your lips the confession ; Bethink ye, before ye make answer !
Think not, O think not with guile to deceive the questioning Teacher.
Sharp is his eye to-day, and a curse ever rests upon falsehood.
Enter not with a lie on Life's journey ; the multitude bears you,
Brothers and sisters and parents, what dear upon earth is and holy
Standeth before your sight as a witness ; the Judge everlasting
Looks from the sun down upon you, and angels in waiting beside him
Grave your confession in letters of fire, upon tablets eternal.
Thus then,—believe ye in God, in the Father who this world created ?
Him who redeemed it, the Son, and the Spirit where both are united ?
Will ye promise me here, (a holy promise !) to cherish
God more than all things earthly, and every man as a brother ?
Will ye promise me here, to confirm your faith by your living,
Th' heavenly faith of affection ! to hope, to forgive, and to suffer,
Be what it may your condition, and walk before God in uprightness ?
Will ye promise me this before God and man ?"—with a clear voice
Answered the young men Yes ! and Yes ! with lips softly-breathing
Answered the maidens eke.   Then dissolved from the brow of the Teacher
Clouds with the thunders therein, and he spake in accents more gentle,
Soft as the evening's breath, as harps by Babylon's rivers.

" Hail, then, hail to you all ! To the heirdom of heaven be ye welcome
Children no more from this day, but by covenant brothers and sisters !
Yet,—for what reason not children ? Of such is the kingdom of heaven.
Here upon earth an assemblage of children, in heaven one Father,
Ruling them all as his household,—forgiving in turn and chastising,
That is of human life a picture, as Scripture has taught us.
Blessed are the pure before God ! Upon purity and upon virtue
Resteth the Christian Faith ; she herself from on high is descended.
Strong as a man and pure as a child, is the sum of the doctrine,

Which the Divine One taught, and suffered and died on the cross for.
O! as ye wander this day from childhood's sacred asylum
Downward and ever downward, and deeper in Age's chill valley,
O! how soon will ye come,—too soon!—and long to turn backward
Up to its hill-tops again, to the sun-illumined, where Judgment
Stood like a father before you, and Pardon, clad like a mother,
Gave you her hand to kiss, and the loving heart was forgiven.
Life was a play, and your hands grasped after the roses of heaven!
Seventy years have I lived already; the Father eternal
Gave me gladness and care; but the loveliest hours of existence,
When I have steadfastly gazed in their eyes, I have instantly known them,
Known them all again;—They were my childhood's acquaintance.
Therefore take from henceforth, as guides in the paths of existence,
Prayer, with their eyes raised to heaven, and Innocence, bride of man's childhood.
Innocence, child beloved, is a guest from the world of the blessed,
Beautiful, and in her hand a lily; on life's roaring billows
Swings she in safety, she heedeth them not, in the ship she is sleeping.
Calmly she gazes around in the turmoil of men; in the desert
Angels descend and minister unto her; she herself knoweth
Nought of her glorious attendance; but follows faithful and humble,
Follows so long as she may her friend; O do not reject her.
For she cometh from God and she holdeth the keys of the heavens.—
Prayer is Innocence' friend; and willingly flieth incessant
'Twixt the earth and the sky, the carrier-pigeon of heaven.
Son of Eternity, fettered in Time, and an exile, the Spirit
Tugs at his chains evermore, and struggles like flames ever upward.
Still he recalls with emotion his Father's manifold mansions,
Thinks of the land of his fathers, where blossomed more freshly the flowers,
Shone a more beautiful sun, and he played with the wingèd angels.
Then grows the earth too narrow, too close; and homesick for heaven
Longs the wanderer again; and the Spirit's longings are worship;
Worship is called his most beautiful hour, and its tongue is entreaty.
Ah! when the infinite burden of life descendeth upon us,
Crushes to earth our hope, and, under the earth, in the grave-yard,—
Then it is good to pray unto God; for his sorrowing children
Turns he ne'er from his door, but he heals and helps and consoles them.
Yet is it better to pray when all things are prosperous with us,
Pray in fortunate days, for life's most beautiful Fortune
Kneels down before the Eternal's throne; and, with hands interfolded,
Praises thankful and moved the only giver of blessings.

Or do ye know, ye children, one blessing that comes not from Heaven?
What has mankind forsooth, the poor! that it has not received?
Therefore, fall in the dust and pray! The seraphs adoring
Cover with pinions six their face in the glory of him who
Hung his masonry pendant on nought, when the world he created.
Earth declareth his might, and the firmament uttereth his glory.
Races blossom and die, and stars fall downward from heaven,
Downward like withered leaves; at the last stroke of midnight, millenniums
Lay themselves down at his feet, and he sees them, but counts them as nothing.
Who shall stand in his presence? The wrath of the judge is terrific,
Casting the insolent down at a glance. When he speaks in his anger
Hillocks skip like the kid, and mountains leap like the roe-buck.
Yet,—why are ye afraid, ye children? This awful avenger,
Ah! is a merciful God! God's voice was not in the earthquake,
Not in the fire, nor the storm, but it was in the whispering breezes.
Love is the root of creation; God's essence; worlds without number
Lie in his bosom like children; he made them for this purpose only,
Only to love and be loved again, he breathed forth his spirit
Into the slumbering dust, and upright standing, it laid its
Hand on its heart, and felt it was warm with a flame out of heaven.
Quench, O quench not that flame! It is the breath of your being.
Love is life, but hatred is death. Not father nor mother
Loved you, as God has loved you; for 'twas that you may be happy
Gave he his only Son. When he bowed down his head in the death-hour
Solemnised Love its triumph; the sacrifice then was completed.
Lo! then was rent on a sudden the vail of the temple, dividing
Earth and heaven apart, and the dead from their sepulchres rising
Whispered with pallid lips and low in the ears of each other
Th' answer, but dreamed of before, to creation's enigma,—Atonement!
Depths of Love are Atonement's depths, for Love is Atonement.
Therefore, child of mortality, love thou the merciful Father;
Wish what the Holy One wishes, and not from fear, but affection;
Fear is the virtue of slaves; but the heart that loveth is willing;
Perfect was before God, and perfect is Love, and Love only.
Lovest thou God as thou oughtest, then lovest thou likewise thy brethren;
One is the sun in heaven, and one, only one, is Love also.
Bears not each human figure the godlike stamp on his forehead?
Readest thou not in his face thine origin? Is he not sailing
Lost like thyself on an ocean unknown, and is he not guided
By the same stars that guide thee? Why shouldst thou hate then thy brother?

Hateth he thee, forgive!   For 'tis sweet to stammer one letter
Of the Eternal's language;—on earth it is called Forgiveness!
Knowest thou Him, who forgave, with the crown of thorns round his temples?
Earnestly prayed for his foes, for his murderers? Say, dost thou know him?
Ah! thou confessest his name, so follow likewise his example,
Think of thy brother no ill, but throw a veil over his failings,
Guide the erring aright; for the good, the heavenly Shepherd
Took the lost lamb in his arms, and bore it back to its mother.
This is the fruit of Love, and it is by its fruits that we know it.
Love is the creature's welfare, with God; but Love among mortals
Is but an endless sigh! He longs, and endures, and stands waiting,
Suffers, and yet rejoices, and smiles with tears on his eyelids.
Hope,—so is called upon earth, his recompense,—Hope, the befriending,
Does what she can, for she points evermore up to heaven, and faithful
Plunges her anchor's peak in the depths of the grave, and beneath it
Paints a more beautiful world, a dim, but a sweet play of shadows!
Races, better than we, have leaned on her wavering promise,
Having nought else but Hope.   Then praise we our Father in heaven,
Him, who has given us more: for to us has Hope been transfigured,
Groping no longer in night; she is Faith, she is living assurance.
Faith is enlightened Hope; she is light, is the eye of affection,
Dreams of the longing interprets, and carves their visions in marble.
Faith is the sun of life; and her countenance shines like the Hebrew's,
For she has looked upon God; the heaven on its stable foundation
Draws she with chains down to earth, and the New Jerusalem sinketh
Splendid with portals twelve in golden vapors descending.
There enraptured she wanders, and looks at the figures majestic,
Fears not the winged crowd, in the midst of them all is her homestead.
Therefore love and believe; for works will follow spontaneous,
Even as day does the sun; the Right from the Good is an offspring,
Love in a bodily shape; and Christian works are no more than
Animate Love and faith, as flowers are the animate spring-tide.
Works do follow us all unto God; there stand and bear witness
Not what they seemed,—but what they were only.   Blessed is he who
Hears their confession secure; they are mute upon earth until Death's hand
Opens the mouth of the silent.   Ye children, does Death e'er alarm you?
Death is the brother of Love, twin-brother is he, and is only
More austere to behold.   With a kiss upon lips that are fading
Takes he the soul and departs, and rocked in the arms of affection,
Places the ransomed child, new born, 'fore the face of its father.

Sounds of its coming already I hear,—see dimly his pinions,
Swart as the night, but with stars strewn upon them! I fear not before him.
Death is only release, and in mercy is mute. On his bosom
Freer breathes, in its coolness, my breast; and face to face standing,
Look I on God as he is, a sun unpolluted by vapors;
Look on the light of the ages I loved, the spirits majestic,
Nobler, better than I; they stand by the throne all transfigured,
Vested in white, and with harps of gold, and are singing an anthem,
Writ in the climate of heaven, in the language spoken by angels.
You, in like manner, ye children beloved, he one day shall gather,
Never forgets he the weary;—then welcome, ye loved ones, hereafter!
Meanwhile forget not the keeping of vows, forget not the promise,
Wander from holiness onward to holiness; earth shall ye heed not;
Earth is but dust and heaven is light; I have pledged you to heaven.
God of the Universe, hear me! thou fountain of Love everlasting,
Hark to the voice of thy servant! I send up my prayer to thy heaven!
Let me hereafter not miss at thy throne one spirit of all these,
Whom thou hast given me here! I have loved them all like a father.
May they bear witness for me, that I taught them the way of salvation,
Faithful, so far as I know of thy word; again may they know me,
Fall on their Teacher's breast, and before thy face may I place them,
Pure as they now are, but only more tried, and exclaiming with gladness,
Father, lo! I am here, and the children, whom thou hast given me!"

Weeping he spake in these words; and now at the beck of the old man
Knee against knee they knitted a wreath round the altar's enclosure.
Kneeling he read then the prayers of the consecration, and softly
With him the children read; at the close, with tremulous accents,
Asked he the peace of heaven, a benediction upon them.
Now should have ended his task for the day; the following Sunday
Was for the young appointed to eat of the Lord's holy Supper.
Sudden, as struck from the clouds, stood the Teacher silent and laid his
Hand on his forehead, and cast his looks upward; while thoughts high and holy
Flew through the midst of his soul, and his eyes glanced with wonderful brightness.
"On the next Sunday, who knows! perhaps I shall rest in the grave-yard!
Some one perhaps of yourselves, a lily broken untimely,
Bow down his head to the earth; why delay I? the hour is accomplished.
Warm is the heart;—I will so! for to-day grows the harvest of heaven.
What I began accomplish I now; for what failing therein is
I, the old man, will answer to God and the reverend father.

Say to me only, ye children, ye denizens new-come in heaven,
Are ye ready this day to eat of the bread of Atonement?
What it denoteth, that know ye full well, I have told it you often.
Of the new covenant a symbol it is, of Atonement a token,
Stablished between earth and heaven. Man by his sins and transgressions
Far has wandered from God, from his essence. 'Twas in the beginning
Fast by the Tree of Knowledge he fell, and it hangs its crown o'er the
Fall to this day; in the Thought is the Fall; in the Heart the Atonement.
Infinite is the Fall, the Atonement infinite likewise.
See! behind me, as far as the old man remembers, and forward,
Far as Hope in her flight can reach with her wearied pinions,
Sin and Atonement incessant go through the life-time of mortals.
Drought forth is sin full-grown; but Atonement sleeps in our bosoms
Still as the cradled babe; and dreams of heaven and of angels,
Cannot awake to sensation; is like the tones in the harp's strings,
Spirits imprisoned, that wait evermore the deliverer's finger.
Therefore, ye children beloved, descended the Prince of Atonement,
Woke the slumberer from sleep, and she stands now with eyes all resplendent,
Bright as the vault of the sky, and battles with sin and o'ercomes her.
Downward to earth he came and transfigured, thence reascended,
Not from the heart in like wise, for there he still lives in the Spirit,
Loves and atones evermore. So long as Time is, is Atonement.
Therefore with reverence receive this day her visible token.
Tokens are dead if the things do not live. The light everlasting
Unto the blind man is not, but is born of the eye that has vision.
Neither in bread nor in wine, but in the heart that is hallowed
Lieth forgiveness enshrined; the intention alone of amendment
Fruits of the earth ennobles to heavenly things, and removes all
Sin and the guerdon of sin. Only Love with his arms wide extended,
Penitence weeping and praying; the Will that is tried, and whose gold flows
Purified forth from the flames; in a word, mankind by Atonement
Breaketh Atonement's bread, and drinketh Atonement's wine-cup.
But he who cometh up hither, unworthy, with hate in his bosom,
Scoffing at men and at God, is guilty of Christ's blessed body,
And the Redeemer's blood! To himself he eateth and drinketh
Death and doom! And from this, preserve us, thou heavenly Father!
Are ye ready, ye children, to eat of the bread of Atonement?"
Thus with emotion he asked, and together answered the children
Yes! with deep sobs interrupted. Then read he the due supplications,
Read the Form of Communion, and in chimed the organ and anthem;

O! Holy Lamb of God, who takest away our transgressions,
Hear us! give us thy peace! have mercy, have mercy upon us!
Th' old man, with trembling hand, and heavenly pearls on his eyelids,
Filled now the chalice and paten, and dealt round the mystical symbols.
O! then seemed it to me, as if God, with the broad eye of mid-day,
Clearer looked in at the windows, and all the trees in the churchyard
Bowed down their summits of green, and the grass on the graves 'gan to shiver.
But in the children, (I noted it well; I know it) there ran a
Tremor of holy rapture along through their icy-cold members.
Decked like an altar before them, there stood the green earth, and above it
Heaven opened itself, as of old before Stephen; they saw there
Radiant in glory the Father, and on his right hand the Redeemer.
Under them hear they the clang of harpstrings, and angels from gold clouds
Beckon to them like brethren, and fan with their pinions of purple.
Closed was the Teacher's task, and with heaven in their hearts and their faces,
Up rose the children all, and each bowed him, weeping full sorely,
Downward to kiss that reverend hand, but all of them pressed ho
Moved to his bosom, and laid, with a prayer, his hands full of blessings,
Now on the holy breast, and now on the innocent tresses.

THE TWO LOCKS OF HAIR.

FROM THE GERMAN OF PFIZER.

A YOUTH, light-hearted and content,
  I wander through the world;
Here, Arab-like, is pitched my tent
  And straight again is furled.

Yet oft I dream, that once a wife
  Close to my heart was locked,
And in the sweet repose of life
  A blessed child I rocked.

I wake! Away that dream,—away!
  Too long did it remain!
So long, that both by night and day
  It ever comes again.

The end lies ever in my thought;
  To a grave so cold and deep
The mother beautiful was brought;
  Then dropt the child asleep.

But now the dream is wholly o'er,
  I bathe mine eyes and see;
And wander through the world once more,
  A youth so light and free.

Two locks,—and they are wondrous fair,—
  Left me that vision mild;
The brown is from the mother's hair,
  The blond is from the child.

And when I see that lock of gold,
  Pale grows the evening-red;
And when the dark lock I behold,
  I wish that I were dead.

THE HEMLOCK-TREE.

FROM THE GERMAN.

O hemlock-tree! O hemlock-tree! how faithful are thy branches!
    Green not alone in summer time,
    But in the winter's frost and rime!
O hemlock-tree! O hemlock-tree! how faithful are thy branches!

O maiden fair! O maiden fair! how faithless is thy bosom!
    To love me in prosperity,
    And leave me in adversity!
O maiden fair! O maiden fair! how faithless is thy bosom!

The nightingale, the nightingale, thou tak'st for thine example!
    So long as summer laughs she sings,
    But in the autumn spreads her wings.
The nightingale, the nightingale, thou tak'st for thine example!

The meadow brook, the meadow brook, is mirror of thy falsehood!
    It flows so long as falls the rain,
    In drought its springs soon dry again.
The meadow brook, the meadow brook, is mirror of thy falsehood!

ANNIE OF THARAW.

FROM THE LOW GERMAN OF SIMON DACH.

Annie of Tharaw, my true love of old,
She is my life, and my goods, and my gold.

Annie of Tharaw, her heart once again
To me has surrendered in joy and in pain.

Annie of Tharaw, my riches, my good,
Thou, O my soul, my flesh and my blood!

Then come the wild weather, come sleet or come snow,
We will stand by each other, however it blow.

Oppression, and sickness, and sorrow, and pain,
Shall be to our true love as links to the chain.

As the palm-tree standeth so straight and so tall,
The more the hail beats, and the more the rains fall,—

So love in our hearts shall grow mighty and strong,
Through crosses, through sorrows, through manifold wrong.

Shouldst thou be torn from me to wander alone
In a desolate land where the sun is scarce known,—

Through forests I'll follow, and where the sea flows,
Through ice, and through iron, through armies of foes.

Annie of Tharaw, my light and my sun,
The threads of our two lives are woven in one.

Whate'er I have bidden thee thou hast obeyed,
Whatever forbidden thou hast not gainsaid.

How in the turmoil of life can love stand,
Where there is not one heart, and one mouth, and one hand?

Some seek for dissension, and trouble, and strife;
Like a dog and a cat live such man and wife.

Annie of Tharaw, such is not our love;
Thou art my lambkin, my chick, and my dove.

Whate'er my desire is, in thine may be seen;
I am king of the household, and thou art its queen.

It is this, O my Annie, my heart's sweetest rest,
That makes of us twain but one soul in one breast.

This turns to a heaven the hut where we dwell;
While wrangling soon changes a home to a hell.

D

THE STATUE OVER THE CATHEDRAL DOOR.

FROM THE GERMAN OF JULIUS MOSEN.

Forms of saints and kings are standing
  The cathedral door above;
Yet I saw but one among them
  Who hath soothed my soul with love.

In his mantle,—wound about him,
  As their robes the sowers wind,—

Bore be swallows and their fledglings,
  Flowers and weeds of every kind.

And so stands he calm and childlike,
  High in wind and tempest wild;
O, were I like him exalted,
  I would be like him, a child!

And my songs,—green leaves and blossoms,—
  To the doors of heaven would bear,
Calling, even in storm and tempest,
  Round me still these birds of air.

THE LEGEND OF THE CROSSBILL.

FROM THE GERMAN OF JULIUS MOSEN.

On the cross the dying Saviour
  Heavenward lifts his eyelids calm,
Feels, but scarcely feels, a trembling
  In his pierced and bleeding palm.

And by all the world forsaken,
  Sees he how with zealous care
At the ruthless nail of iron
  A little bird is striving there.

Stained with blood and never tiring,
  With its beak it doth not cease,
From the cross 'twould free the Saviour,
  Its Creator's Son release.

And the Saviour speaks in mildness:
  " Blest be thou of all the good!
Bear, as token of this moment,
  Marks of blood and holy rood!"

And that bird is called the crossbill;
  Covered all with blood so clear,
In the groves of pine it singeth
  Songs, like legends, strange to hear.

THE SEA HATH ITS PEARLS.

FROM THE GERMAN OF HEINRICH HEINE.

The sea hath its pearls,
  The heaven hath its stars;
But my heart, my heart,
  My heart hath its love.

Great are the sea and the heaven;
  Yet greater is my heart,
And fairer than pearls and stars
  Flashes and beams my love.

Thou little, youthful maiden,
  Come unto my great heart:
My heart, and the sea, and the heaven,
  Are melting away with love!

POETIC APHORISMS.

FROM THE MANUSCRIPTS OF FRIEDRICH VON LOGAU.—SEVENTEENTH CENTURY.

* *

MONEY.

WHEREUNTO is money good?
Who has it not wants hardihood,
Who has it has much trouble and care,
Who once has had it has despair.

THE BEST MEDICINES.

Joy and Temperance and Repose
Slam the door on the doctor's nose.

SIN.

Man-like is it to fall into sin,
Fiend-like is it to dwell therein,
Christ-like is it for sin to grieve,
God-like is it all sin to leave.

POVERTY AND BLINDNESS.

A blind man is a poor man, and blind a poor man is;
For the former seeth no man, and the latter no man sees.

LAW OF LIFE.

Live I, so live I,
To my Lord heartily,
To my Prince faithfully,
To my Neighbour honestly,
Die I, so die I.

CREEDS

Lutheran, Popish, Calvinistic, all these creeds and doctrines three
Extant are; but still the doubt is, where Christianity may be.

THE RESTLESS HEART.

A millstone and the human heart are driven ever round;
If they have nothing else to grind, they must themselves be ground.

CHRISTIAN LOVE.

Whilom Love was like a fire, and warmth and comfort it bespoke;
But, alas! it now is quenched, and only bites us, like the smoke.

ART AND TACT.

Intelligence and courtesy not always are combined;
Often in a wooden house a golden room we find.

RETRIBUTION.

Though the mills of God grind slowly, yet they grind exceeding small;
Though with patience he stands waiting, with exactness grinds he all.

TRUTH.

When by night the frogs are croaking, kindle but a torch's fire,
Ha! how soon they all are silent! Thus Truth silences the liar.

RHYMES.

If perhaps these rhymes of mine should sound not well in strangers' ears,
They have only to bethink them that it happens so with theirs;
For so long as words, like mortals, call a fatherland their own,
They will be most highly valued where they are best and longest known.

THE BLIND GIRL OF CASTÈL-CUILLÈ.

FROM THE GASCON OF JASMIN.

Only the Lowland tongue of Scotland might
Rehearse this little tragedy aright :
Let me attempt it with an English quill ;
And take, O Reader, for the deed the will.

I.

At the foot of the mountain height
Where is perched Castèl-Cuillè,
When the apple, the plum, and the almond tree
In the plain below were growing white,
This is the song one might perceive
On a Wednesday morn of Saint Joseph's Eve :

" The roads should blossom, the roads should bloom,
 So fair a bride shall leave her home !
Should blossom and bloom with garlands gay,
 So fair a bride shall pass to-day ! "

This old Te Deum, rustic rites attending,
  Seemed from the clouds descending :
  When lo ! a merry company
Of rosy village girls, clean as the eye,
  Each one with her attendant swain,
Came to the cliff, all singing the same strain ;
Resembling there, so near unto the sky,
Rejoicing angels, that kind Heaven has sent
For their delight and our encouragement.
    Together blending,
    And soon descending
    The narrow sweep
    Of the hill-side steep,
    They wind aslant
    Toward Saint Amant,
    Through leafy alleys
    Of verdurous valleys
    With merry sallies
    Singing their chant :

" The roads should blossom, the roads should bloom,
 So fair a bride shall leave her home !
Should blossom and bloom with garlands gay,
 So fair a bride shall pass to-day ! "

It is Baptiste, and his affianced maiden,
With garlands for the bridal laden !

The sky was blue ; without one cloud of gloom,
 The sun of March was shining brightly,
And to the air the freshening wind gave lightly
 Its breathings of perfume.

When one beholds the dusky hedges blossom,
A rustic bridal, ah! how sweet it is!
   To sounds of joyous melodies,
That touch with tenderness the trembling bosom,
            A band of maidens
            Gaily frolicking,
            A band of youngsters
            Wildly rollicking!
               Kissing,
               Caressing,
         With fingers pressing,
            Till in the veriest
      Madness of mirth, as they dance,
      They retreat and advance,
         Trying whose laugh shall be loudest and merriest;
   While the bride, with anguish eyes,
Sporting with them, now escapes and cries:
   " Those who catch me
            Married verily
            This year shall be!"

   And all pursue with eager haste,
   And all attain what they pursue,
And touch her pretty apron fresh and new,
   And the linen kirtle round her waist.

   Meanwhile, whence comes it that among
   These youthful maidens fresh and fair,
   So joyous, with such laughing air,
   Baptiste stands sighing, with silent tongue?
   And yet the bride is fair and young!
Is it Saint Joseph would say to us all,
That love, o'er-hasty, precedeth a fall?
   O, no! for a maiden frail, I trow,
   Never bore so lofty a brow!
What lovers! they give not a single caress!
To see them so careless and cold to-day,
   These are grand people, one would say.
What ails Baptiste? what grief doth him oppress?

P

It is, that, half way up the hill,
In yon cottage, by whose walls
Stand the cart-house and the stalls,
Dwelleth the blind orphan still,
Daughter of a veteran old ;
And you must know, one year ago,
That Margaret, the young and tender,
Was the village pride and splendor,
And Baptiste her lover bold.
Love, the deceiver, them ensnared ;
For them the altar was prepared ;
But alas! the summer's blight,
The dread disease that none can stay,
The pestilence that walks by night,
Took the young bride's sight away.

All at the father's stern command was changed ;
Their peace was gone, but not their love estranged ;
Wearied at home, ere long the lover fled ;
Returned but three short days ago,
The golden chain they round him throw,
He is enticed, and onward led
To marry Angela, and yet
Is thinking ever of Margaret.

Then suddenly a maiden cried,
  "Anna, Theresa, Mary, Kate!
Here comes the cripple Jane!" And by a fountain's side
  A woman, bent and gray with years,
  Under the mulberry-trees appears,
  And all towards her run, as fleet
  As had they wings upon their feet.

  It is that Jane, the cripple Jane,
 .Is a soothsayer, wary and kind.
She telleth fortunes, and none complain.
  She promises one a village swain,
  Another a happy wedding-day,
  And the bride a lovely boy straightway.
  All comes to pass as she avers;
  She never deceives, she never errs.

  But for this once the village seer
  Wears a countenance severe,
And from beneath her eyebrows thin and white
  Her two eyes flash like cannons bright

Aimed at the bridegroom in waistcoat blue,
Who, like a statue, stands in view :
Changing color, as well he might,
When the beldame wrinkled and gray
Takes the young bride by the hand,
And, with the tip of her reedy wand
Making the sign of the cross, doth say :—
" Thoughtless Angela, beware !
Lest, when thou weddest this false bridegroom,
Thou diggest for thyself a tomb !"

And she was silent ; and the maidens fair
Saw from each eye escape a swollen tear ;
But on a little streamlet silver-clear,
 What are two drops of turbid rain ?
 Saddened a moment, the bridal train
 Resumed the dance and song again ;
The bridegroom only was pale with fear ;—
  And down green alleys
  Of verdurous valleys,
  With merry sallies,
  They sang the refrain :—

" The roads should blossom, the roads should bloom,
So fair a bride shall leave her home !
Should blossom and bloom with garlands gay,
So fair a bride shall pass to-day !"

II.

 And by suffering worn and weary,
But beautiful as some fair angel yet,
 Thus lamented Margaret,
 In her cottage lone and dreary :—

 " He has arrived ! arrived at last !
Yet Jane has named him not these three days past ;
 Arrived ! yet keeps aloof so far !
And knows that of my night he is the star !

Knows that long months I wait alone, benighted,
And count the moments since he went away!
Come! keep the promise of that happier day,
That I may keep the faith to thee I plighted!
What joy have I without thee? what delight?
Grief wastes my life, and makes it misery;
Day for the others ever, but for me
　　For ever night! for ever night!
When he is gone 'tis dark! my soul is sad!
I suffer! O my God! come, make me glad.
When he is near, no thoughts of day intrude;
Day has blue heavens, but Baptiste has blue eyes!
Within them shines for me a heaven of love,
A heaven all happiness, like that above,
　　No more of grief! no more of lassitude!
Earth I forget,—and heaven, and all distresses,
When seated by my side my hand he presses;
　　But when alone, remember all!
Where is Baptiste? he hears not when I call!
A branch of ivy, dying on the ground,
　　I need some bough to twine around!
In pity come! be to my suffering kind!
True love, they say, in grief doth more abound!
　　What then—when one is blind?

　　" Who knows? perhaps I am forsaken!
Ah! woe is me! then bear me to my grave!
　　O God! what thoughts within me waken!
Away! he will return! I do but rave!
　　He will return! I need not fear!
　　He swore it by our Saviour dear;
　　He could not come at his own will;
　　Is weary, or perhaps is ill!
　　Perhaps his heart, in this disguise,
　　Prepares for me some sweet surprise!
But some one comes! Though blind, my heart can see!
And that deceives me not! 'tis he! 'tis he!"
　　And the door ajar is set,
　　And poor, confiding Margaret
Risen, with outstretched arms, but sightless eyes;
'Tis only Paul, her brother, who thus cries:—

TRANSLATIONS

" Angela the bride has passed !
I saw the wedding guests go by ;
Tell me, my sister, why were we not asked ?
For all are there but you and I !"

" Angela married ! and not send
To tell her secret unto me !
O, speak ! who may the bridegroom be ?"
" My sister, 'tis Baptiste, thy friend !"

A cry the blind girl gave, but nothing said ;
A milky whiteness spreads upon her cheeks ;
An icy hand, as heavy as lead,
Descending, as her brother speaks,
Upon her heart, that has ceased to beat,
Suspends awhile its life and heat.
She stands beside the boy, now sore distressed,
A wax Madonna as a peasant dressed.

At length, the bridal song again
Brings her back to her sorrow and pain.

" Hark ! the joyous airs are ringing !
Sister, dost thou hear them singing ?
How merrily they laugh and jest !
Would we were bidden with the rest !
I would don my hose of homespun gray,
And my doublet of linen striped and gay ;
Perhaps they will come ; for they do not wed
Till to-morrow at seven o'clock, it is said !"
" I know it !" answered Margaret ;
Whom the vision, with aspect black as jet,
Mastered again ; and its hand of ice
Held her heart crushed, as in a vice !
" Paul, be not sad ! 'Tis a holiday ;
To-morrow put on thy doublet gay !
But leave me now for a while alone."
Away, with a hop and a jump, went Paul,
And, as he whistled along the hall,
Entered Jane, the crippled crone.

" Holy Virgin ! what dreadful heat !
  I am faint, and weary, and out of breath !
  But thou art cold,—art chill as death ;
  My little friend ! what ails thee, sweet ? "
" Nothing ! I heard them singing home the bride :
  And, as I listened to the song,
  I thought my turn would come ere long,
  Thou knowest it is at Whitsuntide.
  Thy curls forsooth can never lie,
  To me such joy they prophesy,
  Thy skill shall be vaunted far and wide
  When they behold him at my side.
  And poor Baptiste, what sayest thou ?
It must seem long to him ;—methinks I see him now ! "
    Jane, shuddering, her hand doth press :
  " Thy love I cannot all approve ;
We must not trust too much to happiness ;—
Go, pray to God, that thou mayst love him less ! "
  " The more I pray, the more I love !
It is no sin, for God is on my side ! "
It was enough ; and Jane no more replied.

Now to all hope her heart is barred and cold ;
  But to deceive the beldame old
  She takes a sweet, contented air ;
  Speak of foul weather or of fair,
  At every word the maiden smiles !
  Thus the beguiler she beguiles ;
So that, departing at the evening's close,
  She says, " She may be saved ! she nothing knows ! "

  Poor Jane, the cunning sorceress !
Now that thou wouldst, thou art no prophetess !
This morning, in the fulness of thy heart,
  Thou wast so, far beyond thine art !

III.

Now rings the bell, nine times reverberating,
And the white daybreak, stealing up the sky,
Sees in two cottages two maidens waiting,
     How differently!

Queen of a day, by flatterers caressed,
    The one puts on her cross and crown,
    Decks with a huge bouquet her breast,
    And flaunting, fluttering up and down,
    Looks at herself, and cannot rest.

The other, blind, within her little room,
Has neither crown nor flower's perfume ;
But in their stead for something gropes apart
That in a drawer's recess doth lie,
And, 'neath her boddice of bright scarlet dye,
Convulsive clasps it to her heart.

The one, fantastic, light as air,
'Mid kisses ringing,
And joyous singing,
Forgets to say her morning prayer !

The other, with cold drops upon her brow,
Joins her two hands, and kneels upon the floor,
And whispers, as her brother opes the door,
" O God ! forgive me now ! "

And then the orphan, young and blind,
Conducted by her brother's hand,
Towards the church, through paths unscanned,
With tranquil air, her way doth wind.

Odors of laurel, making her faint and pale,
  Round her at times exhale,
And in the sky as yet no sunny ray,
  But brumal vapors gray.

  Near that castle, fair to see,
Crowded with sculptures old, in every part,
  Marvels of nature and of art,
    And proud of its name of high degree.
  A little chapel, almost bare
  At the base of the rock, is builded there;
  All glorious that it lifts aloof,
  Above each jealous cottage roof,
Its sacred summit, swept by autumn gales,
  And its blackened steeple high in air,
  Round which the osprey screams and sails.

  " Paul, lay thy noisy rattle by!"
Thus Margaret said.   " Where are we? we several!"
    " Yes; seest thou not our journey's end?
Hearest not the osprey from the belfry cry?
The hideous bird, that brings ill luck, we know!
Dost thou remember when our father said,
    The night we watched beside his bed,
  ' O daughter, I am weak and low;
Take care of Paul; I feel that I am dying!'
And thou, and he, and I, all fell to crying?
Then on the roof the osprey screamed aloud;
And here they brought our father in his shroud.
There is his grave; there stands the cross we set;
Why dost thou clasp me so, dear Margaret?
    Come in!   The bride will be here soon:
Thou tremblest!   O my God! thou art going to swoon!"
She could no more,—the blind girl, weak and weary!
A voice seemed crying from that grave so dreary,
" What wouldst thou do, my daughter?"—and she started;
    And quick recoiled, aghast, faint-hearted;
But Paul, impatient, urges ever more
    Her steps towards the open door;
  And when, beneath her feet, the unhappy maid

Crushes the laurel near the house immortal,
And with her head, as Paul talks on again,
  Touches the crown of filigrane
  Suspended from the low-arched portal,
  No more restrained, no more afraid,
  She walks, as for a feast arrayed.
And in the ancient chapel's sombre night
  They both are lost to sight.

            At length the bell,
            With booming sound,
            Sends forth, resounding round,
Its hymeneal peal o'er rock and down the dell.
    It is broad day, with sunshine and with rain ;
    And yet the guests delay not long,
    For soon arrives the bridal train,
    And with it brings the village throng.

In sooth, deceit maketh no mortal gay,
For lo! Baptiste on this triumphant day,
Mute as an idiot, sad as yester-morning,
Thinks only of the beldame's words of warning.

And Angela thinks of her cross, I wis ;
To be a bride is all! The pretty lisper
Feels her heart swell to hear all round her whisper,
" How beautiful! how beautiful she is! "

        But she must calm that giddy head,
        For already the Mass is said ;
        At the holy table stands the priest ;
The wedding ring is blessed ; Baptiste receives it ;
Ere on the finger of the bride he leaves it,
    He must pronounce one word at least !
'Tis spoken ; and sudden at the groomsman's side
" 'Tis he! " a well-known voice has cried.
And while the wedding guests all hold their breath,
Opes the confessional, and the blind girl, see !
" Baptiste," she said, " since thou hast wished my death,
As holy water be my blood for thee! "
    And calmly in the air a knife suspended !
    Doubtless her guardian angel near attended,

For anguish did its work so well,
That, ere the fatal stroke descended,
      Lifeless she fell!

At eve, instead of bridal verse,
The De Profundis filled the air;
Decked with flowers a single bearse
To the church-yard forth they bear;
Village girls in robes of snow
Follow, weeping as they go:
Nowhere was a smile that day,
No, ah no! for each one seemed to say :—

  " The roads shall mourn and be veiled in gloom,
    So fair a corpse shall leave its home!
    Should mourn and should weep, ah, well-away!
    So fair a corpse shall pass to-day!"

JASMIN, the author of this beautiful poem, is to the South of France what Burns is to the North of Scotland,—the representative of the heart of the people,—one of those happy bards who are born with their mouths full of birds (la bouche pleine d'oiseaux). He has written his own biography in a poetic form, and the simple narrative of his poverty, his struggles and his triumphs, is very touching. He still lives at Agen, on the Garonne; and long may he live there to delight his native land with native songs!

Those who may feel interested in knowing something about " Jasmin, Coiffeur "— for such is his calling—will find a description of his person and mode of life in the graphic pages of Bears and the Pyrenees (Vol. I. p. 369, et seq.), by Louisa Stuart Costello, whose charming pen has done so much to illustrate the French provinces and their literature

A CHRISTMAS CAROL.[*]

FROM THE NOEL BOURGUIGNON DE GUI BAROZAI

I steal along our street
Pass the minstrel throngs;
Hark! they play so sweet,
On their hautboys, Christmas songs!
Let us by the fire
Ever higher
Sing them till the night expire!

In December ring
Every day the chimes;
Loud the gleemen sing
In the streets their merry rhymes,

* For an interesting and minute description of Christmas in Burgundy, the curious reader is referred to M. Perthault's *Coup d'œil sur les Noels en Bourgogne*, prefixed to the Paris edition of *Les Noels Bourguignons de Bernard de la Monnoye* (Gui Barozai), 1842.

Let us by the fire
Ever higher
Sing them till the night expire.

Shepherds at the grange,
Where the Babe was born,
Sang, with many a change,
Christmas carols until morn.
Let us by the fire
Ever higher
Sing them till the night expire!

These good people sang
Songs devout and sweet;
While the rafters rang,
There they stood with freezing feet.
Let us by the fire
Ever higher
Sing them till the night expire.

Nuns in frigid cells
At this holy tide,
For want of something else,
Christmas songs at times have tried
Let us by the fire
Ever higher
Sing them till the night expire!

Washerwomen old,
To the sound they beat,
Sing by rivers cold,
With uncovered heads and feet.
Let us by the fire
Ever higher
Sing them till the night expire.

Who by the fireside stands
Stamps his feet and sings;
But he who blows his hands
Not so gay a carol brings.
Let us by the fire
Ever higher
Sing them till the night expire!

BALLADS.

THE SKELETON IN ARMOUR.

PREFATORY NOTE.

THE following Ballad was suggested to me while riding on the sea-shore at Newport. A year or two previous a skeleton had been dug up at Fall River, clad in broken and corroded armour; and the idea occurred to me of connecting it with the Round Tower at Newport, generally known hitherto as the Old Windmill, though now claimed by the Danes as a work of their early ancestors. Professor Rafn, in the *Mémoires de la Société Royale des Antiquaires du Nord*, for 1838-9, says,—

"There is no mistaking in this instance the style in which the more ancient stone edifices of the North were constructed, the style which belongs to the Roman or Ante-Gothic architecture, and which, especially after the time of Charlemagne, diffused itself from Italy over the whole of the West and North of Europe, where it continued to predominate until the close of the twelfth century; that style which some authors have, from one of its most striking characteristics, called the round arch style, the same which in England is denominated Saxon and sometimes Norman architecture.

"On the ancient structure in Newport there are no ornaments remaining, which might possibly have served to guide us in assigning the probable date of its erection. That no vestige whatever is found of the pointed arch, nor any approximation to it, is indicative of an earlier rather than of a later period. From such characteristics as remain, however, we can scarcely form any other inference than one, in which I am persuaded that all, who are familiar with Old-Northern architecture, will concur, THAT THIS BUILDING WAS ERECTED AT A PERIOD DECIDEDLY NOT LATER THAN THE TWELFTH CENTURY. This remark applies, of course, to the original building only, and not to the alterations that it subsequently received; for there are several such alterations in the upper part of the building which cannot be mistaken, and which were most likely occasioned by its being adapted in modern times to various uses, for example, as the substructure of a windmill, and latterly as a hay magazine. To the same times may be referred the windows, the galleries, and the apertures made above the columns. That this building could not have been erected for a windmill is what an architect will easily discern."

I will not enter into a discussion of the point. It is sufficiently well established for the purpose of a ballad, though doubtless many an honest citizen of Newport, who has passed his days within sight of the Round Tower, will be ready to exclaim with Sancho, "God bless me! did I not warn you to have a care of what you were doing, for that it was nothing but a windmill? and nobody could mistake it, but one who had the like in his head."

THE SKELETON IN ARMOUR.

" Speak ! speak ! thou fearful guest !
  Who, with thy hollow breast
  Still in rude armour drest,
      Comest to daunt me !

Wrapt not in Eastern balms,
But with thy fleshless palms
Stretched, as if asking alms,
    Why dost thou haunt me ? "

Then, from those cavernous eyes
Pale flashes seemed to rise,
As when the Northern skies
  Gleam in December;
And, like the water's flow
Under December's snow,
Came a dull voice of woe
  From the heart's chamber.

"I was a Viking old!
My deeds, though manifold,
No Skald in song has told,
  No Saga taught thee!
Take heed, that in thy verse
Thou dost the tale rehearse,
Else dread a dead man's curse!
  For this I sought thee.

"Far in the Northern Land,
By the wild Baltic's strand,
I, with my childish hand,
  Tamed the gerfalcon;
And, with my skates fast-bound,
Skimmed the half-frozen Sound,
That the poor whimpering hound
  Trembled to walk on.

"Oft to his frozen lair
Tracked I the grisly bear,
While from my path the hare
  Fled like a shadow;
Oft through the forest dark
Followed the were-wolf's bark,
Until the soaring lark
  Sang from the meadow.

"But when I older grew,
Joining a corsair's crew,
O'er the dark sea I flew
  With the marauders.
Wild was the life we led;
Many the souls that sped,
Many the hearts that bled,
  By our stern orders.

"Many a wassail-bout
Wore the long Winter out;
Often our midnight shout
  Set the cocks crowing,
As we the Berserk's tale
Measured in cups of ale,
Draining the oaken pail,
  Filled to o'erflowing.

"Once as I told in glee
Tales of the stormy sea,
Soft eyes did gaze on me,
  Burning yet tender;
And as the white stars shine
On the dark Norway pine,
On that dark heart of mine
  Fell their soft splendour.

"I wooed the blue-eyed maid,
Yielding, yet half afraid,
And in the forest's shade
  Our vows were plighted.
Under its loosened vest
Fluttered her little breast,
Like birds within their nest
  By the hawk frighted.

"Bright in her father's hall
Shields gleamed upon the wall,
Loud sang the minstrels all,
  Chaunting his glory;
When of old Hildebrand
I asked his daughter's hand,
Mute did the minstrels stand
  To hear my story.

"While the brown ale he quaffed,
Loud then the champion laughed,
And as the wind-gusts waft
  The sea-foam brightly,
So the loud laugh of scorn,
Out of those lips unshorn,
From the deep drinking-horn
  Blew the foam lightly.

" She was a Prince's child,
  I but a Viking wild,
And though she blushed and smiled,
    I was discarded !
Should not the dove so white
Follow the sea-mew's flight,
Why did they leave that night
    Her nest unguarded ?

" Scarce had I put to sea,
Bearing the maid with me,—
Fairest of all was she
    Among the Norsemen !—
When on the white-sea strand,
Waving his armèd hand,
Saw we old Hildebrand,
    With twenty horsemen

" Then launched they to the blast,
Bent like a reed each mast,
Yet we were gaining fast,
    When the wind failed us ;
And with a sudden flaw
Came round the gusty Skaw,
So that our foe we saw
    Laugh as he hailed us.

" And as to catch the gale
Round veered the flapping sail,
Death ! was the helmsman's hail,
    Death without quarter !
Mid-ships with iron keel
Struck we her ribs of steel ;
Down her black hulk did reel
    Through the black water !

" As with his wings aslant,
Sails the fierce cormorant,
Seeking some rocky haunt,
    With his prey laden ;

So toward the open main,
Beating to sea again,
Through the wild hurricane,
    Bore I the maiden.

" Three weeks we westward bore,
And when the storm was o'er,
Cloud-like we saw the shore
    Stretching to lee-ward ;
There for my lady's bower
Built I the lofty tower,
Which, to this very hour,
    Stands looking sea-ward.

" There lived we many years ;
Time dried the maiden's tears ;
She had forgot her fears,
    She was a mother ;
Death closed her mild blue eyes,
Under that tower she lies ;
Ne'er shall the sun arise
    On such another !

" Still grew my bosom then,
Still as a stagnant fen !
Hateful to me were men,
    The sun-light hateful !
In the vast forest here,
Clad in my warlike gear,
Fell I upon my spear,
    O, death was grateful !

" Thus, seamed with many scars
Bursting these prison bars,
Up to its native stars
    My soul ascended !
There from the flowing bowl
Deep drinks the warrior's soul,
Skoal ! to the Northland ! skoal !"*
    —Thus the tale ended.

---

* In Scandinavia this is the customary salutation when drinking a health. I have slightly
changed the orthography of the word, in order to preserve the correct pronunciation.

THE WRECK OF THE HESPERUS.

It was the schooner Hesperus,
    That sailed the wintry sea;
And the skipper had taken his little daughter,
    To bear him company.

Blue were her eyes as the fairy-flax,
    Her cheeks like the dawn of day,
And her bosom white as the hawthorn buds,
    That ope in the mouth of May.

The skipper he stood beside the helm,
    His pipe was in his mouth,
And he watched how the veering flaw did blow
    The smoke now West, now South.

Then up and spake an old Sailor,
    Had sailed the Spanish Main,
"I pray thee, put into yonder port,
    For I fear a hurricane.

"Last night, the moon had a golden ring,
    And to-night no moon we see!"
The skipper, he blew a whiff from his pipe,
    And a scornful laugh laughed he.

Colder and louder blew the wind,
    A gale from the North-east;
The snow fell hissing in the brine,
    And the billows frothed like yeast.

Down came the storm, and smote amain
    The vessel in its strength;
She shuddered and paused, like a frighted steed,
    Then leaped her cable's length.   .

"Come hither! come hither! my little daughter,
    And do not tremble so;
For I can weather the roughest gale
    That ever wind did blow."

He wrapped her warm in his seaman's coat
    Against the stinging blast;
He cut a rope from a broken spar,
    And bound her to the mast.

"O father! I hear the church-bells ring,
    O say, what may it be?"
  "'Tis a fog-bell on a rock-bound coast!"
    And he steered for the open sea.

"O father! I hear the sound of guns,
    O say, what may it be?"
"Some ship in distress, that cannot live
    In such an angry sea!"

"O father! I see a gleaming light,
    O say, what may it be?"
But the father answered never a word,
    A frozen corpse was he.

Lashed to the helm, all stiff and stark,
    With his face turned to the skies,
The lantern gleamed through the gleaming snow
    On his fixed and glassy eyes.

Then the maiden clasped her hands and prayed
    That saved she might be;
And she thought of Christ, who stilled the wave,
    On the Lake of Galilee.

And fast through the midnight dark and drear,
    Through the whistling sleet and snow,
Like a sheeted ghost, the vessel swept
    Towards the reef of Norman's Woe.

And ever the fitful gusts between
    A sound came from the land;
It was the sound of the trampling surf,
    On the rocks and the hard sea-sand.

The breakers were right beneath her bows,
    She drifted a dreary wreck,
And a whooping billow swept the crew
    Like icicles from her deck.

She struck where the white and fleecy waves
    Looked soft as carded wool,
But the cruel rocks, they gored her side
    Like the horns of an angry bull.

Her rattling shrouds, all sheathed in ice,
    With the masts went by the board;
Like a vessel of glass, she stove and sank,
    Ho! ho! the breakers roared!

At daybreak, on the bleak sea-beach,
    A fisherman stood aghast,
To see the form of a maiden fair,
    Lashed close to a drifting mast.

The salt sea was frozen on her breast,
    The salt tears in her eyes;
And he saw her hair, like the brown sea-weed,
    On the billows fall and rise.

Such was the wreck of the Hesperus,
    In the midnight and the snow!
Christ save us all from a death like this,
    On the reef of Norman's Woe!

THE LUCK OF EDENHALL.

FROM THE GERMAN OF UHLAND.

Of Edenhall, the youthful Lord
Bids sound the festal trumpet's call;
He rises at the banquet board,
And cries, 'mid the drunken revellers all,
"Now bring me the Luck of Edenhall!"

The butler hears the words with pain,
The house's oldest seneschal,
Takes slow from its silken cloth again
The drinking glass of crystal tall;
They call it The Luck of Edenhall.

Then said the Lord; "This glass to praise,
Fill with red wine from Portugal!"
The gray-beard with trembling hand obeys:
A purple light shines over all,
It beams from the Luck of Edenhall.

Then speaks the Lord, and waves it light,
"This glass of flashing crystal tall
Gave to my sires the Fountain-Sprite;
She wrote in it; *If this glass doth fall,*
Farewell then, O Luck of Edenhall!

"'Twas right a goblet the Fate should be
Of the joyous race of Edenhall!
Deep draughts drink we right willingly;
And willingly ring, with merry call,
Kling! klang! to the Luck of Edenhall!"

First rings it deep, and full, and mild,
Like to the song of a nightingale;
Then like the roar of a torrent wild;
Then mutters at last like the thunder's fall,
The glorious Luck of Edenhall.

" For its keeper takes a race of might,
The fragile goblet of crystal tall;
It has lasted longer than is right;
Kling! klang!—with a harder blow than all
Will I try the Luck of Edenhall!"

As the goblet ringing flies apart,
Suddenly cracks the vaulted hall;
And through the rift, the wild flames start;
The guests in dust are scattered all,
With the Breaking Luck of Edenhall!

In storms the foe, with fire and sword;
He in the night had scaled the wall,
Slain by the sword lies the youthful Lord,
But holds in his hand the crystal tall,
The shattered Luck of Edenhall.

On the morrow the butler gropes alone,
The gray-beard in the desert hall,
He seeks his Lord's burnt skeleton,
He seeks in the dismal ruin's fall
The shards of the Luck of Edenhall.

" The stone wall," saith he, " doth fall aside,
Down must the stately columns fall;
Glass is this earth's Luck and Pride;
In atoms shall fall this earthly hall
One day like the Luck of Edenhall!"

[The tradition upon which this ballad is founded, and the "shards of the Luck of Edenhall," still exist in England. The goblet is in the possession of Sir Christopher Musgrave, Bart. of Eden Hall, Cumberland; and is not so entirely shattered as the ballad leaves it.]

THE ELECTED KNIGHT.

FROM THE DANISH.

Sir Oluf he rideth over the plain,
  Full seven miles broad and seven miles wide,
But never, ah never can meet with the man
  A tilt with him dare ride.

He saw under the hill-side
  A Knight full well equipped :
His steed was black, his helm was barred ;
  He was riding at full speed.

He wore upon his spurs
  Twelve little golden birds ;
Anon he spurred his steed with a clang,
  And there sat all the birds and sang.

He wore upon his mail
  Twelve little golden wheels ;
Anon in eddies the wild wind blew,
  And round and round the wheels they flew.

He wore before his breast
  A lance that was poised in rest ;
And it was sharper than diamond-stone,
  It made Sir Oluf's heart to groan.

He wore upon his helm
  A wreath of ruddy gold ;
And that gave him the Maidens Three,
  The youngest was fair to behold.

Sir Oluf questioned the Knight eftsoon
  If he were come from heaven down ;
" Art thou Christ of Heaven," quoth he,
  " So will I yield me unto thee."

" I am not Christ the Great,
  Thou shalt not yield thee yet ;
I am an Unknown Knight,
  Three maidens have me bedight."

" Art thou a Knight elected,
  And have three Maidens thee bedight ;
So shalt thou ride a tilt this day,
  For all the Maidens' honor !"

The first tilt they together rode,
  They put their steeds to the test ;
The second tilt they together rode,
  They proved their manhood best ;

The third tilt they together rode,
  Neither of them would yield ;
The fourth tilt they together rode,
  They both fell on the field.

Now lie the lords upon the plain,
  And their blood runs unto death ;
Now sit the Maidens in the high tower,
  The youngest sorrows till death.

———   ———

[This strange and somewhat mystical ballad is from Syrup and Nahlek's *Danske Viser* of the Middle Ages. It seems to refer to the first preaching of Christianity in the North, and to the institution of Knight-Errantry. The three maidens I suppose to be Faith, Hope, and Charity. The irregularities of the original have been carefully preserved in the translation.]

POEMS ON SLAVERY.

1842.

— —

[The following Poems with one exception, were written at sea, in the latter part of October. I had not then heard of Dr. Channing's death. Since that event the poem addressed to him is no longer appropriate. I have decided, however, to let it remain as it was written, a feeble testimony of my admiration for a great and good man.]

— —

TO WILLIAM E. CHANNING.

The pages of thy book I read,
  And as I closed each one,
My heart, responding, ever said,
  "Servant of God! well done!"

Well done! Thy words are great and bold;
  At times they seem to me,
Like Luther's, in the days of old,
  Half-battles for the free.

Go on, until this land revokes
  The old and chartered Lie,
The feudal curse, whose whips and yokes
  Insult humanity.

A voice is ever at thy side
  Speaking in tones of might,
Like the prophetic voice, that cried,
  To John in Patmos, "Write!"

Write! and tell out this bloody tale:
  Record this dire eclipse,
This Day of Wrath, this Endless Wail,
  This dread Apocalypse.

THE SLAVE'S DREAM.

Beside the ungathered rice he lay,
  His sickle in his hand;
His breast was bare, his matted hair
  Was buried in the sand,
Again, in the mist and shadow of sleep,
  He saw his Native Land.

Wide through the landscape of his dreams
  The lordly Niger flowed;
Beneath the palm-trees on the plain
  Once more a king he strode;
And heard the tinkling caravans
  Descend the mountain-road.

He saw once more his dark-eyed queen
  Among her children stand;
They clasped his neck, they kissed his cheeks,
  They held him by the hand!—
A tear burst from the sleeper's lids
  And fell into the sand.

And then at furious speed he rode
  Along the Niger's bank;
His bridle-reins were golden chains,
  And, with a martial clank,
At each leap he could feel his scabbard of steel
  Smiting his stallion's flank.

Before him, like a blood-red flag,
  The bright flamingoes flew;
From morn till night he followed their flight,
  O'er plains where the tamarind grew,
Till he saw the roofs of Caffre huts,
  And the ocean rose to view.

At night he heard the lion roar,
  And the hyena scream;
And the river-horse, as he crushed the reeds
  Beside some hidden stream;
And it passed, like a glorious roll of drums,
  Through the triumph of his dream.

The forests, with their myriad tongues,
  Shouted of liberty;
And the Blast of the Desert cried aloud,
  With a voice so wild and free,
That he started in his sleep and smiled
  At their tempestuous glee.

He did not feel the driver's whip,
  Nor the burning heat of day;
For Death had illumined the Land of Sleep,
  And his lifeless body lay
A worn-out fetter, that the soul
  Had broken and thrown away!

—

THE GOOD PART,

THAT SHALL NOT BE TAKEN AWAY.

She dwells by Great Kenhawa's side,
  In valleys green and cool;
And all her hope and all her pride
  Are in the village school.

Her soul, like the transparent air
  That robes the hills above,
Though not of earth, encircles there
  All things with arms of love.

And thus she walks among her girls
  With praise and mild rebukes;
Subduing e'en rude village churls
  By her angelic looks.

She reads to them at eventide
  Of one who came to save;
To cast the captive's chains aside,
  And liberate the slave.

And oft the blessed time foretells
  When all men shall be free;
And musical, as silver bells,
  Their falling chains shall be.

And following her beloved Lord,
  In decent poverty,
She makes her life one sweet record
  And deed of charity.

For she was rich, and gave up all
  To break the iron bands
Of those who waited in her hall,
  And labored in her lands.

Long since beyond the Southern sea
  Their outbound sails have sped,
While she, in meek humility,
  Now earns her daily bread.

It is their prayers, which never cease,
  That clothe her with such grace;
Their blessing is the light of peace
  That shines upon her face.

THE SLAVE IN THE DISMAL SWAMP.

In dark fens of the Dismal Swamp
  The hunted Negro lay;
He saw the fire of the midnight camp,
And heard at times a horse's tramp
  And a bloodhound's distant bay.

Where will-o'-the-wisps and glow-worms shine,
  In bulrush and in brake;
Where waving mosses shroud the pine,
And the cedar grows, and the poisonous vine
  Is spotted like the snake;

Where hardly a human foot could pass,
  Or a human heart would dare,
On the quaking turf of the green morass
He crouched in the rank and tangled grass,
  Like a wild beast in his lair.

A poor old slave, infirm and lame;
  Great scars deformed his face;
On his forehead he bore the brand of shame,
And the rags, that hid his mangled frame,
  Were the livery of disgrace.

All things above were bright and fair,
  All things were glad and free;
Lithe squirrels darted here and there,
And wild birds filled the echoing air
  With songs of Liberty!

On him alone was the doom of pain,
  From the morning of his birth;
On him alone the curse of Cain
Fell, like a flail on the garnered grain,
  And struck him to the earth!

*

THE WITNESSES.

In Ocean's wide domains,
  Half buried in the sands,
Lie skeletons in chains,
  With shackled feet and hands.

T

POEMS ON SLAVERY.

Beyond the fall of dews,
    Deeper than plummet lies,
Float ships with all their crews,
    No more to sink nor rise.

There the black Slave-ship swims,
    Freighted with human forms,
Whose fettered, fleshless limbs
    Are not the sport of storms.

These are the bones of Slaves;
    They gleam from the abyss;
They cry, from yawning waves,
    "We are the Witnesses!"

Within Earth's wide domains
    Are markets for men's lives;
Their necks are galled with chains,
    Their wrists are cramped with gyves.

Dead bodies, that the kite
    In deserts makes its prey;
Murders, that with affright
    Scare schoolboys from their play!

All evil thoughts and deeds;
    Anger, and lust, and pride;
The foulest, rankest weeds,
    That choke Life's groaning tide!

These are the woes of Slaves;
    They glare from the abyss;
They cry, from unknown graves,
    "We are the Witnesses!"

THE SLAVE SINGING AT MIDNIGHT.

Loud he sang the Psalm of David!
He, a Negro and enslaved,
Sang of Israel's victory,
Sang of Zion, bright and free.

In that hour, when night is calmest,
Sang he from the Hebrew Psalmist,
In a voice so sweet and clear
That I could not choose but hear.

Songs of triumph, and ascriptions,
Such as reached the swart Egyptians,
When upon the Red Sea coast
Perished Pharaoh and his host.

And the voice of his devotion
Filled my soul with strange emotion:
For its tones by turns were glad,
Sweetly solemn, wildly sad.

Paul and Silas, in their prison,
Sang of Christ, the Lord arisen,
And an earthquake's arm of might
Broke their dungeon-gates at night.

But, alas! what holy angel
Brings the Slave this glad evangel?
And what earthquake's arm of might
Breaks his dungeon-gates at night?

THE QUADROON GIRL.

THE Slaver in the broad lagoon
    Lay moored with idle sail;
He waited for the rising moon,
    And for the evening gale.

Under the shore his boat was tied,
    And all her listless crew
Watched the gray alligator slide
    Into the still bayou.

Odors of orange-flowers, and spice,
    Reached them from time to time,
Like airs that breathe from Paradise
    Upon a world of crime.

The Planter, under his roof of thatch,
    Smoked thoughtfully and slow;
The Slaver's thumb was on the latch,
    He seemed in haste to go.

He said, "My ship at anchor rides
  In yonder broad lagoon;
I only wait the evening tides,
  And the rising of the moon."

Before them, with her face upraised,
  In timid attitude,
Like one half curious, half amazed,
  A Quadroon maiden stood.

Her eyes were large, and full of light,
  Her arms and neck were bare;
No garment she wore, save a kirtle bright,
  And her own long, raven hair.

And on her lips there played a smile
  As holy, meek, and faint,
As lights in some cathedral aisle
  The features of a saint.

"The soil is barren,—the farm is old;"
  The thoughtful Planter said;
Then looked upon the Slaver's gold,
  And then upon the maid.

His heart within him was at strife
  With such accursed gains;
For he knew whose passions gave her life,
  Whose blood ran in her veins.

But the voice of nature was too weak;
  He took the glittering gold!
Then pale as death grew the maiden's cheek,
  Her hands as icy cold.

The Slaver led her from the door,
  He led her by the hand,
To be his slave and paramour
  In a strange and distant land!

THE WARNING.

Beware! The Israelite of old, who tore
    The lion in his path,—when, poor and blind,
He saw the blessed light of heaven no more,
    Shorn of his noble strength and forced to grind
In prison, and at last led forth to be
A pander to Philistine revelry,—

Upon the pillars of the temple laid
    His desperate hands, and in its overthrow
Destroyed himself, and with him those who made
    A cruel mockery of his sightless woe;
The poor, blind Slave, the scoff and jest of all,
Expired, and thousands perished in the fall!

There is a poor, blind Samson in this land,
    Shorn of his strength, and bound in bonds of steel,
Who may, in some grim revel, raise his hand,
    And shake the pillars of this Commonweal,
Till the vast Temple of our liberties
A shapeless mass of wreck and rubbish lies.

SONGS

·

SEA-WEED.

When descends on the Atlantic
    The gigantic
Storm-wind of the equinox,
Landward in his wrath he scourges
    The toiling surges,
Laden with sea-weed from the rocks:

From Bermuda's reefs; from edges
    Of sunken ledges,
In some far-off, bright Azore;
From Bahama, and the dashing,
    Silver-flashing
Surges of San Salvador;

From the tumbling surf, that buries
 The Orkneyan skerries,
Answering the hoarse Hebrides;
And from wrecks of ships, and drifting
 Spars, uplifting
On the desolate, rainy seas;—

Ever drifting, drifting, drifting
 On the shifting
Currents of the restless main;
Till in sheltered coves, and reaches
 Of sandy beaches,
All have found repose again.

So when storms of wild emotion
 Strike the ocean
Of the poet's soul, ere long
From each cave and rocky fastness,
 In its vastness,
Floats some fragment of a song:

From the far-off isles enchanted,
 Heaven has planted
With the golden fruit of Truth;
From the flashing surf, whose vision
 Gleams Elysian
In the tropic clime of Youth;

From the strong Will, and the Endeavour
 That forever
Wrestle with the tides of Fate;
From the wreck of Hopes far-scattered,
 Tempest-shattered,
Floating waste and desolate;—

Ever drifting, drifting, drifting
 On the shifting
Currents of the restless heart;
Till at length in books recorded,
 They, like hoarded
Household words, no more depart.

THE DAY IS DONE.

The day is done, and the darkness
    Falls from the wings of Night,
As a feather is wafted downward
    From an eagle in his flight.

I see the lights of the village
    Gleam through the rain and the mist,
And a feeling of sadness comes o'er me,
    That my soul cannot resist:

A feeling of sadness and longing,
    That is not akin to pain,
And resembles sorrow only
    As the mist resembles the rain.

Come, read to me some poem,
  Some simple and heartfelt lay,
That shall soothe this restless feeling.
  And banish the thoughts of day.

Not from the grand old masters,
  Not from the bards sublime,
Whose distant footsteps echo
  Through the corridors of Time.

For, like strains of martial music.
  Their mighty thoughts suggest
Life's endless toil and endeavour;
  And to-night I long for rest.

Read from some humbler poet,
  Whose songs gushed from his heart.
As showers from the clouds of summer,
  Or tears from the eyelids start;

Who, through long days of labour,
  And nights devoid of ease,
Still heard in his soul the music
  Of wonderful melodies.

Such songs have power to quiet
  The restless pulse of care,
And come like the benediction
  That follows after prayer.

Then read from the treasured volume
  The poem of thy choice,
And lend to the rhyme of the poet
  The beauty of thy voice.

And the night shall be filled with music,
  And the cares, that infest the day,
Shall fold their tents, like the Arabs,
  And as silently steal away.

AFTERNOON IN FEBRUARY.

Tur day is ending,
The night is descending;
Tho marsh is frozen,
   The river dead.

Through clouds like ashes,
The red sun flashes
On village windows
   That glimmer red.

The snow recommences:
The buried fences
Mark no longer
   The road o'er the plain;

While through the meadows,
Like fearful shadows,
Slowly passes
   A funeral train.

The bell is pealing,
And every feeling
Within me responds
   To the dismal knell;

Shadows are trailing,
My heart is bewailing
And tolling within
   Like a funeral bell.

TO AN OLD DANISH SONG-BOOK.

Welcome, my old friend,
Welcome to a foreign fireside,
While the sullen gales of autumn
Shake the windows.

The ungrateful world
Has, it seems, dealt harshly with thee,
Since, beneath the skies of Denmark,
First I met thee.

There are marks of age,
There are thumb-marks on thy margin,
Made by hands that clasped thee rudely,
At the alehouse.

Soiled and dull thou art;
Yellow are thy time-worn pages,
As the russet, rain-molested
Leaves of autumn.

Thou art stained with wine
Scattered from hilarious goblets.
As these leaves with the libations
Of Olympus.

Yet dost thou recall
Days departed, half-forgotten,
When in dreamy youth I wandered
By the Baltic,—

When I paused to hear
The old ballad of King Christian
Shouted from suburban taverns
In the twilight.

Thou recallest bards,
Who, in solitary chambers,
And with hearts by passion wasted,
Wrote thy pages.

Thou recallest homes
Where thy songs of love and friendship
Made the gloomy Northern winter
Bright as summer.

Once some ancient Scald,
In his bleak, ancestral Iceland,
Chanted staves of these old ballads
To the Vikings.

Once in Elsinore,
At the court of old King Hamlet,
Yorick and his low companions
Sang these ditties.

Once Prince Frederick's Guard
Sang them in their smoky barracks :—
Suddenly the English cannon
Joined the chorus !

Peasants in the field,
Sailors on the roaring ocean,
Students, tradesmen, pale mechanics,
All have sung them.

Thou hast been their friend ;
They, alas, have left thee friendless !
Yet at least by one warm fireside
Art thou welcome.

And, as swallows build
In these wide, old-fashioned chimneys,
So thy twittering songs shall nestle
In my bosom,—

Quiet, close, and warm,
Sheltered from all molestation,
And recalling by their voices
Youth and travel.

WALTER VON DER VOGELWEID[1]

Vogelweid the Minnesinger,
  When he left this world of ours,
Laid his body in the cloister,
  Under Würtzburg's minster towers.

And he gave the monks his treasures,
  Gave them all with this behest:
They should feed the birds at noontide
  Daily on his place of rest;

Saying, " From these wandering minstrels
  I have learned the art of song;
Let me now repay the lessons
  They have taught so well and long."

Thus the bard of love departed;
  And, fulfilling his desire,
On his tomb the birds were feasted
  By the children of the choir.

Day by day, o'er tower and turret,
  In foul weather and in fair,
Day by day, in vaster numbers,
  Flocked the poets of the air.

On the tree whose heavy branches
  Overshadowed all the place,
On the pavement, on the tombstone,
  On the poet's sculptured face,

(1) Walter von der Vogelweid, or Bird-Meadow, was one of the principal Minnesingers of the thirteenth century. He triumphed over Heinrich von Ofterdingen in that poetic contest at Wartburg Castle, known in literary history as the War of Wartburg.

On the cross-bars of each window,
  On the lintel of each door,
They renewed the War of Wartburg,
  Which the bard had fought before.

There they sang their merry carols,
  Sang their lauds on every side;
And the name their voices uttered
  Was the name of Vogelweid.

Till at length the portly abbot
  Murmured, "Why this waste of food?
Be it changed to loaves henceforward
  For our fasting brotherhood."

Then in vain o'er tower and turret,
  From the walls and woodland nests,
When the minster bell rang noontide,
  Gathered the unwelcome guests.

Then in vain, with cries discordant,
  Clamorous round the Gothic spire,
Screamed the feathered Minnesingers
  For the children of the choir.

Time has long effaced the inscriptions
  On the cloister's funeral stones,
And tradition only tells us
  Where repose the poet's bones.

But around the vast cathedral,
  By sweet echoes multiplied,
Still the birds repeat the legend,
  And the name of Vogelweid.

DRINKING SONG.

INSCRIPTION FOR AN ANTIQUE PITCHER

COME, old friend! sit down and listen!
From the pitcher, placed between us,
How the waters laugh and glisten
In the head of old Silenus;

X

SONG.

Old Silenus, bloated, drunken,
  Led by his inebriate Satyrs;
On his breast his head is sunken,
  Vacantly he leers and chatters.

Fauns with youthful Bacchus follow;
  Ivy crowns that brow supernal
As the forehead of Apollo,
  And possessing youth eternal.

Round about him, fair Bacchantes,
  Bearing cymbals, flutes, and thyrses.
Wild from Nœian groves, or Zante's
  Vineyards, sing delirious verses.

Thus he won, through all the nations,
  Bloodless victories, and the farmer
Bore, as trophies and oblations,
  Vines for banners, ploughs for armour.

Judged by no o'erzealous rigor,
  Much this mystic throng expresses:
Bacchus was the type of vigor,
  And Silenus of excesses.

These are ancient ethnic revels,
  Of a faith long since forsaken:
Now the Satyrs, changed to devils,
  Frighten mortals wine-o'ertaken.

Now to rivulets from the mountains
  Point the rods of fortune-tellers;
Youth perpetual dwells in fountains,—
  Not in flasks, and casks, and cellars.

Claudius, though he sang of flagons
  And huge tankards filled with Rhenish,
From that fiery blood of dragons
  Never would his own replenish.

Even Redi, though he chaunted
    Bacchus in the Tuscan valleys,
Never drank the wine he vaunted
    In his dithyrambic sallies.

Then with water fill the pitcher
    Wreathed about with classic fables:
Ne'er Falernian threw a richer
    Light upon Lucullus' tables.

Come, old friend, sit down and listen!
    As it passes thus between us,
How its wavelets laugh and glisten
    In the head of old Silenus!

THE ARROW AND THE SONG.

I shot an arrow into the air,
It fell to earth, I knew not where;
For, so swiftly it flew, the sight
Could not follow it in its flight.

I breathed a song into the air,
It fell to earth, I knew not where;
For who has sight so keen and strong,
That it can follow the flight of song?

Long, long afterward, in an oak
I found the arrow, still unbroke;
And the song from beginning to end,
I found again in the heart of a friend.

THE OLD CLOCK ON THE STAIRS.

L'éternité est une pendule, dont le balancier dit et redit sans cesse ces deux mots seulement, dans le silence des tombeaux : "Toujours ! jamais ! Jamais ! toujours !"—JACQUES BRIDAINE.

SOMEWHAT back from the village street
Stands the old-fashioned country-seat,
Across its antique portico
Tall poplar trees their shadows throw,
And from its station in the hall
An ancient timepiece says to all,—
     "Forever—never !
       Never—forever !"

Halfway up the stairs it stands,
And points and beckons with its hands
From its case of massive oak,
Like a monk, who, under his cloak,
Crosses himself, and sighs alas !
With sorrowful voice to all who pass,—
    " Forever—never !
        Never—forever ! "

By day its voice is low and light ;
But in the silent dead of night,
Distinct as a passing footstep's fall,
It echoes along the vacant hall,
Along the ceiling, along the floor,
And seems to say at each chamber-door,—
    " Forever—never ;
        Never—forever ! "

Through days of sorrow and of mirth,
Through days of death and days of birth,
Through every swift vicissitude
Of changeful time, unchanged it has stood,
And as if, like God, it all things saw,
It calmly repeats those words of awe,—
    " Forever—never !
        Never—forever ! "

In that mansion used to be
Free-hearted Hospitality ;
His great fires up the chimney roared ;
The stranger feasted at his board ;
But, like the skeleton at the feast,
That warning timepiece never ceased,—
    " Forever—never !
        Never—forever ! "

There groups of merry children played,
There youths and maidens dreaming strayed;
O precious hours! O golden prime,
And affluence of love and time!
Even as a miser counts his gold,
Those hours the ancient timepiece told,—
        "Forever—never!
          Never—forever!"

From that chamber, clothed in white,
The bride came forth on her wedding night;
There, in that silent room below,
The dead lay in his shroud of snow;
And in the hush that followed the prayer,
Was heard the old clock on the stair,—
        "Forever—never!
          Never—forever!"

All are scattered now and fled,
Some are married, some are dead;
And when I ask, with throbs of pain,
"Ah! when shall they all meet again?"
As in the days long-since gone by,
The ancient time-piece makes reply,—
        "Forever—never!
          Never—forever!"

Never here, forever there,
Where all parting, pain, and care,
And death, and time shall disappear,—
Forever there, but never here!
The horologe of Eternity
Sayeth this incessantly,—
        "Forever—never!
          Never—forever!"

SONNETS.

AUTUMN.

Thou comest, Autumn, heralded by the rain,
With banners, by great gales incessant fanned,

Brighter than brightest silks of Samarcand,
And stately oxen harnessed to thy wain !
Thou standest, like imperial Charlemagne,[1]
Upon thy bridge of gold ; thy royal hand
Outstretched with benedictions o'er the land,
Blessing the farms through all thy vast domain.
Thy shield is the red harvest moon, suspended
So long beneath the heaven's o'erhanging eaves ;
Thy steps are by the farmer's prayers attended ;
Like flames upon an altar shine the sheaves ;
And, following thee, in thy ovation splendid,
Thine almoner, the wind, scatters the golden leaves !

DANTE.

Tuscan, that wanderest through the realms of gloom,
With thoughtful pace, and sad majestic eyes,
Stern thoughts and awful from thy soul arise,
Like Farinata from his fiery tomb,
Thy sacred song is like the trump of doom ;
Yet in thy heart what human sympathies,
What soft compassion glows, as in the skies
The tender stars their clouded lamps relume !
Methinks I see thee stand, with pallid cheeks,
By Fra Hilario in his diocese,
As up the convent-walls, in golden streaks,
The ascending sunbeams mark the day's decrease ;
And, as he asks what there the stranger seeks,
Thy voice along the cloister whispers, " Peace !"

---

(1) Charlemagne may be called by preeminence the monarch of farmers.
According to the German tradition, in seasons of great abundance his spirit
crosses the Rhine on a golden bridge at Bingen, and blesses the cornfields and
the vineyards.

THE EVENING STAR.

Lo! in the painted oriel of the West,
Whose panes the sunken sun incarnadines,
Like a fair lady at her casement, shines
The Evening Star, the star of love and rest!
And then anon she doth herself divest
Of all her radiant garments, and reclines
Behind the sombre screen of yonder pines,
With slumber and soft dreams of love oppressed.
O my beloved, my sweet Hesperus!
My morning and my evening star of love!
My best and gentlest lady! even thus,
As that fair planet in the sky above,
Dost thou retire unto thy rest at night,
And from thy darkened window fades the light.

PREFATORY NOTE.

The story of "Evangeline" is founded on a painful occurrence which took place in the early period of British colonization in the northern part of America.

In the year 1713, Acadia, or as it is now named, Nova Scotia, was ceded to Great Britain by the French. The wishes of the inhabitants seem to have been little consulted in the change, and they with great difficulty were induced to take the oaths of allegiance to the British government. Some time after this, war having again broken out between the French and British in Canada, the Acadians were accused of having assisted the French, from whom they were descended, and connected by many ties of friendship, with provisions and ammunition, at the siege of Beau Sejour. Whether the accusation was founded on fact or not, has not been satisfactorily ascertained; the result, however, was most disastrous to the primitive, simple-minded Acadians. The British government ordered them to be removed from their homes, and dispersed throughout the other colonies, at a distance from their much-loved land. This resolution was not communicated to the inhabitants till measures had been matured to carry it into immediate effect; when the Governor of the colony, having issued a summons calling the whole people to a meeting, informed them that their lands, tenements, and cattle of all kinds were forfeited to the British crown, that he had orders to remove them to remote to distant colonies, and they must remain in custody till their embarkation.

The poem is descriptive of the fate of some of the persons involved in these calamitous proceedings.

EVANGELINE.

A TALE OF ACADIE.

This is the forest primeval.   The murmuring pines and the hemlocks,
Bearded with moss, and in garments green, indistinct in the twilight,
Stand like Druids of old, with voices sad and prophetic,
Stand like harpers hoar, with beards that rest on their bosoms.
Loud from its rocky caverns, the deep-voiced neighbouring ocean
Speaks, and in accents disconsolate answers the wail of the forest.

This is the forest primeval; but where are the hearts that beneath it
Leaped like the roe, when he hears in the woodland the voice of the huntsman?
Where is the thatch-roofed village, the home of Acadian farmers,—
Men whose lives glided on like rivers that water the woodlands,
Darkened by shadows of earth, but reflecting an image of heaven?
Waste are those pleasant farms, and the farmers forever departed!
Scattered like dust and leaves, when the mighty blasts of October
Seize them, and whirl them aloft, and sprinkle them far o'er the ocean.
Nought but tradition remains of the beautiful village of Grand-Pré.

Ye who believe in affection that hopes, and endures, and is patient,
Ye who believe in the beauty and strength of woman's devotion,
List to the mournful tradition still sung by the pines of the forest;
List to a Tale of Love in Acadie, home of the happy.

PART THE FIRST.

I.

In the Acadian land, on the shores of the Basin of Minas,
Distant, secluded, still, the little village of Grand-Pré
Lay in the fruitful valley. Vast meadows stretched to the eastward,
Giving the village its name, and pasture to flocks without number.
Dikes, that the hands of the farmers had raised with labor incessant,
Shut out the turbulent tides; but at stated seasons the flood-gates
Opened, and welcomed the sea to wander at will o'er the meadows.
West and south there were fields of flax, and orchards and cornfields
Spreading afar and unfenced o'er the plain, and away to the northward
Blomidon rose, and the forests old, and aloft on the mountains
Sea-fogs pitched their tents, and mists from the mighty Atlantic

Looked on the happy valley, but ne'er from their station descended.
There, in the midst of its farms, reposed the Acadian village.
Strongly built were the houses, with frames of oak and of chestnut,
Such as the peasants of Normandy built in the reign of the Henries.
Thatched were the roofs, with dormer-windows; and gables projecting
Over the basement below protected and shaded the door-way.
There in the tranquil evenings of summer, when brightly the sunset
Lighted the village street, and gilded the vanes on the chimneys,
Matrons and maidens sat in snow-white caps and in kirtles
Scarlet and blue and green, with distaffs spinning the golden
Flax for the gossiping looms, whose noisy shuttles within doors
Mingled their sound with the whir of the wheels and the songs of the maidens.
Solemnly down the street came the parish priest, and the children
Paused in their play to kiss the hand he extended to bless them.
Reverend walked he among them; and up rose matrons and maidens,

Hailing his slow approach with words of affectionate welcome.
Then came the laborers home from the field, and serenely the sun sank
Down to his rest, and twilight prevailed. Anon from the belfry
Softly the Angelus sounded, and over the roofs of the village
Columns of pale blue smoke, like clouds of incense ascending.
Rose from a hundred hearths, the homes of peace and contentment.
Thus dwelt together in love these simple Acadian farmers,—

Dwelt in the love of God and of man. Alike were they free from
Fear, that reigns with the tyrant, and envy, the voice of republics.
Neither locks had they to their doors, nor bars to their windows;
But their dwellings were open as day and the hearts of the owners;
There the richest was poor, and the poorest lived in abundance.

Somewhat apart from the village, and nearer the Basin of Minas,
Benedict Bellefontaine, the wealthiest farmer of Grand-Pré,

Dwelt on his goodly acres; and with him, directing his household,
Gentle Evangeline lived, his child, and the pride of the village.
Stalworth and stately in form was the man of seventy winters;
Hearty and hale was he, an oak that is covered with snow-flakes;
White as the snow were his locks, and his cheeks as brown as the oak-leaves.
Fair was she to behold, that maiden of seventeen summers.
Black were her eyes as the berry that grows on the thorn by the way-side,
Black, yet how softly they gleamed beneath the brown shade of her tresses!

Sweet was her breath as the breath of kine that feed in the meadows.
When in the harvest heat she bore to the reapers at noontide
Flagons of home-brewed ale, ah! fair in sooth was the maiden.
Fairer was she when, on Sunday morn, while the bell from its turret
Sprinkled with holy sounds the air, as the priest with his hyssop
Sprinkles the congregation, and scatters blessings upon them,

Down the long street she passed, with her chaplet of beads and her missal,
Wearing her Norman cap, and her kirtle of blue, and the ear-rings,
Brought in the olden time from France, and since, as an heirloom,
Handed down from mother to child, through long generations.
But a celestial brightness—a more ethereal beauty—
Shone on her face and encircled her form, when, after confession,
Homeward serenely she walked with God's benediction upon her.
When she had passed, it seemed like the ceasing of exquisite music,
Firmly builded with rafters of oak, the house of the farmer
Stood on the side of a hill commanding the sea; and a shady

Sycamore grew by the door, with a woodbine wreathing around it.
Rudely carved was the porch, with seats beneath; and a footpath
Led through an orchard wide, and disappeared in the meadow,
Under the sycamore-tree were hives overhung by a penthouse,
Such as the traveller sees in regions remote by the road-side,
Built o'er a box for the poor, or the blessed image of Mary.
Farther down, on the slope of the hill, was the well with its moss-grown
Bucket, fastened with iron, and near it a trough for the horses.
Shielding the house from storms, on the north, were the barns and the farm-yard

There stood the broad-wheeled wains and the antique ploughs and the harrows;
There were the folds for the sheep; and there, in his feathered seraglio,
Strutted the lordly turkey, and crowed the cock, with the selfsame
Voice that in ages of old had startled the penitent Peter.
Bursting with hay were the barns, themselves a village.   In each one
Far o'er the gable projected a roof of thatch; and a staircase,
Under the sheltering eaves, led up to the odorous corn-loft.
There too the dove-cot stood, with its meek and innocent inmates
Murmuring ever of love; while above in the variant breezes
Numberless noisy weathercocks rattled and sang of mutation.

Thus, at peace with God and the world, the farmer of Grand-Pré
Lived on his sunny farm, and Evangeline governed his household.
Many a youth, as he knelt in the church and opened his missal,
Fixed his eyes upon her, as the saint of his deepest devotion;
Happy was he who might touch her hand or the hem of her garment!
Many a suitor came to her door, by the darkness befriended,
And as he knocked and waited to hear the sound of her footsteps,
Knew not which beat the louder, his heart or the knocker of iron;
Or at the joyous feast of the Patron Saint of the village,
Bolder grew, and pressed her hand in the dance as he whispered
Hurried words of love, that seemed a part of the music.
But, among all who came, young Gabriel only was welcome;
Gabriel Lajeunesse, the son of Basil the blacksmith,
Who was a mighty man in the village, and honored of all men;
For since the birth of time, throughout all ages and nations,
Has the craft of the smith been held in repute by the people.
Basil was Benedict's friend.   Their children from earliest childhood
Grew up together as brother and sister; and Father Felician,
Priest and pedagogue both in the village, had taught them their letters
Out of the selfsame book, with the hymns of the church and the plain-song.
But when the hymn was sung, and the daily lesson completed,
Swiftly they hurried away to the forge of Basil the blacksmith.
There at the door they stood, with wondering eyes to behold him
Take in his leathern lap the hoof of the horse as a plaything,
Nailing the shoe in its place; while near him the tire of the cart-wheel
Lay like a fiery snake, coiled round in a circle of cinders.
Oft on autumnal eves, when without in the gathering darkness
Bursting with light seemed the smithy, through every cranny and crevice,
Warm by the forge within they watched the laboring bellows,

And as its panting ceased, and the sparks expired in the ashes,
Merrily laughed, and said they were nuns going into the chapel.
Oft on sledges in winter, as swift as the swoop of the eagle,
Down the hill-side bounding, they glided away o'er the meadow.
Oft in the barns they climbed to the populous nests on the rafters,
Seeking with eager eyes that wondrous stone, which the swallow
Brings from the shore of the sea to restore the sight of its fledglings:
Lucky was he who found that stone in the nest of the swallow!
Thus passed a few swift years, and they no longer were children.
He was a valiant youth, and his face, like the face of the morning,
Gladdened the earth with its light, and ripened thought into action.
She was a woman now, with the heart and hopes of a woman.
"Sunshine of Saint Eulalie" was she called; for that was the sunshine
Which, as the farmers believed, would load their orchards with apples;
She, too, would bring to her husband's house delight and abundance,
Filling it full of love and the ruddy faces of children.

II.

Now had the season returned, when the nights grow colder and longer,
And the retreating sun the sign of the Scorpion enters.
Birds of passage sailed through the leaden air, from the ice-bound,
Desolate northern bays to the shores of tropical islands.
Harvests were gathered in; and wild with the winds of September
Wrestled the trees of the forest, as Jacob of old with the angel.
All the signs foretold a winter long and inclement.
Bees, with prophetic instinct of want, had hoarded their honey
Till the hives overflowed; and the Indian hunters asserted
Cold would the winter be, for thick was the fur of the foxes.
Such was the advent of autumn. Then followed that beautiful season,
Called by the pious Acadian peasants the Summer of All-Saints!
Filled was the air with a dreamy and magical light; and the landscape
Lay as if new-created in all the freshness of childhood.
Peace seemed to reign upon earth, and the restless heart of the ocean
Was for a moment consoled. All sounds were in harmony blended.
Voices of children at play, the crowing of cocks in the farm-yards,
Whir of wings in the drowsy air, and the cooing of pigeons,
All were subdued and low as the murmurs of love, and the great sun
Looked with the eye of love through the golden vapors around him;
While arrayed in its robes of russet and scarlet and yellow,
Bright with the sheen of the dew, each glittering tree of the forest
Flashed like the plane-tree the Persian adorned with mantles and jewels.

Now recommenced the reign of rest and affection and stillness.
Day with its burden and heat had departed, and twilight descending
Brought back the evening star to the sky, and the herds to the homestead.
Pawing the ground they came, and resting their necks on each other,
And with their nostrils distended inhaling the freshness of evening.
Foremost, bearing the bell, Evangeline's beautiful heifer,
Proud of her snow-white hide, and the ribbon that waved from her collar,
Quietly paced and slow, as if conscious of human affection.

Then came the shepherd back with his bleating flocks from the sea-side,
Where was their favourite pasture.   Behind them followed the watch-dog,
Patient, full of importance, and grand in the pride of his instinct,
Walking from side to side with a lordly air, and superbly
Waving his bushy tale, and urging forward the stragglers;
Regent of flocks was he when the shepherd slept; their protector,
When from the forest at night, through the starry silence, the wolves howled.

Late, with the rising moon, returned the wains from the marshes,
Laden with briny hay, that filled the air with its odor.
Cheerily neighed the steeds, with dew on their manes and their fetlocks,
While aloft on their shoulders the wooden and ponderous saddles,
Painted with brilliant dyes, and adorned with tassels of crimson,
Nodded in bright array, like hollyhocks heavy with blossoms.
Patiently stood the cows meanwhile, and yielded their udders
Unto the milkmaid's hand; whilst loud and in regular cadence
Into the sounding pails the foaming streamlets descended.
Lowing of cattle and peals of laughter were heard in the farm-yard,
Echoed back by the barns. Anon they sank into stillness;
Heavily closed, with a jarring sound, the valves of the barn-doors,
Rattled the wooden bars, and all for a season was silent.

In-doors, warm by the wide-mouthed fire-place, idly the farmer
Sat in his elbow-chair, and watched how the flames and the smoke-wreaths
Struggled together like foes in a burning city. Behind him,
Nodding and mocking along the wall, with gestures fantastic.

Darted his own huge shadow, and vanished away into darkness.
Faces, clumsily carved in oak, on the back of his arm-chair
Laughed in the flickering light, and the pewter plates on the dresser
Caught and reflected the flame, as shields of armies the sunshine.
Fragments of song the old man sang, and carols of Christmas,
Such as at home, in the olden time, his fathers before him
Sung in their Norman orchards and bright Burgundian vineyards.
Close at her father's side was the gentle Evangeline seated,
Spinning flax for the loom, that stood in the corner behind her.
Silent awhile were its treadles, at rest was its diligent shuttle,
While the monotonous drone of the wheel, like the drone of a bagpipe,
Followed the old man's song, and united the fragments together.
As in a church, when the chant of the choir at intervals ceases,
Footfalls are heard in the aisles, or words of the priest at the altar.
So, in each pause of the song, with measured motion the clock clicked.

Thus as they sat, there were footsteps heard, and, suddenly lifted,
Sounded the wooden latch, and the door swung back on its hinges.
Benedict knew by the hob-nailed shoes it was Basil the blacksmith.
And by her beating heart Evangeline knew who was with him.
" Welcome ! " the farmer exclaimed, as their footsteps paused on the threshold,
" Welcome, Basil, my friend ! Come, take thy place on the settle
Close by the chimney-side, which is always empty without thee ;
Take from the shelf overhead thy pipe and the box of tobacco ;
Never so much thyself art thou as when through the curling
Smoke of the pipe or the forge thy friendly and jovial face gleams
Round and red as the harvest moon through the mist of the marshes."
Then, with a smile of content, thus answered Basil the blacksmith,
Taking with easy air the accustomed seat by the fireside :—
" Benedict Bellefontaine, thou hast ever thy jest and thy ballad !
Ever in cheerfullest mood art thou, when others are filled with
Gloomy forebodings of ill, and see only ruin before them.
Happy art thou, as if every day thou hadst picked up a horseshoe."
Pausing a moment, to take the pipe that Evangeline brought him,
And with a coal from the embers had lighted, he slowly continued :—
" Four days now are passed since the English ships at their anchors
Ride in the Gaspereau's mouth, with their cannon pointed against us.
What their design may be is unknown : but all are commanded
On the morrow to meet in the church, where his Majesty's mandate
Will be proclaimed as law in the land.   Alas ! in the meantime

Many surmises of evil alarm the hearts of the people."
Then made answer the farmer :—" Perhaps some friendlier purpose
Brings these ships to our shores.   Perhaps the harvests in England
By the untimely rains or untimelier heat have been blighted,
And from our bursting barns they would feed their cattle and children."
" Not so thinketh the folk in the village," said, warmly, the blacksmith,
Shaking his head, as in doubt ; then, heaving a sigh, he continued :—
" Louisburg is not forgotten, nor Beau Séjour, nor Port Royal.
Many already have fled to the forest, and lurk on its outskirts,
Waiting with anxious hearts the dubious fate of to-morrow.
Arms have been taken from us, and warlike weapons of all kinds ;
Nothing is left but the blacksmith's sledge and the scythe of the mower."
Then with a pleasant smile made answer the jovial farmer :—
" Safer are we unarmed, in the midst of our flocks and our cornfields,
Safer within these peaceful dikes, besieged by the ocean,
Than were our fathers in forts, besieged by the enemy's cannon.
Fear no evil, my friend, and to-night may no shadow of sorrow
Fall on this house and hearth ; for this is the night of the contract.
Built are the house and the barn.   The merry lads of the village
Strongly have built them and well ; and, breaking the glebe round about them,
Filled the barn with hay, and the house with food for a twelvemonth.
René Leblanc will be here anon, with his papers and inkhorn.
Shall we not then be glad, and rejoice in the joy of our children ? "
As apart by the window she stood, with her hand in her lover's,
Blushing Evangeline heard the words that her father had spoken,
And as they died on his lips the worthy notary entered.

III.

BENT like a laboring oar, that toils in the surf of the ocean,
Bent, but not broken, by age was the form of the notary public ;
Shocks of yellow hair, like the silken floss of the maize, hung
Over his shoulders ; his forehead was high ; and glasses with horn bows
Sat astride on his nose, with a look of wisdom supernal.
Father of twenty children was he, and more than a hundred
Children's children rode on his knee, and heard his great watch tick.
Four long years in the times of the war had he languished a captive.
Suffering much in an old French fort as the friend of the English.

Now, though warier grown, without all guile or suspicion,
Ripe in wisdom was he, but patient, and simple, and childlike.
He was beloved by all, and most of all by the children;
For he told them tales of the Loup-garou in the forest,
And of the goblin that came in the night to water the horses,
And of the white Létiche, the ghost of a child who unchristened
Died, and was doomed to haunt unseen the chambers of children;
And how on Christmas eve the oxen talked in the stable,
And how the fever was cured by a spider shut up in a nutshell,
And of the marvellous powers of four-leaved clover and horseshoes,
With whatsoever else was writ in the lore of the village.
Then up rose from his seat by the fireside Basil the blacksmith,
Knocked from his pipe the ashes, and slowly extending his right hand,
" Father Leblanc," he exclaimed, " thou hast heard the talk in the village,
And, perchance, canst tell us some news of these ships and their errand."
Then with modest demeanour made answer the notary public,—
" Gossip enough have I heard, in sooth, yet am never the wiser;
And what their errand may be I know not better than others.

A A

Yet am I not of those who imagine some evil intention
Brings them here, for we are at peace; and why then molest us?"
" God's name!" shouted the hasty and somewhat irascible blacksmith;
" Must we in all things look for the how, and the why, and the wherefore?
Daily injustice is done, and might is the right of the strongest!"
But, without heeding his warmth, continued the notary public,—
" Man is unjust, but God is just; and finally justice
Triumphs; and well I remember a story, that often consoled me,
When as a captive I lay in the old French fort at Port Royal."

This was the old man's favorite tale, and he loved to repeat it
When his neighbours complained that any injustice was done them.
" Once in an ancient city, whose name I no longer remember,
Raised aloft on a column, a brazen statue of Justice
Stood in the public square, upholding the scales in its left hand,
And in its right a sword, as an emblem that justice presided
Over the laws of the land, and the hearts and homes of the people.
Even the birds had built their nests in the scales of the balance,
Having no fear of the sword that flashed in the sunshine above them.
But in the course of time the laws of the land were corrupted ;
Might took the place of right, and the weak were oppressed, and the mighty
Ruled with an iron rod.   Then it chanced in a nobleman's palace
That a necklace of pearls was lost, and ere long a suspicion
Fell on an orphan girl who lived as maid in the household.
She, after form of trial condemned to die on the scaffold,
Patiently met her doom at the foot of the statue of Justice.
As to her Father in heaven her innocent spirit ascended,
Lo ! o'er the city a tempest rose ; and the bults of the thunder
Smote the statue of bronze, and hurled in wrath from its left hand
Down on the pavement below the clattering scales of the balance,
And in the hollow thereof was found the nest of a magpie,
Into whose clay-built walls the necklace of pearls was inwoven."
Silenced, but not convinced, when the story was ended, the blacksmith
Stood like a man who fain would speak, but findeth no language :
All his thoughts were congealed into lines on his face, as the vapours
Freeze in fantastic shapes on the window-panes in the winter.

Then Evangeline lighted the brazen lamp on the table,
Filled, till it overflowed, the pewter tankard with home-brewed
Nut-brown ale, that was famed for its strength in the village of Grand-Pré ;
While from his pocket the notary drew his papers and ink-horn,
Wrote with a steady hand the date and the age of the parties,
Naming the dower of the bride in flocks of sheep and in cattle.
Orderly all things proceeded, and duly and well were completed,
And the great seal of the law was set like a sun on the margin.
Then from his leathern pouch the farmer threw on the table
Three times the old man's fee in solid pieces of silver ;
And the notary rising, and blessing the bride and the bridegroom,
Lifted aloft the tankard of ale and drank to their welfare.
Wiping the foam from his lip, he solemnly bowed and departed

While in silence the others sat and mused by the fireside,
Till Evangeline brought the draught-board out of its corner.
Soon was the game begun.   In friendly contention the old men
Laughed at each lucky hit, or unsuccessful manœuvre,
Laughed when a man was crowned, or a breach was made in the king-row.
Meanwhile apart, in the twilight gloom of a window's embrasure,
Sat the lovers, and whispered together, beholding the moon rise
Over the pallid sea and the silvery mist of the meadows.
Silently one by one, in the infinite meadows of heaven,
Blossomed the lovely stars, the forget-me-nots of the angels.

Thus passed the evening away.   Anon the bell from the belfry
Rang out the hour of nine, the village curfew, and straightway
Rose the guests and departed ; and silence reigned in the household.
Many a farewell word and sweet good-night on the door-step
Lingered long in Evangeline's heart, and filled it with gladness.
Carefully then were covered the embers that glowed on the hearth-stone,
And on the oaken stairs resounded the tread of the farmer.
Soon with a soundless step the foot of Evangeline followed.
Up the staircase moved a luminous space in the darkness,
Lighted less by the lamp than the shining face of the maiden.
Silent she passed through the hall, and entered the door of her chamber.
Simple that chamber was, with its curtains of white, and its clothes-press
Ample and high, on whose spacious shelves were carefully folded
Linen and woollen stuffs, by the hand of Evangeline woven.
This was the precious dower she would bring to her husband in marriage,
Better than flocks and herds, being proofs of her skill as a housewife.
Soon she extinguished her lamp, for the mellow and radiant moonlight
Streamed through the windows, and lighted the room, till the heart of the maiden
Swelled and obeyed its power, like the tremulous tides of the ocean.
Ah ! she was fair, exceeding fair to behold, as she stood with
Naked snow-white feet on the gleaming floor of her chamber !
Little she dreamed that below, among the trees of the orchard,
Waited her lover and watched for the gleam of her lamp and her shadow.
Yet were her thoughts of him, and at times a feeling of sadness
Passed o'er her soul, as the sailing shade of clouds in the moonlight
Flitted across the floor and darkened the room for a moment.
And as she gazed from the window she saw serenely the moon pass
Forth from the folds of a cloud, and one star follow her footsteps,
As out of Abraham's tent young Ishmael wandered with Hagar !

IV.

PLEASANTLY rose next morn the sun on the village of Grand-Pré.
Pleasantly gleamed in the soft, sweet air the Basin of Minas,
Where the ships, with their wavering shadows, were riding at anchor.
Life had long been astir in the village, and clamorous labor
Knocked with its hundred hands at the golden gates of the morning.
Now from the country around, from the farms and the neighbouring hamlets,
Came in their holiday dresses the blithe Acadian peasants.
Many a glad good-morrow and jocund laugh from the young folk
Made the bright air brighter, as up from the numerous meadows,
Where no path could be seen but the track of wheels in the greensward,
Group after group appeared, and joined, or passed on the highway.
Long ere noon, in the village all sounds of labor were silenced.
Thronged were the streets with people; and noisy groups at the house-doors
Sat in the cheerful sun, and rejoiced and gossipped together.
Every house was an inn, where all were welcomed and feasted;
For with this simple people, who lived like brothers together,
All things were held in common, and what one had was another's.

Yet under Benedict's roof hospitality seemed more abundant:
For Evangeline stood among the guests of her father;
Bright was her face with smiles, and words of welcome and gladness
Fell from her beautiful lips, and blessed the cup as she gave it.

Under the open sky, in the odorous air of the orchard,
Bending with golden fruit, was spread the feast of betrothal.
There in the shade of the porch were the priest and the notary seated;

There good Benedict sat, and sturdy Basil the blacksmith.
Not far withdrawn from these, by the cider-press and the beehives,
Michael the fiddler was placed, with the gayest of hearts and of waistcoats.
Shadow and light from the leaves alternately played on his snow-white
Hair, as it waved in the wind; and the jolly face of the fiddler
Glowed like a living coal when the ashes are blown from the embers.
Gaily the old man sang to the vibrant sound of his fiddle,
Tous les Bourgeois de Chartres, and *Le Carillon de Dunkerque.*

And anon with his wooden shoes beat time to the music.
Merrily, merrily whirled the wheels of the dizzying dances
Under the orchard-trees and down the path to the meadows;
Old folk and young together, and children mingled among them.
Fairest of all the maids was Evangeline, Benedict's daughter!
Noblest of all the youths was Gabriel, son of the blacksmith!

So passed the morning away. And lo! with a summons sonorous
Sounded the bell from its tower, and over the meadows a drum beat.

Thronged ere long was the church with men.   Without, in the churchyard,
Waited the women.   They stood by the graves, and hung on the head-stones
Garlands of autumn-leaves and evergreens fresh from the forest.
Then came the guard from the ships, and marching proudly among them
Entered the sacred portal.   With loud and dissonant clangor
Echoed the sound of their brazen drums from ceiling and casement,
Echoed a moment only, and slowly the ponderous portal
Closed, and in silence the crowd awaited the will of the soldiers.
Then uprose their commander, and spake from the steps of the altar,
Holding aloft in his hands, with its seals, the royal commission.
" You are convened this day," he said, " by his Majesty's orders.

Clement and kind has he been; but how you have answered his kindness,
Let your own hearts reply! To my natural make and my temper
Painful the task is I do, which to you I know must be grievous.
Yet must I bow and obey, and deliver the will of our monarch;
Namely, that all your lands, and dwellings, and cattle of all kinds,
Forfeited be to the crown; and that you yourselves from this province
Be transported to other lands. God grant you may dwell there
Ever as faithful subjects, a happy and peaceable people!
Prisoners now I declare you; for such is his Majesty's pleasure!"
As, when the air is serene in the sultry solstice of summer,
Suddenly gathers a storm, and the deadly sling of the hailstones
Beats down the farmer's corn in the field and shatters his windows,
Hiding the sun, and strewing the ground with thatch from the house-roofs,
Bellowing fly the herds, and seek to break their inclosures;
So on the hearts of the people descended the words of the speaker.
Silent a moment they stood in speechless wonder, and then rose
Louder and ever louder a wail of sorrow and anger,
And, by one impulse moved, they madly rushed to the doorway.
Vain was the hope of escape; and cries and fierce imprecations
Rang through the house of prayer; and high o'er the heads of the others
Rose, with his arms uplifted, the figure of Basil the blacksmith,
As, on a stormy sea, a spar is tossed by the billows.
Flushed was his face and distorted with passion; and wildly he shouted,—
" Down with the tyrants of England! we never have sworn them allegiance
Death to these foreign soldiers, who seize on our homes and our harvests!"
More he fain would have said, but the merciless hand of a soldier
Smote him upon the mouth, and dragged him down to the pavement.

In the midst of the strife and tumult of angry contention,
Lo! the door of the chancel opened, and Father Felician
Entered, with serious mien, and ascended the steps of the altar.
Raising his reverend hand, with a gesture he awed into silence
All that clamorous throng; and thus he spake to his people.
Deep were his tones and solemn; in accents measured and mournful
Spake he, as, after the tocsin's alarum, distinctly the clock strikes.
" What is this that ye do, my children? what madness has seized you?
Forty years of my life have I labored among you, and taught you,
Not in word alone, but in deed, to love one another!
Is this the fruit of my toils, of my vigils and prayers and privations?
Have you so soon forgotten all lessons of love and forgiveness?

This is the house of the Prince of Peace, and would you profane it
Thus with violent deeds and hearts overflowing with hatred?
Lo! where the crucified Christ from his cross is gazing upon you!
See! in those sorrowful eyes what meekness and holy compassion!
Hark! how those lips still repeat the prayer, 'O Father, forgive them!'
Let us repeat that prayer in the hour when the wicked assail us,
Let us repeat it now, and say, 'O Father, forgive them!'"
Few were his words of rebuke, but deep in the hearts of his people
Sank they, and sobs of contrition succeeded that passionate outbreak;
And they repeated his prayer, and said, "O Father, forgive them!"

Then came the evening service. The tapers gleamed from the altar.
Fervent and deep was the voice of the priest, and the people responded,
Not with their lips alone, but their hearts; and the Ave Maria
Sang they, and fell on their knees, and their souls, with devotion translated,
Rose on the ardor of prayer, like Elijah ascending to heaven.

Meanwhile had spread in the village the tidings of ill, and on all sides
Wandered, wailing, from house to house the women and children.
Long at her father's door Evangeline stood, with her right hand
Shielding her eyes from the level rays of the sun, that, descending,
Lighted the village street with mysterious splendor, and roofed each
Peasant's cottage with golden thatch, and emblazoned its windows.
Long within had been spread the snow-white cloth on the table;
There stood the wheaten loaf, and the honey fragrant with wild flowers;
There stood the tankard of ale, and the cheese fresh brought from the dairy;
And at the head of the board the great arm-chair of the farmer.
Thus did Evangeline wait at her father's door, as the sunset
Threw the long shadows of trees o'er the broad ambrosial meadows.
Ah! on her spirit within a deeper shadow had fallen,
And from the fields of her soul a fragrance celestial ascended,—
Charity, meekness, love, and hope, and forgiveness, and patience!
Then, all-forgetful of self, she wandered into the village,
Cheering with looks and words the disconsolate hearts of the women,
As o'er the darkening fields with lingering steps they departed,
Urged by their household cares, and the weary feet of their children.
Down sank the great red sun, and in golden, glimmering vapors
Veiled the light of his face, like the Prophet descending from Sinai.
Sweetly over the village the bell of the Angelus sounded.

Meanwhile, amid the gloom, by the church Evangeline lingered.
All was silent within; and in vain at the door and the windows
Stood she, and listened and looked, until, overcome by emotion,
"Gabriel!" cried she aloud with tremulous voice; but no answer
Came from the graves of the dead; nor the gloomier grave of the living.
Slowly at length she returned to the tenantless house of her father.
Smouldered the fire on the hearth, on the board stood the supper untasted,
Empty and drear was each room, and haunted with phantoms of terror.

Sadly echoed her step on the stair and the floor of her chamber.
In the dead of the night she heard the whispering rain fall
Loud on the withered leaves of the sycamore-tree by the window.
Keenly the lightning flashed; and the voice of the echoing thunder
Told her that God was in heaven, and governed the world he created!
Then she remembered the tale she had heard of the justice of heaven;
Soothed was her troubled soul, and she peacefully slumbered till morning.

V.

Four times the sun had risen and set; and now on the fifth day
Cheerily called the cock to the sleeping maids of the farm-house.
Soon o'er the yellow fields, in silent and mournful procession,
Came from the neighbouring hamlets and farms the Acadian women,
Driving in ponderous wains their household goods to the sea-shore,
Pausing and looking back to gaze once more on their dwellings,
Ere they were shut from sight by the winding road and the woodland.
Close at their sides their children ran, and urged on the oxen,
While in their little hands they clasped some fragments of playthings.

Thus to the Gaspereau's mouth they hurried ; and there on the sea-beach
Piled in confusion lay the household goods of the peasants.
All day long between the shore and the ships did the boats ply ;
All day long the wains came laboring down from the village.
Late in the afternoon, when the sun was near to his setting,
Echoing far o'er the fields came the roll of drums from the church-yard.
Thither the women and children thronged. On a sudden the church-doors
Opened, and forth came the guard, and marching in gloomy procession
Followed the long-imprisoned, but patient, Acadian farmers.
Even as pilgrims, who journey afar from their homes and their country,
Sing as they go, and in singing forget they are weary and way-worn,
So with songs on their lips the Acadian peasants descended
Down from the church to the shore, amid their wives and their daughters.
Foremost the young men came ; and, raising together their voices,
Sang they with tremulous lips a chant of the Catholic Missions :—
"Sacred heart of the Saviour ! O inexhaustible fountain !
Fill our hearts this day with strength and submission and patience !"
Then the old men, as they marched, and the women that stood by the way-side,
Joined in the sacred psalm, and the birds in the sunshine above them
Mingled their notes therewith, like voices of spirits departed.

Half-way down to the shore Evangeline waited in silence,
Not overcome with grief, but strong in the hour of affliction,—
Calmly and sadly waited, until the procession approached her.
And she beheld the face of Gabriel pale with emotion.
Tears then filled her eyes, and, eagerly running to meet him,
Clasped she his hands, and laid her head on his shoulder, and whispered,—
"Gabriel ! be of good cheer ! for if we love one another,
Nothing, in truth, can harm us, whatever mischances may happen !"
Smiling she spake these words ; then suddenly paused, for her father
Saw she slowly advancing. Alas ! how changed was his aspect !
Gone was the glow from his cheek, and the fire from his eye, and his footstep
Heavier seemed with the weight of the weary heart in his bosom.
But with a smile and a sigh, she clasped his neck and embraced him,
Speaking words of endearment where words of comfort availed not.
Thus to the Gaspereau's mouth moved on that mournful procession.

There disorder prevailed, and the tumult and stir of embarking.
Busily plied the freighted boats : and in the confusion
Wives were torn from their husbands, and mothers, too late, saw their children

Left on the land, extending their arms, with wildest entreaties.
So unto separate ships were Basil and Gabriel carried,
While in despair on the shore Evangeline stood with her father.
Half the task was not done when the sun went down, and the twilight
Deepened and darkened around; and in haste the refluent ocean
Fled away from the shore, and left the line of the sand-beach
Covered with waifs of the tide, with kelp and the slippery sea-weed.
Farther back in the midst of the household goods and the wagons,
Like to a gipsy camp, or a leaguer after a battle,
All escape cut off by the sea, and the sentinels near them,
Lay encamped for the night the houseless Acadian farmers.
Back to its nethermost caves retreated the bellowing ocean,
Dragging adown the beach the rattling pebbles, and leaving
Inland and far up the shore the stranded boats of the sailors.
Then, as the night descended, the herds returned from their pastures;
Sweet was the moist still air with the odor of milk from their udders;
Lowing they waited, and long, at the well-known bars of the farm-yard. —
Waited and looked in vain for the voice and the hand of the milkmaid.
Silence reigned in the streets; from the church no Angelus sounded,
Rose no smoke from the roofs, and gleamed no lights from the windows.

But on the shore meanwhile the evening fires had been kindled,
Built of the drift-wood thrown on the sands from wrecks in the tempest.
Round them shapes of gloom and sorrowful faces were gathered,
Voices of women were heard, and of men, and the crying of children.
Onward from fire to fire, as from hearth to hearth in his parish,
Wandered the faithful priest, consoling and blessing and cheering,
Like unto shipwrecked Paul on Melita's desolate sea-shore.
Thus he approached the place where Evangeline sat with her father,
And in the flickering light beheld the face of the old man,
Haggard and hollow and wan, and without either thought or emotion,
E'en as the face of a clock from which the hands have been taken.
Vainly Evangeline strove with words and caresses to cheer him,
Vainly offered him food; yet he moved not, he looked not, he spake not.
But, with a vacant stare, ever gazed at the flickering fire-light.
" Benedicite!" murmured the priest, in tones of compassion.
More he fain would have said, but his heart was full, and his accents
Faltered and paused on his lips, as the feet of a child on a threshold,
Hushed by the scene he beholds, and the awful presence of sorrow.
Silently, therefore, he laid his hand on the head of the maiden,

Raising his eyes, full of tears, to the silent stars that above them
Moved on their way, unperturbed by the wrongs and sorrows of mortals.
Then sat he down at her side, and they wept together in silence.

Suddenly rose from the south a light, as in autumn the blood-red
Moon climbs the crystal walls of heaven, and o'er the horizon
Titan-like stretches its hundred hands upon mountain and meadow,

Seizing the rocks and the rivers, and piling huge shadows together.
Broader and ever broader it gleamed on the roofs of the village,
Gleamed on the sky and the sea, and the ships that lay in the roadstead.
Columns of shining smoke uprose, and flashes of flame were
Thrust through their folds and withdrawn, like the quivering hands of a martyr.
Then as the wind seized the gleeds and the burning thatch, and, uplifting,
Whirled them aloft through the air, at once from a hundred house-tops
Started the sheeted smoke with flashes of flame intermingled.

These things beheld in dismay the crowd on the shore and on shipboard.
Speechless at first they stood, then cried aloud in their anguish,
" We shall behold no more our homes in the village of Grand-Pré!"
Loud on a sudden the cocks began to crow in the farm-yards,
Thinking the day had dawned; and anon the lowing of cattle
Came on the evening breeze, by the barking of dogs interrupted.
Then rose a sound of dread, such as startles the sleeping encampments
Far in the western prairies or forests that skirt the Nebraska,
When the wild horses affrighted sweep by with the speed of the whirlwind,
Or the loud bellowing herds of buffaloes rush to the river.
Such was the sound that arose on the night, as the herds and the horses
Broke through their folds and fences, and madly rushed o'er the meadows.

Overwhelmed with the night, yet speechless, the priest and the maiden
Gazed on the scene of terror that reddened and widened before them ;
And as they turned at length to speak to their silent companion,
Lo! from his seat he had fallen, and stretched abroad on the sea-shore
Motionless lay his form, from which the soul had departed.
Slowly the priest uplifted the lifeless head, and the maiden
Knelt at her father's side, and wailed aloud in her terror.
Then in a swoon she sank, and lay with her head on his bosom.
Through the long night she lay in deep, oblivious slumber ;
And when she woke from the trance, she beheld a multitude near her.
Faces of friends she beheld, that were mournfully gazing upon her.
Pallid, with tearful eyes, and looks of saddest compassion.
Still the blaze of the burning village illumined the landscape,
Reddened the sky overhead, and gleamed on the faces around her,
And like the day of doom it seemed to her wavering senses.
Then a familiar voice she heard, as it said to the people.—
" Let us bury him here by the sea. When a happier season
Brings us again to our homes from the unknown land of our exile,

Then shall his sacred dust be piously laid in the church-yard."
Such were the words of the priest.   And there in haste by the sea-side,
Having the glare of the burning village for funeral torches,
But without bell or book, they buried the farmer of Grand-Pré.
And as the voice of the priest repeated the service of sorrow,
Lo! with a mournful sound, like the voice of a vast congregation,
Solemnly answered the sea, and mingled its roar with the dirges.
'Twas the returning tide, that afar from the waste of the ocean,
With the first dawn of the day, came heaving and hurrying landward.
Then recommenced once more the stir and noise of embarking;
And with the ebb of that tide the ships sailed out of the harbour,
Leaving behind them the dead on the shore, and the village in ruins.

PART THE SECOND.

I.

Many a weary year had passed since the burning of Grand-Pré,
When on the falling tide the freighted vessels departed,

Bearing a nation, with all its household gods, into exile,
Exile without an end, and without an example in story.
Far asunder, on separate coasts, the Acadians landed;
Scattered were they, like flakes of snow, when the wind from the north-east
Strikes aslant through the fogs that darken the Banks of Newfoundland.
Friendless, homeless, hopeless, they wandered from city to city,
From the cold lakes of the North to sultry Southern savannas,—
From the bleak shores of the sea to the lands where the Father of Waters
Seizes the hills in his hands, and drags them down to the ocean,
Deep in their sands to bury the scattered bones of the mammoth.
Friends they sought and homes; and many, despairing, heart-broken,
Asked of the earth but a grave, and no longer a friend nor a fireside.
Written their history stands on tablets of stone in the church-yards.
Long among them was seen a maiden who waited and wandered,
Lowly and meek in spirit, and patiently suffering all things.
Fair was she and young; but, alas! before her extended,
Dreary and vast and silent, the desert of life, with its pathway
Marked by the graves of those who had sorrowed and suffered before her,
Passions long extinguished, and hopes long dead and abandoned,
As the emigrant's way o'er the Western desert is marked by
Camp-fires long consumed, and bones that bleach in the sunshine.
Something there was in her life incomplete, imperfect, unfinished;
As if a morning of June, with all its music and sunshine,
Suddenly paused in the sky, and, fading, slowly descended
Into the east again, from whence it late had arisen.
Sometimes she lingered in towns, till, urged the fever within her,
Urged by a restless longing, the hunger and thirst of the spirit,
She would commence again her endless search and endeavour;
Sometimes in church-yards strayed, and gazed on the crosses and tombstones,
Sat by some nameless grave, and thought that perhaps in its bosom
He was already at rest, and she longed to slumber beside him.
Sometimes a rumor, a hearsay, an inarticulate whisper,
Came with its airy hand to point and beckon her forward.
Sometimes she spake with those who had seen her beloved and known him,
But it was long ago, in some far-off place or forgotten.
"Gabriel Lajeunesse!" said others; "O, yes! we have seen him.
He was with Basil the blacksmith, and both have gone to the prairies;
Coureurs-des-Bois are they, and famous hunters and trappers."
"Gabriel Lajeunesse!" said others; "O, yes! we have seen him.
He is a Voyageur in the lowlands of Louisiana."

Then would they say,—" Dear child! why dream and wait for him longer?
Are there not other youths as fair as Gabriel? others
Who have hearts as tender and true, and spirits as loyal?
Here is Baptiste Leblanc, the notary's son, who has loved thee
Many a tedious year; come, give him thy hand and be happy!
Thou art too fair to be left to braid St. Catherine's tresses."
Then would Evangeline answer, serenely but sadly,—" I cannot!
Whither my heart has gone, there follows my hand, and not elsewhere.
For when the heart goes before, like a lamp, and illumines the pathway,
Many things are made clear, that else lie hidden in darkness."
And thereupon the priest, her friend and father-confessor,
Said, with a smile,—" O daughter! thy God thus speaketh within thee!
Talk not of wasted affection, affection never was wasted;
If it enrich not the heart of another, its waters, returning
Back to their springs, like the rain, shall fill them full of refreshment;
That which the fountain sends forth returns again to the fountain.
Patience; accomplish thy labor; accomplish thy work of affection!
Sorrow and silence are strong, and patient endurance is godlike,
Therefore accomplish thy labor of love, till the heart is made godlike,
Purified, strengthened, perfected, and rendered more worthy of heaven!"
Cheered by the good man's words, Evangeline labored and waited.
Still in her heart she heard the funeral dirge of the ocean,
But with its sound there was mingled a voice that whispered, " Despair not!"
Thus did that poor soul wander in want and cheerless discomfort,
Bleeding, barefooted, over the shards and thorns of existence.
Let me essay, O Muse! to follow the wanderer's footsteps;—
Not through each devious path, each changeful year of existence;
But as a traveller follows a streamlet's course through the valley;
Far from its margin at times, and seeing the gleam of its water
Here and there, in some open space, and at intervals only;
Then drawing nearer its banks, through sylvan glooms that conceal it,
Though he behold it not, he can hear its continuous murmur;
Happy, at length, if he find the spot where it reaches an outlet.

II.

It was the month of May. Far down the Beautiful River,
Past the Ohio shore and past the mouth of the Wabash,
Into the golden stream of the broad and swift Mississippi,
Floated a cumbrous boat, that was rowed by Acadian boatmen.
It was a band of exiles: a raft, as it were, from the shipwrecked
Nation, scattered along the coast, now floating together,
Bound by the bonds of a common belief and a common misfortune;
Men and women and children, who, guided by hope or by hearsay,
Sought for their kith and their kin among the few-acred farmers
On the Acadian coast, and the prairies of fair Opelousas.
With them Evangeline went, and her guide, the Father Felician.
Onward o'er sunken sands, through a wilderness sombre with forests,
Day after day they glided adown the turbulent river;
Night after night, by their blazing fires, encamped on its borders.

Now through rushing chutes, among green islands, where plumelike
Cotton-trees nodded their shadowy crests, they swept with the current,
Then emerged into broad lagoons, where silvery sand-bars
Lay in the stream, and along the wimpling waves of their margin,
Shining with snow-white plumes, large flocks of pelicans waded.
Level the landscape grew, and along the shores of the river,
Shaded by china-trees, in the midst of luxuriant gardens,
Stood the houses of planters, with negro-cabins and dove-cots.
They were approaching the region where reigns perpetual summer,
Where through the Golden Coast, and groves of orange and citron,
Sweeps with majestic curve the river away to the eastward.
They, too, swerved from their course; and, entering the Bayou of Plaquemine,
Soon were lost in a maze of sluggish and devious waters,
Which, like a network of steel, extended in every direction.
Over their heads the towering and tenebrous boughs of the cypress
Met in a dusky arch, and trailing mosses in mid air
Waved like banners that hang on the walls of ancient cathedrals.
Deathlike the silence seemed, and unbroken, save by the herons
Home to their roosts in the cedar-trees returning at sunset,
Or by the owl, as he greeted the moon with demoniac laughter.
Lovely the moonlight was as it glanced and gleamed on the water,
Gleamed on the columns of cypress and cedar sustaining the arches,
Down through whose broken vaults it fell as through chinks in a ruin.
Dreamlike, and indistinct, and strange were all things around them ;
And o'er their spirits there came a feeling of wonder and sadness,—
Strange forebodings of ill, unseen and that cannot be compassed.
As, at the tramp of a horse's hoof on the turf of the prairies,
Far in advance are closed the leaves of the shrinking mimosa,
So, at the hoof-beats of fate, with sad forebodings of evil,
Shrinks and closes the heart, ere the stroke of doom has attained it.
But Evangeline's heart was sustained by a vision, that faintly
Floated before her eyes, and beckoned her on through the moonlight.
It was the thought of her brain that assumed the shape of a phantom.
Through those shadowy aisles had Gabriel wandered before her,
And every stroke of the oar now brought him nearer and nearer.

Then in his place, at the prow of the boat, rose one of the oarsmen,
And, as a signal sound, if others like them peradventure
Sailed on those gloomy and midnight streams, blew a blast on his bugle.
Wild through the dark colonnades and corridors leafy the blast rang,

Breaking the seal of silence, and giving tongues to the forest.
Soundless above them the banners of moss just stirred to the music.
Multitudinous echoes awoke and died in the distance,
Over the watery floor, and beneath the reverberant branches;
But not a voice replied; no answer came from the darkness;
And when the echoes had ceased, like a sense of pain was the silence.
Then Evangeline slept : but the boatmen rowed through the midnight,
Silent at times, then singing familiar Canadian boat-songs,
Such as they sang of old on their own Acadian rivers.

And through the night were heard the mysterious sounds of the desert,
Far off, indistinct, as of wave or wind in the forest,
Mixed with the whoop of the crane and the roar of the grim alligator.

  Thus ere another noon they emerged from those shades; and before them
Lay, in the golden sun, the lakes of the Atchafalaya.
Water-lilies in myriads rocked on the slight undulations
Made by the passing oars, and, resplendent in beauty, the lotus
Lifted her golden crown above the heads of the boatmen.
Faint was the air with the odorous breath of magnolia blossoms,
And with the heat of noon; and numberless sylvan islands,
Fragrant and thickly embowered with blossoming hedges of roses,
Near to whose shores they glided along, invited to slumber.
Soon by the fairest of these their weary oars were suspended.
Under the boughs of Wachita willows, that grew by the margin,
Safely their boat was moored; and scattered about on the greensward,
Tired with their midnight toil, the weary travellers slumbered.
Over them vast and high extended the cope of a cedar.
Swinging from its great arms, the trumpet-flower and the grape-vine
Hung their ladder of ropes aloft like the ladder of Jacob,
On whose pendulous stairs the angels ascending, descending,
Were the swift humming-birds, that flitted from blossom to blossom.
Such was the vision Evangeline saw as she slumbered beneath it.
Filled was her heart with love, and the dawn of an opening heaven
Lighted her soul in sleep with the glory of regions celestial.

  Nearer and ever nearer, among the numberless islands,
Darted a light, swift boat, that sped away o'er the water,
Urged on its course by the sinewy arms of hunters and trappers.
Northward its prow was turned, to the land of the bison and beaver.
At the helm sat a youth, with countenance thoughtful and careworn.
Dark and neglected locks overshadowed his brow, and a sadness
Somewhat beyond his years on his face was legibly written.
Gabriel was it, who, weary with waiting, unhappy and restless,
Sought in the Western wilds oblivion of self and of sorrow.
Swiftly they glided along, close under the lee of the island,
But by the opposite bank, and behind a screen of palmettos,
So that they saw not the boat, where it lay concealed in the willows,
And undisturbed by the dash of their oars, and unseen, were the sleepers;
Angel of God was there none to awaken the slumbering maiden.

Swiftly they glided away, like the shade of a cloud on the prairie.
After the sound of their oars on the tholes had died in the distance,
As from a magic trance the sleepers awoke, and the maiden
Said with a sigh to the friendly priest,—" O Father Felician !
Something says in my heart that near me Gabriel wanders.
Is it a foolish dream, an idle and vague superstition ?
Or has an angel passed, and revealed the truth to my spirit ? "
Then, with a blush, she added,—" Alas for my credulous fancy !
Unto ears like thine such words as these have no meaning."
But made answer the reverend man, and he smiled as he answered,—
" Daughter, thy words are not idle ; nor are they to me without meaning.
Feeling is deep and still ; and the word that floats on the surface
Is as the tossing buoy, that betrays where the anchor is hidden.
Therefore trust to thy heart, and to what the world calls illusions.
Gabriel truly is near thee ; for not far away to the southward,
On the banks of the Têche, are the towns of St. Maur and St. Martin.
There the long-wandering bride shall be given again to her bridegroom,
There the long-absent pastor regain his flock and his sheepfold.
Beautiful is the land, with its prairies and forests of fruit-trees ;
Under the feet a garden of flowers, and the bluest of heavens
Bending above, and resting its dome on the walls of the forest.
They who dwell there have named it the Eden of Louisiana."

And with these words of cheer they arose and continued their journey.
Softly the evening came.   The sun from the western horizon
Like a magician extended his golden wand o'er the landscape ;
Twinkling vapors arose ; and sky and water and forest
Seemed all on fire at the touch, and melted and mingled together.
Hanging between two skies, a cloud with edges of silver,
Floated the boat, with its dripping oars, on the motionless water.
Filled was Evangeline's heart with inexpressible sweetness.
Touched by the magic spell, the sacred fountains of feeling
Glowed with the light of love, as the skies and waters around her.
Then from a neighbouring thicket the mocking-bird, wildest of singers,
Swinging aloft on a willow spray that hung o'er the water,
Shook from his little throat such floods of delirious music,
That the whole air and the woods and the waves seemed silent to listen.
Plaintive at first were the tones and sad ; then soaring to madness
Seemed they to follow or guide the revel of frenzied Bacchantes.
Single notes were then heard, in sorrowful, low lamentation ;

D D

Till, having gathered them all, he flung them abroad in derision,
As when, after a storm, a gust of wind through the tree-tops
Shakes down the rattling rain in a crystal shower on the branches.
With such a prelude as this, and hearts that throbbed with emotion,
Slowly they entered the Têche, where it flows through the green Opelousas,
And through the amber air, above the crest of the woodland,
Saw the column of smoke that arose from a neighbouring dwelling;—
Sounds of a horn they heard, and the distant lowing of cattle.

III.

Near to the bank of the river, o'ershadowed by oaks, from whose branches
Garlands of Spanish moss and of mystic mistletoe flaunted,
Such as the Druids cut down with golden hatchets at Yule-tide,
Stood, secluded and still, the house of the herdsman.   A garden
Girded it round about with a belt of luxuriant blossoms,
Filling the air with fragrance.   The house itself was of timbers
Hewn from the cypress-tree, and carefully fitted together.
Large and low was the roof; and on slender columns supported,
Rose-wreathed, vine-encircled, a broad and spacious veranda,
Haunt of the humming-bird and the bee, extended around it.
At each end of the house, amid the flowers of the garden,
Stationed the dove-cots were, as love's perpetual symbol,
Scenes of endless wooing, and endless contentions of rivals.
Silence reigned o'er the place.   The line of shadow and sunshine
Ran near the tops of the trees; but the house itself was in shadow,
And from its chimney-top, ascending and slowly expanding
Into the evening air, a thin blue column of smoke rose.
In the rear of the house, from the garden gate, ran a pathway
Through the great groves of oak to the skirts of the limitless prairie,
Into whose sea of flowers the sun was slowly descending.
Full in his track of light, like ships with shadowy canvas
Hanging loose from their spars in a motionless calm in the tropics,
Stood a cluster of trees, with tangled cordage of grape-vines.

   Just where the woodlands met the flowery surf of the prairie,
Mounted upon his horse, with Spanish saddle and stirrups,

Sat a herdsman, arrayed in gaiters and doublet of deerskin.
Broad and brown was the face that from under the Spanish sombrero
Glazed on the peaceful scene, with the lordly look of its master.

Round about him were numberless herds of kine, that were grazing
Quietly in the meadows, and breathing the vapory freshness
That uprose from the river, and spread itself over the landscape.
Slowly lifting the horn that hung at his side, and expanding
Fully his broad, deep chest, he blew a blast, that resounded
Wildly and sweet and far, through the still damp air of the evening.
Suddenly out of the grass the long white horns of the cattle
Rose like flakes of foam on the adverse currents of ocean.
Silent a moment they gazed, then bellowing rushed o'er the prairie,
And the whole mass became a cloud, a shade in the distance.
Then, as the herdsman turned to the house, through the gate of the garden
Saw he the forms of the priest and the maiden advancing to meet him.
Suddenly down from his horse he sprang in amazement, and forward
Rushed with extended arms and exclamations of wonder;
When they beheld his face, they recognised Basil the Blacksmith.
Hearty his welcome was, as he led his guests to the garden.
There in an arbour of roses with endless question and answer
Gave they vent to their hearts, and renewed their friendly embraces,
Laughing and weeping by turns, or sitting silent and thoughtful.
Thoughtful, for Gabriel came not; and now dark doubts and misgivings
Stole o'er the maiden's heart; and Basil, somewhat embarrassed,
Broke the silence and said,—"If you came by the Atchafalaya,
How have you nowhere encountered my Gabriel's boat on the bayous?"
Over Evangeline's face at the words of Basil a shade passed.
Tears came into her eyes, and she said, with a tremulous accent,—
"Gone? is Gabriel gone?" and, concealing her face on his shoulder,
All her o'erburdened heart gave way, and she wept and lamented.
Then the good Basil said,—and his voice grew blithe as he said it,—
"Be of good cheer, my child; it is only to-day he departed.
Foolish boy! he has left me alone with my herds and my horses.
Moody and restless grown, and tried and troubled, his spirit
Could no longer endure the calm of this quiet existence.
Thinking ever of thee, uncertain and sorrowful ever,
Ever silent, or speaking only of thee and his troubles,
He at length had become so tedious to men and to maidens,
Tedious even to me, that at length I bethought me, and sent him
Unto the town of Adayes to trade for mules with the Spaniards.
Thence he will follow the Indian trails to the Ozark Mountains,
Hunting for furs in the forests, on rivers trapping the beaver.
Therefore be of good cheer; we will follow the fugitive lover;

He is not far on his way, and the Fates and the streams are against him.
Up and away to-morrow, and through the red dew of the morning
We will follow him fast, and bring him back to his prison."

Then glad voices were heard, and up from the banks of the river,
Borne aloft on his comrades' arms, came Michael the fiddler.
Long under Basil's roof had he lived like a god on Olympus,
Having no other care than dispensing music to mortals.

Far renowned was he for his silver locks and his fiddle.
"Long live Michael," they cried, "our brave Acadian minstrel!"
As they bore him aloft in triumphal procession; and straightway
Father Felician advanced with Evangeline, greeting the old man
Kindly and oft, and recalling the past, while Basil, enraptured,
Hailed with hilarious joy his old companions and gossips,
Laughing loud and long, and embracing mothers and daughters.
Much they marvelled to see the wealth of the ci-devant blacksmith,
All his domains and his herds, and his patriarchal demeanour;
Much they marvelled to hear his tales of the soil and the climate,
And of the prairies, whose numberless herds were his who would take them;
Each one thought in his heart, that he, too, would go and do likewise.
Thus they ascended the steps, and, crossing the airy veranda,
Entered the hall of the house, where already the supper of Basil
Waited his late return; and they rested and feasted together.

Over the joyous feast the sudden darkness descended.
All was silent without, and, illuming the landscape with silver,
Fair rose the dewy moon and the myriad stars, but within doors,
Brighter than these, shone the faces of friends in the glimmering lamplight.
Then from his station aloft, at the head of the table, the herdsman
Poured forth his heart and his wine together in endless profusion.
Lighting his pipe, that was filled with sweet Natchitoches tobacco,
Thus he spake to his guests, who listened, and smiled as they listened:—
"Welcome once more, my friends, who so long have been friendless and homeless,
Welcome once more to a home, that is better perchance than the old one!
Here no hungry winter congeals our blood like the rivers;
Here no stony ground provokes the wrath of the farmer.
Smoothly the ploughshare runs through the soil as a keel through the water.
All the year round the orange-groves are in blossom; and grass grows
More in a single night than a whole Canadian summer.
Here, too, numberless herds run wild and unclaimed in the prairies;
Here, too, lands may be had for the asking, and forests of timber
With a few blows of the axe are hewn and framed into houses.
After your houses are built, and your fields are yellow with harvests,
No King George of England shall drive you away from your homesteads,
Burning your dwellings and barns, and stealing your farms and your cattle."
Speaking these words, he blew a wrathful cloud from his nostrils,
And his huge, brawny hand came thundering down on the table,
So that the guests all started; and Father Felician, astounded,

Suddenly paused, with a pinch of snuff half-way to his nostrils.
But the brave Basil resumed, and his words were milder and gayer:—
" Only beware of the fever, my friends, beware of the fever!
For it is not like that of our cold Acadian climate,
Cured by wearing a spider hung round one's neck in a nutshell!"
Then there were voices heard at the door, and footsteps approaching
Sounded upon the stairs and the floor of the breezy veranda.
It was the neighbouring Creoles and small Acadian planters,
Who had been summoned all to the house of Basil the Herdsman.
Merry the meeting was of ancient comrades and neighbours:
Friend clasped friend in his arms; and they who before were as strangers,
Meeting in exile, became straightway as friends to each other,
Drawn by the gentle bond of a common country together.
But in the neighbouring hall a strain of music, proceeding
From the accordant strings of Michael's melodious fiddle,
Broke up all further speech.   Away, like children delighted,
All things forgotten beside, they gave themselves to the maddening
Whirl of the dizzy dance, as it swept and swayed to the music,
Dreamlike, with beaming eyes and the rush of fluttering garments.

Meanwhile, apart, at the head of the hall, the priest and the herdsman
Sat, conversing together of past and present and future;
While Evangeline stood like one entranced, for within her
Olden memories rose, and loud in the midst of the music
Heard she the sound of the sea, and an irrepressible sadness
Came o'er her heart, and unseen she stole forth into the garden.
Beautiful was the night. Behind the black wall of the forest,
Tipping its summit with silver, arose the moon. On the river
Fell here and there through the branches a tremulous gleam of the moonlight,
Like the sweet thoughts of love on a darkened and devious spirit.
Nearer and round about her, the manifold flowers of the garden
Poured out their souls in odors, that were their prayers and confessions
Unto the night, as it went its way, like a silent Carthusian.
Fuller of fragrance than they, and as heavy with shadows and night-dews,
Hung the heart of the maiden. The calm and the magical moonlight
Seemed to inundate her soul with indefinable longings,
As, through the garden gate, beneath the brown shade of the oak-trees,
Passed she along the path to the edge of the measureless prairie.

Silent it lay, with a silvery haze upon it, and fire-flies
Gleaming and floating away in mingled and infinite numbers.
Over her head the stars, the thoughts of God in the heavens,
Shone on the eyes of man, who had ceased to marvel and worship,
Save when a blazing comet was seen on the walls of that temple,
As if a hand had appeared and written upon them, " Upharsin."
And the soul of the maiden, between the stars and the fire-flies,
Wandered alone, and she cried,—" O Gabriel ! O my beloved !
Art thou so near unto me, and yet I cannot behold thee ?
Art thou so near unto me, and yet thy voice does not reach me ?
Ah ! how often thy feet have trod this path to the prairie !
Ah ! how often thine eyes have looked on the woodlands around me !
Ah ! how often beneath this oak, returning from labor,
Thou hast lain down to rest, and to dream of me in thy slumbers,
When shall these eyes behold, these arms be folded about thee ?"
Loud and sudden and near the note of a whippoorwill sounded
Like a flute in the woods ; and anon, through the neighbouring thickets,
Farther and farther away it floated and dropped into silence.
" Patience !" whispered the oaks from oracular caverns of darkness ;
And, from the moonlit meadow, a sigh responded, " To-morrow !"

Bright rose the sun next day ; and all the flowers of the garden
Bathed his shining feet with their tears, and anointed his tresses
With the delicious balm that they bore in their vases of crystal.
" Farewell !" said the priest, as he stood at the shadowy threshold ;
" See that you bring us the Prodigal Son from his fasting and famine,
And, too, the Foolish Virgin, who slept when the bridegroom was coming."
" Farewell !" answered the maiden, and, smiling, with Basil descended
Down to the river's brink, where the boatmen already were waiting.
Thus beginning their journey with morning, and sunshine, and gladness,
Swiftly they followed the flight of him who was speeding before them,
Blown by the blast of fate like a dead leaf over the desert.
Not that day, nor the next, nor yet the day that succeeded,
Found they trace of his course, in lake or forest or river,
Nor, after many days, had they found him ; but vague and uncertain
Rumors alone were their guides through a wild and desolate country ;
Till, at the little inn of the Spanish town of Adayes,
Weary and worn, they alighted, and learned from the garrulous landlord,
That on the day before, with horses and guides and companions,
Gabriel left the village, and took the road of the prairies,

IV.

Far in the West there lies a desert land, where the mountains
Lift, through perpetual snows, their lofty and luminous summits.
Down from their jagged, deep ravines, where the gorge, like a gateway,
Opens a passage rude to the wheels of the emigrant's wagon,
Westward the Oregon flows and the Walleway and the Owyhee.
Eastward, with devious course, among the Wind-river Mountains,
Through the Sweet-water Valley precipitate leaps the Nebraska;
And to the south, from Fontaine-qui-bout and the Spanish sierras,
Fretted with sands and rocks, and swept by the wind of the desert,
Numberless torrents, with ceaseless sound, descend to the ocean,
Like the great chords of a harp, in loud and solemn vibrations.
Spreading between these streams are the wondrous, beautiful prairies,
Billowy bays of grass ever rolling in shadow and sunshine,
Bright with luxuriant clusters of roses and purple amorphas.

Over them wander the buffalo herds, and the elk and the roebuck ;
Over them wander the wolves, and herds of riderless horses ;
Fires that blast and blight, and winds that are weary with travel ;
Over them wander the scattered tribes of Ishmael's children,
Staining the desert with blood ; and above their terrible war-trails
Circles and sails aloft, on pinions majestic, the vulture,

Like the implacable soul of a chieftain slaughtered in battle,
By invisible stairs ascending and scaling the heavens.
Here and there rise smokes from the camps of these savage marauders;
Here and there rise groves from the margins of swift-running rivers;
And the grim, taciturn bear, the anchorite monk of the desert,
Climbs down their dark ravines to dig for roots by the brook-side,
And over all is the sky, the clear and crystalline heaven,
Like the protecting hand of God inverted above them.

Into this wonderful land, at the base of the Ozark Mountains,
Gabriel far had entered, with hunters and trappers behind him.
Day after day, with their Indian guides, the maiden and Basil
Followed his flying steps, and thought each day to o'ertake him.
Sometimes they saw, or thought they saw, the smoke of his camp-fire
Rise in the morning air from the distant plain; but at nightfall,
When they had reached the place, they found only embers and ashes.
And, though their hearts were sad at times and their bodies were weary,
Hope still guided them on, as the magic Fata Morgana
Showed them her lakes of light, that retreated and vanished before them.

Once, as they sat by their evening fire, there silently entered
Into the little camp an Indian woman, whose features
Wore deep traces of sorrow, and patience as great as her sorrow.
She was a Shawnee woman returning home to her people,
From the far-off hunting-grounds of the cruel Camanches,
Where her Canadian husband, a Coureur-des-Bois, had been murdered.
Touched were their hearts at her story, and warmest and friendliest welcome
Gave they, with words of cheer, and she sat and feasted among them
On the buffalo-meat and the venison cooked on the embers.
But when their meal was done, and Basil and all his companions,
Worn with the long day's march and the chase of the deer and the bison,
Stretched themselves on the ground, and slept where the quivering fire-light
Flashed on their swarthy cheeks, and their forms wrapped up in their blankets,
Then at the door of Evangeline's tent she sat and repeated
Slowly, with soft, low voice, and the charm of her Indian accent,
All the tale of her love, with its pleasures, and pains, and reverses.
Much Evangeline wept at the tale, and to know that another
Hapless heart like her own had loved and had been disappointed
Moved to the depths of her soul by pity and woman's compassion.
Yet in her sorrow pleased that one who had suffered was near her,

She in turn related her love and all its disasters.
Mute with wonder the Shawnee sat, and when she had ended
Still was mute; but at length, as if a mysterious horror
Passed through her brain, she spake, and repeated the tale of the Mowis;
Mowis, the bridegroom of snow, who won and wedded a maiden,
But, when the morning came, arose and passed from the wigwam,
Fading and melting away and dissolving into the sunshine,
Till she beheld him no more, though she followed far into the forest.
Then, in those sweet, low tones, that seemed like a weird incantation,
Told she the tale of the fair Lilinau, who was wooed by a phantom,
That, through the pines o'er her father's lodge, in the hush of the twilight,
Breathed like the evening wind, and whispered love to the maiden,
Till she followed his green and waving plume through the forest,
And never more returned, nor was seen again by her people.
Silent with wonder and strange surprise, Evangeline listened
To the soft flow of her magical words, till the region around her
Seemed like enchanted ground, and her swarthy guest the enchantress.
Slowly over the tops of the Ozark Mountains the moon rose,
Lighting the little tent, and with a mysterious splendor
Touching the sombre leaves, and embracing and filling the woodland.

With a delicious sound the brook rushed by, and the branches
Swayed and sighed overhead in scarcely audible whispers.
Filled with the thoughts of love was Evangeline's heart, but a secret,
Subtile sense crept in of pain and indefinite terror,
As the cold, poisonous snake creeps into the nest of the swallow.
It was no earthly fear.   A breath from the region of spirits
Seemed to float in the air of night; and she felt for a moment
That, like the Indian maid, she, too, was pursuing a phantom.
And with this thought she slept, and the fear and the phantom had vanished.

Early upon the morrow the march was resumed; and the Shawnee
Said, as they journeyed along,—" On the western slope of these mountains
Dwells in his little village the Black Robe chief of the Mission.
Much he teaches the people, and tells them of Mary and Jesus;
Loud laugh their hearts with joy, and weep with pain, as they hear him."
Then, with a sudden and secret emotion, Evangeline answered,—
" Let us go to the Mission, for there good tidings await us !"
Thither they turned their steeds; and behind a spur of the mountains,
Just as the sun went down, they heard a murmur of voices,
And in a meadow green and broad, by the bank of a river,
Saw the tents of the Christians, the tents of the Jesuit Mission.
Under a towering oak, that stood in the midst of the village,
Knelt the Black Robe chief with his children.   A crucifix fastened
High on the trunk of the tree, and overshadowed by grape-vines,
Looked with its agonized face on the multitude kneeling beneath it.
This was their rural chapel.   Aloft, through the intricate arches
Of its aërial roof, arose the chant of their vespers,
Mingling its notes with the soft susurrus and sighs of the branches.
Silent, with heads uncovered, the travellers, nearer approaching,
Knelt on the swarded floor, and joined in the evening devotions.
But when the service was done, and the benediction had fallen
Forth from the hands of the priest, like seed from the hands of the sower,
Slowly the reverend man advanced to the strangers, and bade them
Welcome; and when they replied, he smiled with benignant expression,
Hearing the homelike sounds of his mother-tongue in the forest,
And with words of kindness conducted them into his wigwam.
There upon mats and skins they reposed, and on cakes of the maize-ear
Feasted, and slaked their thirst from the water-gourd of the teacher.
Soon was their story told; and the priest with solemnity answered :—
" Not six suns have risen and set since Gabriel, seated

On this mat by my side, where now the maiden reposes,
Told me this same sad tale; then arose and continued his journey!"
Soft was the voice of the priest, and he spake with an accent of kindness;
But on Evangeline's heart fell his words as in winter the snow-flakes
Fall into some lone nest from which the birds have departed.
" Far to the north he has gone," continued the priest; " but in autumn,
When the chase is done, will return again to the Mission."
Then Evangeline said, and her voice was meek and submissive,—
" Let me remain with thee, for my soul is sad and afflicted."
So seemed it wise and well unto all; and betimes on the morrow,
Mounting his Mexican steed, with his Indian guides and companions,
Homeward Basil returned, and Evangeline stayed at the Mission.

Slowly, slowly, slowly the days succeeded each other,—
Days and weeks and months; and the fields of maize that were springing
Green from the ground when a stranger she came, now waving above her,
Lifted their slender shafts, with leaves interlacing, and forming
Cloisters for mendicant crows and granaries pillaged by squirrels.
Then in the golden weather the maize was husked, and the maidens
Blushed at each blood-red ear, for that betokened a lover,
But at the crooked laughed, and called it a thief in the corn-field.
Even the blood-red ear to Evangeline brought not her lover.
" Patience!" the priest would say; " have faith, and thy prayer will be answered!
Look at this delicate plant that lifts its head from the meadow,
See how its leaves all point to the north, as true as the magnet;
It is the compass-flower, that the finger of God has suspended
Here on its fragile stalk, to direct the traveller's journey
Over the sea-like, pathless, limitless waste of the desert.
Such in the soul of man is faith.   The blossoms of passion,
Gay and luxuriant flowers, are brighter and fuller of fragrance,
But they beguile us, and lead us astray, and their odor is deadly.
Only this humble plant can guide us here, and hereafter
Crown us with asphodel flowers, that are wet with the dews of nepenthe."

So came the autumn, and passed, and the winter,—yet Gabriel came not;
Blossomed the opening spring, and the voice of the robin and blue-bird
Sounded sweet upon wold and in wood, yet Gabriel came not.
But on the breath of the summer winds a rumor was wafted
Sweeter than song of bird, or hue or odor of blossom.
Far to the north and east, it said, in the Michigan forests,

Gabriel had his lodge by the banks of the Saginaw river.
And, with returning guides, that sought the lakes of St. Lawrence,
Saying a sad farewell, Evangeline went from the Mission.
When over weary ways, by long and perilous marches,
She had attained at length the depths of the Michigan forests,
Found she the hunter's lodge deserted and fallen to ruin!

Thus did the long sad years glide on, and in seasons and places
Divers and distant far was seen the wandering maiden;—
Now in the tents of grace of the meek Moravian Missions,
Now in the noisy camps and the battle-fields of the army,
Now in secluded hamlets, in towns and populous cities,
Like a phantom she came, and passed away unremembered.
Fair was she and young, when in hope began the long journey:
Faded was she and old, when in disappointment it ended.
Each succeeding year stole something away from her beauty,
Leaving behind it, broader and deeper, the gloom and the shadow.
Then there appeared and spread faint streaks of gray o'er her forehead,
Dawn of another life, that broke o'er her earthly horizon,
As in the eastern sky the first faint streaks of the morning.

V.

In that delightful land which is washed by the Delaware's waters,
Guarding in sylvan shades the name of Penn the apostle,
Stands on the banks of its beautiful stream the city he founded.
There all the air is balm, and the peach is the emblem of beauty,
And the streets still re-echo the names of the trees of the forest,
As if they fain would appease the Dryads whose haunts they molested.
There from the troubled sea had Evangeline landed, an exile,
Finding among the children of Penn a home and a country.
There old René Leblanc had died; and when he departed,
Saw at his side only one of all his hundred descendants.
Something at least there was in the friendly streets of the city,
Something that spake to her heart, and made her no longer a stranger
And her ear was pleased with the Thee and Thou of the Quakers,
For it recalled the past, the old Acadian country,

Where all men were equal, and all were brothers and sisters.
So, when the fruitless search, the disappointed endeavour,
Ended, to recommence no more upon earth, uncomplaining,
Thither, as leaves to the light, were turned her thoughts and her footsteps
As from a mountain's top the rainy mists of the morning
Roll away, and afar we behold the landscape below us,

Sun-illumined, with shining rivers and cities and hamlets,
So fell the mists from her mind, and she saw the world far below her,
Dark no longer, but all illumined with love; and the pathway
Which she had climbed so far, lying smooth and fair in the distance.
Gabriel was not forgotten. Within her heart was his image,
Clothed in the beauty of love and youth, as last she beheld him,
Only more beautiful made by his deathlike silence and absence.
Into her thoughts of him time entered not, for it was not.
Over him years had no power; he was not changed, but transfigured;
He had become to her heart as one who is dead, and not absent;
Patience and abnegation of self, and devotion to others,
This was the lesson a life of trial and sorrow had taught her.
So was her love diffused, but, like to some odorous spices,
Suffered no waste nor loss, though filling the air with aroma.
Other hope had she none, nor wish in life, but to follow
Meekly, with reverent steps, the sacred feet of her Saviour.
Thus many years she lived as a Sister of Mercy; frequenting
Lonely and wretched roofs in the crowded lanes of the city,
Where distress and want concealed themselves from the sunlight,
Where disease and sorrow in garrets languished neglected.
Night after night, when the world was asleep, as the watchman repeated
Loud, through the gusty streets, that all was well in the city,
High at some lonely window he saw the light of her taper.
Day after day, in the gray of the dawn, as slow through the suburbs
Plodded the German farmer, with flowers and fruits for the market,
Met he that meek, pale face, returning home from its watchings.

    Then it came to pass that a pestilence fell on the city,
Presaged by wondrous signs, and mostly by flocks of wild pigeons,
Darkening the sun in their flight, with nought in their craws but an acorn.
And, as the tides of the sea arise in the month of September,
Flooding some silver stream, till it spreads to a lake in the meadow,
So death flooded life, and, o'erflowing its natural margin,
Spread to a brackish lake, the silver stream of existence.
Wealth had no power to bribe, nor beauty to charm, the oppressor;
But all perished alike beneath the scourge of his anger;—
Only, alas! the poor, who had neither friends nor attendants,
Crept away to die in the almshouse, home of the homeless.
Then in the suburbs it stood, in the midst of meadows and woodlands;—
Now the city surrounds it; but still, with its gateway and wicket

Meek, in the midst of splendour, its humble walls seem to echo
Softly the words of the Lord:—"The poor ye always have with you."
Thither, by night and by day, came the Sister of Mercy. The dying
Looked up into her face, and thought, indeed, to behold there
Gleams of celestial light encircle her forehead with splendor,
Such as the artist paints o'er the brows of saints and apostles,
Or such as hangs by night o'er a city seen at a distance.
Unto their eyes it seemed the lamps of the city celestial,
Into whose shining gates ere long their spirits would enter.

Thus, on a Sabbath morn, through the streets, deserted and silent,
Wending her quiet way, she entered the door of the almshouse.
Sweet on the summer air was the odor of flowers in the garden ;
And she paused on her way to gather the fairest among them,
That the dying once more might rejoice in their fragrance and beauty.
Then, as she mounted the stairs to the corridors, cooled by the east wind,
Distant and soft on her ear fell the chimes from the belfry of Christ Church,
While, intermingled with these, across the meadows were wafted
Sounds of psalms, that were sung by the Swedes in their church at Wicaco.
Soft as descending wings fell the calm of the hour on her spirit ;
Something within her said,—"At length thy trials are ended ;"
And, with light in her looks, she entered the chambers of sickness,
Noiselessly moved about the assiduous careful attendants,
Moistening the feverish lip, and the aching brow, and in silence
Closing the sightless eyes of the dead, and concealing their faces,
Where on their pallets they lay, like drifts of snow by the road-side.
Many a languid head, upraised as Evangeline entered,
Turned on its pillow of pain to gaze while she passed, for her presence
Fell on their hearts like a ray of the sun on the walls of a prison.
And, as she looked around, she saw how Death, the consoler,
Laying his hand upon many a heart, had healed it for ever.
Many familiar forms had disappeared in the night-time ;
Vacant their places were, or filled already by strangers.

Suddenly, as if arrested by fear or a feeling of wonder,
Still she stood, with her colorless lips apart, while a shudder
Ran through her frame, and, forgotten, the flowerets dropped from her fingers,
And from her eyes and cheeks the light and bloom of the morning.
Then there escaped from her lips a cry of such terrible anguish,
That the dying heard it, and started up from their pillows.

On the pallet before her was stretched the form of an old man.
Long, and thin, and gray were the locks that shaded his temples;
But, as he lay in the morning light, his face for a moment
Seemed to assume once more the forms of its earlier manhood;
So are wont to be changed the faces of those who are dying.
Hot and red on his lips still burned the flush of the fever,

As if life, like the Hebrew, with blood had besprinkled its portals,
That the Angel of Death might see the sign, and pass over.
Motionless, senseless, dying, he lay, and his spirit exhausted
Seemed to be sinking down through infinite depths in the darkness,
Darkness of slumber and death, for ever sinking and sinking.
Then through those realms of shade, in multiplied reverberations,
Heard he that cry of pain, and through the hush that succeeded
Whispered a gentle voice, in accents tender and saint-like,
"Gabriel! O my beloved!" and died away into silence.
Then he beheld, in a dream, once more the home of his childhood;
Green Acadian meadows, with sylvan rivers among them,
Village, and mountain, and woodlands; and, walking under their shadow,
As in the days of her youth, Evangeline rose in his vision.
Tears came into his eyes; and as slowly he lifted his eyelids,
Vanished the vision away, but Evangeline knelt by his bedside.
Vainly he strove to whisper her name, for the accents unuttered
Died on his lips, and their motion revealed what his tongue would have spoken.
Vainly he strove to rise; and Evangeline, kneeling beside him,
Kissed his dying lips, and laid his head on her bosom.
Sweet was the light of his eyes; but it suddenly sank into darkness,
As when a lamp is blown out by a gust of wind at a casement.

All was ended now, the hope, and the fear, and the sorrow,
All the aching of heart, the restless unsatisfied longing,
All the dull, deep pain, and constant anguish of patience!
And, as she pressed once more the lifeless head to her bosom,
Meekly she bowed her own, and murmured, "Father, I thank thee!"

STILL stands the forest primeval; but far away from its shadow,
Side by side, in their nameless graves, the lovers are sleeping.
Under the humble walls of the little Catholic church-yard,
In the heart of the city, they lie, unknown and unnoticed.
Daily the tides of life go ebbing and flowing beside them,
Thousands of throbbing hearts, where theirs are at rest and for ever,
Thousands of aching brains, where theirs no longer are busy,
Thousands of toiling hands, where theirs have ceased from their labors,
Thousands of weary feet, where theirs have completed their journey!

Still stands the forest primeval; but under the shade of its branches
Dwells another race, with other customs and language.
Only along the shore of the mournful and misty Atlantic
Linger a few Acadian peasants, whose fathers from exile
Wandered back to their native land to die in its bosom.
In the fisherman's cot the wheel and the loom are still busy;
Maidens still wear their Norman caps and their kirtles of homespun,
And by the evening fire repeat Evangeline's story,
While from its rocky caverns the deep-voiced, neighbouring ocean
Speaks, and in accents disconsolate answers the wail of the forest.

THE SEASIDE AND THE FIRESIDE

—

DEDICATION.

As one who, walking in the twilight gloom,
   Hears round about him voices as it darkens,
And seeing not the forms from which they come,
   Pauses from time to time, and turns and hearkens:

So walking here in twilight, O my friends!
   I hear your voices, softened by the distance,
And pause, and turn to listen, as each sends
   His words of friendship, comfort, and assistance.

If any thought of mine, or sung or told,
   Has ever given delight or consolation,
Ye have repaid me back a thousand fold,
   By every friendly sign and salutation.

Thanks for the sympathies that ye have shown!
   Thanks for each kindly word, each silent token,
That teaches me, when seeming most alone,
   Friends are around us, though no word be spoken.

Kind messages, that pass from land to land;
   Kind letters, that betray the heart's deep history,
In which we feel the pressure of a hand,—
   One touch of fire,—and all the rest is mystery!

The pleasant books, that silently among
  Our household treasures take familiar places,
And are to us as if a living tongue
  Spake from the printed leaves or pictured faces!

Perhaps on earth I never shall behold,
  With eye of sense, your outward form and semblance;
Therefore to me ye never will grow old,
  But live for ever young in my remembrance.

Never grow old, nor change, nor pass away!
  Your gentle voices will flow on for ever,
When life grows bare and tarnished with decay,
  As through a leafless landscape flows a river.

Not chance of birth or place has made us friends,
  Being oftentimes of different tongues and nations,
But the endeavour for the selfsame ends,
  With the same hopes, and fears, and aspirations.

Therefore I hope to join your seaside walk,
  Saddened, and mostly silent, with emotion;
Not interrupting with intrusive talk
  The grand, majestic symphonies of ocean.

Therefore I hope, as no unwelcome guest,
  At your warm fireside, when the lamps are lighted,
To have my place reserved among the rest,
  Nor stand as one unsought and uninvited!

BY THE SEASIDE.

✦

THE BUILDING OF THE SHIP.

" BUILD me straight, O worthy Master!
    Staunch and strong, a goodly vessel,
That shall laugh at all disaster,
    And with wave and whirlwind wrestle!"

The merchant's word
Delighted the Master heard;

For his heart was in his work, and the heart
Giveth grace unto every Art.
A quiet smile played round his lips,
As the eddies and dimples of the tide
Play round the bows of ships,
That steadily at anchor ride.
And with a voice that was full of glee,
He answered, " Ere long we will launch
A vessel as goodly, and strong, and staunch,
As ever weathered a wintry sea!"

And first with nicest skill and art,
Perfect and finished in every part,
A little model the Master wrought,
Which should be to the larger plan
What the child is to the man,
Its counterpart in miniature:
That with a hand more swift and sure
The greater labor might be brought
To answer to his inward thought,
And as he labored, his mind ran o'er
The various ships that were built of yore,
And above them all, and strangest of all
Towered the Great Harry, crank and tall,
Whose picture was hanging on the wall,
With bows and stern raised high in air,
And balconies hanging here and there,
And signal lanterns and flags afloat,
And eight round towers, like those that frown
From some old castle, looking down
Upon the drawbridge and the moat.
And he said with a smile, "Our ship, I wis,
Shall be of another form than this!"

It was of another form, indeed:
Built for freight, and yet for speed,
A beautiful and gallant craft;
Broad in the beam, that the stress of the blast,
Pressing down upon sail and mast,
Might not the sharp bows overwhelm;

Broad in the beam, but sloping aft
With graceful curve and slow degrees,
That she might be docile to the helm,
And that the currents of parted seas,
Closing behind, with mighty force,
Might aid and not impede her course.

In the ship-yard stood the Master,
  With the model of the vessel,
That should laugh at all disaster,
  And with wave and whirlwind wrestle!

Covering many a rood of ground,
Lay the timber piled around;
Timber of chestnut, and elm, and oak,
And scattered here and there, with these,
The knarred and crooked cedar knees;
Brought from regions far away,
From Pascagoula's sunny bay,
And the banks of the roaring Roanoke!
Ah! what a wondrous thing it is
To note how many wheels of toil
One thought, one word, can set in motion!
There's not a ship that sails the ocean,
But every climate, every soil,
Must bring its tribute, great or small,
And help to build the wooden wall!

The sun was rising o'er the sea,
And long the level shadows lay,
As if they, too, the beams would be
Of some great, airy argosy,
Framed and launched in a single day.
That silent architect, the sun,
Had hewn and laid them every one,
Ere the work of man was yet begun.
Beside the Master, when he spoke,
A youth, against an anchor leaning,
Listened, to catch his slightest meaning.
Only the long waves, as they broke

In ripples on the pebbly beach,
Interrupted the old man's speech.

Beautiful they were, in sooth,
The old man and the fiery youth!
The old man, in whose busy brain
Many a ship that sailed the main
Was modelled o'er and o'er again;--
The fiery youth, who was to be
The heir of his dexterity,
The heir of his house, and his daughter's hand,
When he had built and launched from land
What the elder head had planned.

"Thus," said he, "will we build this ship!
Lay square the blocks upon the slip,
And follow well this plan of mine.
Choose the timbers with greatest care;
Of all that is unsound beware;
For only what is sound and strong
To this vessel shall belong.
Cedar of Maine and Georgia pine
Here together shall combine.
A goodly frame, and a goodly fame,
And the Union be her name!
For the day that gives her to the sea
Shall give my daughter unto thee!"

The Master's word
Enraptured the young man heard;
And as he turned his face aside,
With a look of joy and a thrill of pride,
Standing before
Her father's door,
He saw the form of his promised bride.
The sun shone on her golden hair,
And her cheek was glowing fresh and fair,
With the breath of morn and the soft sea-air.
Like a beauteous barge was she,
Still at rest on the sandy beach,
Just beyond the billow's reach;

But lo!
Was the restless, seething, stormy sea!

Ah, how skilful grows the hand
That obeyeth Love's command!
It is the heart and not the brain,
That to the highest doth attain,
And he who followeth Love's behest
Far exceedeth all the rest!

Thus with the rising of the sun
Was the noble task begun,
And soon throughout the ship-yard's bounds
Were heard the intermingled sounds
Of axes and of mallets, plied
With vigorous arms on every side;
Plied so deftly and so well,
That, ere the shadows of evening fell,
The keel of oak for a noble ship,
Scarfed and bolted, straight and strong,
Was lying ready, and stretched along
The blocks, well placed upon the slip.
Happy, thrice happy, every one
Who sees his labor well begun,
And not perplexed and multiplied,
By idly waiting for time and tide!

And when the hot, long day was o'er,
The young man at the Master's door
Sat with the maiden calm and still.
And within the porch, a little more
Removed beyond the evening chill,
The father sat, and told them tales
Of wrecks in the great September gales,
Of pirates upon the Spanish Main,
And ships that never came back again,
The chance and change of a sailor's life,
Want and plenty, rest and strife,
His roving fancy, like the wind,
That nothing can stay and nothing can bind,

And the magic charm of foreign lands,
With shadows of palms, and shining sands,
Where the tumbling surf,
O'er the coral reefs of Madagascar,
Washes the feet of the swarthy Lascar,
As he lies alone and asleep on the turf.
And the trembling maiden held her breath
At the tales of that awful, pitiless sea,
With all its terror and mystery,
The dim, dark sea, so like unto Death,
That divides and yet unites mankind!
And whenever the old man paused, a gleam
From the bowl of his pipe would awhile illume
The silent group in the twilight gloom,
And thoughtful faces, as in a dream;
And for a moment one might mark
What had been hidden by the dark,
That the head of the maiden lay at rest,
Tenderly, on the young man's breast!

Day by day the vessel grew,
With timbers fashioned strong and true,
Stemson and keelson and sternson-knee,
Till, framed with perfect symmetry,
A skeleton ship rose up to view!
And around the bows and along the side
The heavy hammers and mallets plied,
Till after many a week, at length,
Wonderful for form and strength,
Sublime in its enormous bulk,
Loomed aloft the shadowy hulk!
And around it columns of smoke, upwreathing,
Rose from the boiling, bubbling, seething
Caldron, that glowed,
And overflowed
With the black tar, heated for the sheathing.
And amid the clamors
Of clattering hammers,
He who listened heard now and then
The song of the Master and his men :--

" Build me straight, O worthy Master,
  Staunch and strong, a goodly vessel,
That shall laugh at all disaster,
  And with wave and whirlwind wrestle "

With oaken brace and copper band,
Lay the rudder on the sand,
That, like a thought, should have control
Over the movement of the whole ;
And near it the anchor, whose giant hand
Would reach down and grapple with the land,
And immovable and fast
Hold the great ship against the bellowing blast !
And at the bows an image stood,
By a cunning artist carved in wood,
With robes of white, that far behind
Seemed to be fluttering in the wind.
It was not shaped in a classic mould,
Not like a Nymph or Goddess of old,
Or Naiad rising from the water,
But modelled from the Master's daughter !
On many a dreary and misty night,
'Twill be seen by the rays of the signal light,
Speeding along through the rain and the dark,
Like a ghost in its snow-white sark,
The pilot of some phantom bark,
Guiding the vessel, in its flight,
By a path none other knows aright !
Behold, at last,*
Each tall and tapering mast
Is swung into its place ;

* Vessels are sometimes, though not usually, launched fully rigged. I have
availed myself of the exception, as better suited to my purpose than the general
rule ; but the reader will see by the following extract of a letter from a friend
in Portland, Maine, that it is neither a blunder nor a poetic license.

" In this State, and also, I am told, in New York, ships are sometimes rigged upon
the stocks, in order to save time, or to make a show. There was a fine, large ship
launched last summer at Ellsworth, fully rigged and sparred   Some years ago a ship
was launched here, with her rigging, spars, sails, and cargo aboard. She sailed the
next day, and—was never heard of again ! I hope this will not be the fate of your
poem ! "

Shrouds and stays
Holding it firm and fast!

Long ago,
In the deer-haunted forests of Maine,
When upon mountain and plain
Lay the snow,
They fell,—those lordly pines!
Those grand, majestic pines!
'Mid shouts and cheers
The jaded steers,
Panting beneath the goad,
Dragged down the weary, winding road
Those captive kings so straight and tall,
To be shorn of their streaming hair,
And, naked and bare,
To feel the stress and the strain
Of the wind and the reeling main,
Whose roar
Would remind them for evermore
Of their native forests they should not see again.

And everywhere
The slender, graceful spars
Poise aloft in the air,
And at the mast head,
White, blue, and red,
A flag unrolls the stripes and stars.
Ah! when the wanderer, lonely, friendless,
In foreign harbours shall behold
That flag unrolled,
'Twill be as a friendly hand
Stretched out from his native land,
Filling his heart with memories sweet and endless!
All is finished! and at length
Has come the bridal day
Of beauty and of strength.
To-day the vessel shall be launched!
With fleecy clouds the sky is blanched,
And o'er the bay,

Slowly, in all his splendors dight,
The great sun rises to behold the sight.

The ocean old,
Centuries old,
Strong as youth, and as uncontrolled,
Paces restless to and fro,
Up and down the sands of gold.
His beating heart is not at rest;
And far and wide,
With ceaseless flow,
His beard of snow
Heaves with the heaving of his breast.
He waits impatient for his bride.
There she stands,
With her foot upon the sands,
Decked with flags and streamers gay,
In honor of her marriage day.
Her snow-white signals fluttering, blending,
Round her like a veil descending,
Ready to be
The bride of the gray, old sea.

On the deck another bride
Is standing by her lover's side.
Shadows from the flags and shrouds,
Like the shadows cast by clouds,
Broken by many a sunny fleck,
Fall around them on the deck.

The prayer is said,
The service read,
The joyous bridegroom bows his head;
And in tears the good old Master
Shakes the brown hand of his son,
Kisses his daughter's glowing cheek
In silence, for he cannot speak,
And ever faster
Down his own the tears begin to run.
The worthy pastor—

The shepherd of that wandering flock,
That has the ocean for its wold,
That has the vessel for its fold,
Leaping ever from rock to rock—
Spake, with accents mild and clear,
Words of warning, words of cheer,
But tedious to the bridegroom's ear.
He knew the chart
Of the sailor's heart,
All its pleasures and its griefs,
All its shallows and rocky reefs,
All those secret currents, that flow
With such resistless undertow,
And lift and drift, with terrible force,
The will from its moorings and its course.
Therefore he spake, and thus said he:—

"Like unto ships far off at sea,
Outward or homeward bound, are we.
Before, behind, and all around,
Floats and swings the horizon's bound,
Seems at its distant rim to rise
And climb the crystal wall of the skies,
And then again to turn and sink,
As if we could slide from its outer brink.
Ah! it is not the sea,
It is not the sea that sinks and shelves,
But ourselves
That rock and rise
With endless and uneasy motion,
Now touching the very skies,
Now sinking into the depths of ocean.
Ah! if our souls but poise and swing
Like the compass in its brazen ring,
Ever level and ever true
To the toil and the task we have to do,
We shall sail securely, and safely reach
The Fortunate Isles, on whose shining beach
The sights we see, and the sounds we hear,
Will be those of joy and not of fear!"

Then the Master,
With a gesture of command,
Waved his hand;
And at the word,
Loud and sudden there was heard,
All around them and below,
The sound of hammers, blow on blow,
Knocking away the shores and spurs.
And see! she stirs!
She starts,—she moves,—she seems to feel
The thrill of life along her keel.
And, spurning with her foot the ground,
With one exulting, joyous bound,
She leaps into the ocean's arms!

And lo! from the assembled crowd
There rose a shout, prolonged and loud,
That to the ocean seemed to say,—
"Take her, O bridegroom, old and gray,
Take her to thy protecting arms,
With all her youth and all her charms!"

How beautiful she is! How fair
She lies within those arms, that press
Her form within many a soft caress
Of tenderness and watchful care!
Sail forth into the sea, O ship!
Through wind and wave, right onward steer!
The moistened eye, the trembling lip,
Are not the signs of doubt or fear.

Sail forth into the sea of life,
O gentle, loving, trusting wife,
And safe from all adversity
Upon the bosom of that sea
Thy comings and thy goings be!
For gentleness and love and trust
Prevail o'er angry wave and gust;
And in the wreck of noble lives
Something immortal still survives!

Thou, too, sail on, O Ship of State!
Sail on, O Union, strong and great!
Humanity with all its fears,
With all the hopes of future years,
Is hanging breathless on thy fate!
We know what Master laid thy keel,
What Workmen wrought thy ribs of steel,
Who made each mast, and sail, and rope,
What anvils rang, what hammers beat,
In what a forge and what a heat
Were shaped the anchors of thy hope!
Fear not each sudden sound and shock,
'Tis of the wave and not the rock;
'Tis but the flapping of the sail,
And not a rent made by the gale!
In spite of rock and tempest's roar,
In spite of false lights on the shore,
Sail on, nor fear to breast the sea!
Our hearts, our hopes, are all with thee,
Our hearts, our hopes, our prayers, our tears,
Our faith triumphant o'er our fears,
Are all with thee,—are all with thee!

THE EVENING STAR.

Just above yon sandy bar,
    As the day grows fainter and dimmer,
Lonely and lovely, a single star
    Lights the air with a dusky glimmer.

Into the ocean faint and far
    Falls the trail of its golden splendor,
And the gleam of that single star
    Is ever refulgent, soft, and tender.

Chrysaor rising out of the sea,
  Showed thus glorious and thus emulous,
Leaving the arms of Callirrhoe,
  For ever tender, soft, and tremulous.

Thus o'er the ocean faint and far
  Trailed the gleam of his falchion brightly:
Is it a God, or is it a star
  . That, entranced, I gaze on nightly!

—

THE SECRET OF THE SEA.

AH! what pleasant visions haunt me
  As I gaze upon the sea!
All the old romantic legends,
  All my dreams, come back to me.

Sails of silk and ropes of sendal,
  Such as gleam in ancient lore;
And the singing of the sailors,
  And the answer from the shore!

Most of all, the Spanish ballad
  Haunts me oft, and tarries long,
Of the noble Count Arnaldos
  And the sailor's mystic song.

Like the long waves on a sea-beach,
  Where the sand as silver shines,
With a soft, monotonous cadence,
  Flow its unrhymed lyric lines:—

BY THE SEASIDE

Telling how the Count Arnaldos,
  With his hawk upon his hand,
Saw a fair and stately galley,
  Steering onward to the land;—

How he heard the ancient helmsman
  Chant a song so wild and clear,
That the sailing sea-bird slowly
  Poised upon the mast to hear,

Till his soul was full of longing,
  And he cried, with impulse strong,—
"Helmsman! for the love of heaven,
  Teach me, too, that wondrous song!"

"Wouldst thou,"—so the helmsman answered
  "Learn the secret of the sea?
Only those who brave its dangers
  Comprehend its mystery!"

In each sail that skims the horizon,
  In each landward-blowing breeze,
I behold that stately galley,
  Hear those mournful melodies;

Till my soul is full of longing
  For the secret of the sea.
And the heart of the great ocean
  Sends a thrilling pulse through me.

TWILIGHT.

THE twilight is sad and cloudy,
　The wind blows wild and free,
And like the wings of sea-birds
　Flash the white caps of the sea.

But in the fisherman's cottage
　There shines a ruddier light,
And a little face at the window
　Peers out into the night.

Close, close it is pressed to the window,
　As if those childish eyes
Were looking into the darkness,
　To see some form arise.

And a woman's waving shadow
  Is passing to and fro,
Now rising to the ceiling,
  Now bowing and bending low.

What tale do the roaring ocean,
  And the night-wind, bleak and wild,
As they beat at the crazy casement,
  Tell to that little child?

And why do the roaring ocean,
  And the night-wind, wild and bleak,
As they beat at the heart of the mother,
  Drive the color from her cheek?

SIR HUMPHREY GILDERT.[*]

SOUTHWARD with fleet of ice
  Sailed the corsair Death;
Wild and fast blow the blast,
  And the east-wind was his breath.

His lordly ships of ice
  Glistened in the sun;
On each side, like pennons wide,
  Flashing crystal streamlets run.

[*] "When the wind abated and the vessels were near enough, the Admiral was seen constantly sitting in the stern, with a book in his hand. On the 9th of September he was seen for the last time, and was heard by the people of the Hind to say, 'We are as near heaven by sea as by land.' In the following night, the lights of the ship suddenly disappeared. The people in the other vessel kept a good look-out for him during the remainder of the voyage. On the 23d of September they arrived, through much tempest and peril, at Falmouth. But nothing more was seen or heard of the Admiral."—BELKNAP'S American Biography, 1. 203.

His sails of white sea-mist
  Dripped with silver rain;
But where he passed there were cast
  Leaden shadows o'er the main.

Eastward from Campobello
  Sir Humphrey Gilbert sailed;
Three days or more seaward he bore,
  Then, alas! the land-wind failed.

Alas! the land-wind failed,
  And ice-cold grew the night;
And never more, on sea or shore,
  Should Sir Humphrey see the light.

He sat upon the deck,
  The Book was in his hand;
"Do not fear! Heaven is as near,"
  He said, "by water as by land!"

In the first watch of the night,
  Without a signal's sound,
Out of the sea, mysteriously,
  The fleet of Death rose all around.

The moon and the evening star
  Were hanging in the shrouds;
Every mast, as it passed,
  Seemed to rake the passing clouds.

They grappled with their prize,
  At midnight black and cold!
As of a rock was the shock;
  Heavily the ground-swell rolled.

Southward through day and dark,
  They drift in close embrace,
With mist and rain, to the Spanish Main;
  Yet there seems no change of place.

Southward, for ever southward,
  They drift through dark and day;
And like a dream, in the Gulf-Stream
  Sinking, vanish all away.

T I

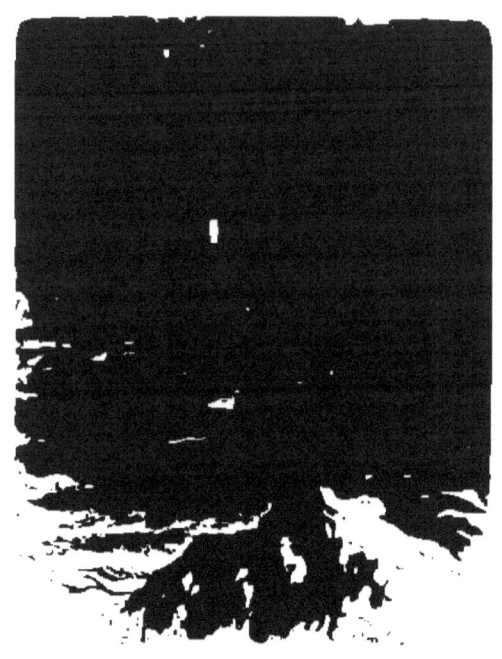

THE LIGHTHOUSE.

The rocky ledge runs far into the sea,
  And on its outer point, some miles away,
The Lighthouse lifts its massive masonry,
  A pillar of fire by night, of cloud by day.

Even at this distance I can see the tides,
  Upbearing, break unheard along its base,
A speechless wrath, that rises and subsides
  In the white lip and tremor of the face.

And as the evening darkens, lo! how bright,
  Through the deep purple of the twilight air,
Beams forth the sudden radiance of its light
  With strange, unearthly splendor in its glare!

Not one alone ; from each projecting cape
  And perilous reef along the ocean's verge,
Starts into life a dim, gigantic shape,
  Holding its lantern o'er the restless surge.

Like the great giant Christopher it stands
  Upon the brink of the tempestuous wave,
Wailing far out among the rocks and sands,
  The night-o'ertaken mariner to save.

And the great ships sail outward and return,
  Bending and bowing o'er the billowy swells,
And ever joyful, as they see it burn,
  They wave their silent welcomes and farewells.

They come forth from the darkness, and their sails
  Gleam for a moment only in the blaze,
And eager faces, as the light unveils,
  Gaze at the tower, and vanish while they gaze.

The mariner remembers when a child,
  On his first voyage, he saw it fade and sink ;
And when, returning from adventures wild,
  He saw it rise again o'er ocean's brink.

Steadfast, serene, immovable, the same
  Year after year, through all the silent night
Burns on for evermore that quenchless flame,
  Shines on that inextinguishable light !

It sees the ocean to its bosom clasp
  The rocks and sea-sand with the kiss of peace ;
It sees the wild winds lift it in their grasp,
  And hold it up, and shake it like a fleece.

The startled waves leap over it ; the storm
  Smites it with all the scourges of the rain,
And steadily against its solid form
  Press the great shoulders of the hurricane.

The sea-bird wheeling round it, with the din
  Of wings and winds and solitary cries,
Blinded and maddened by the light within,
  Dashes himself against the glare, and dies.

A new Prometheus, chained upon the rock,
  Still grasping in his hand the fire of Jove,
It does not hear the cry, nor heed the shock,
  But hails the mariner with words of love.

"Sail on!" it says, "sail on, ye stately ships!
  And with your floating bridge the ocean span;
Be mine to guard this light from all eclipse,
  Be yours to bring man nearer unto man!"

THE FIRE OF DRIFT-WOOD.

WE sat within the farm-house old,
  Whose windows, looking o'er the bay,
Gave to the sea-breeze, damp and cold,
  An easy entrance, night and day.

Not far away we saw the port,—
  The strange, old-fashioned, silent town,—
The lighthouse,—the dismantled fort,—
  The wooden houses, quaint and brown.

We sat and talked until the night,
  Descending, filled the little room;
Our faces faded from the sight,
  Our voices only broke the gloom.

We spake of many a vanished scene,
  Of what we once had thought and said,
Of what had been, and might have been,
  And who was changed, and who was dead;

And all that fills the hearts of friends,
　　When first they feel, with secret pain,
Their lives thenceforth have separate ends,
　　And never can be one again;

The first slight swerving of the heart,
　　That words are powerless to express,
And leave it still unsaid in part,
　　Or say it in too great excess.

The very tones in which we spake
　　Had something strange, I could but mark;
The leaves of memory seemed to make
　　A mournful rustling in the dark.

Oft died the words upon our lips,
　　As suddenly, from out the fire
Built of the wreck of stranded ships,
　　The flames would leap and then expire.

And, as their splendor flashed and failed,
　　We thought of wrecks upon the main,—
Of ships dismasted, that were hailed
　　And sent no answer back again.

The windows, rattling in their frames,—
　　The ocean, roaring up the beach,—
The gusty blast,—the bickering flames,—
　　All mingled vaguely in our speech;

Until they made themselves a part
　　Of fancies floating through the brain,—
The long-lost ventures of the heart,
　　That send no answer back again.

O flames that glowed! O hearts that yearned!
　　They were indeed too much akin,
The drift-wood fire without that burned,
　　The thoughts that burned and glowed within.

BY THE FIRESIDE

RESIGNATION.

THERE is no flock, however watched and tended,
  But one dead lamb is there!
There is no fireside, howsoe'er defended,
  But has one vacant chair!

The air is full of farewells to the dying,
  And mournings for the dead;
The heart of Rachel, for her children crying,
  Will not be comforted!

Let us be patient! These severe afflictions
   Not from the ground arise,
But oftentimes celestial benedictions
   Assume this dark disguise.

We see but dimly through the mists and vapors,
   Amid these earthly damps;
What seem to us but sad, funereal tapers,
   May be heaven's distant lamps.

There is no Death! What seems so is transition;
   This life of mortal breath
Is but a suburb of the life elysian,
   Whose portal we call death.

She is not dead,—the child of our affection,—
   But gone unto that school
Where she no longer needs our poor protection,
   And Christ himself doth rule.

In that great cloister's stillness and seclusion,
   By guardian angels led,
Safe from temptation, safe from sin's pollution,
   She lives, whom we call dead.

Day after day we think what she is doing
   In those bright realms of air;
Year after year, her tender steps pursuing,
   Behold her grown more fair.

Thus do we walk with her, and keep unbroken
   The bond which nature gives,
Thinking that our remembrance, though unspoken,
   May reach her where she lives.

Not as a child shall we again behold her;
   For when with rapture wild
In our embraces we again enfold her,
   She will not be a child;

But a fair maiden, in her Father's mansion,
  Clothed with celestial grace;
And beautiful with all the soul's expansion
  Shall we behold her face.

And though at times impetuous with emotion
  And anguish long suppressed,
The swelling heart heaves moaning like the ocean,
  That cannot be at rest,—

We will be patient, and assuage the feeling
  We may not wholly stay;
By silence sanctifying, not concealing,
  The grief that must have way.

THE BUILDERS.

ALL are architects of Fate,
  Working in these walls of Time;
Some with massive deeds and great,
  Some with ornaments of rhyme.

Nothing useless is, or low;
  Each thing in its place is best;
And what seems but idle show
  Strengthens and supports the rest.

For the structure that we raise,
  Time is with materials filled;
Our to-days and yesterdays
  Are the blocks with which we build.

Truly shape and fashion these;
  Leave no yawning gaps between;
Think not, because no man sees,
  Such things will remain unseen.

In the elder days of Art,
  Builders wrought with greatest care
Each minute and unseen part;
  For the Gods see everywhere.

Let us do our work as well,
　　Both the unseen and the seen;
Make the house, where Gods may dwell,
　　Beautiful, entire, and clean.

Else our lives are incomplete,
　　Standing in these walls of Time,
Broken stairways, where the feet
　　Stumble as they seek to climb.

Build to-day, then, strong and sure,
　　With a firm and ample base;
And ascending and secure
　　Shall to-morrow find its place.

Thus alone can we attain
　　To those turrets, where the eye
Sees the world as one vast plain,
　　And one boundless reach of sky.

SONNET

ON MRS. KEMBLE'S READINGS FROM SHAKSPEARE.

O precious evenings! all too swiftly sped!
Leaving us heirs to amplest heritages
Of all the best thoughts of the greatest sages,
And giving tongues unto the silent dead!
How our hearts glowed and trembled as she read,
Interpreting by tones the wondrous pages
Of the great poet who foreruns the ages,
Anticipating all that shall be said!
O happy Reader! having for thy text
The magic book, whose Sibylline leaves have caught
The rarest essence of all human thought!
O happy Poet! by no critic vext!
How must thy listening spirit now rejoice
To be interpreted by such a voice!

SAND OF THE DESERT IN AN HOUR-GLASS.

A HANDFUL of red sand, from the hot clime
    Of Arab deserts brought,
Within this glass becomes the spy of Time,
    The minister of Thought.

How many weary centuries has it been
    About those deserts blown!
How many strange vicissitudes has seen,
    How many histories known!

Perhaps the camels of the Ishmaelite
    Trampled and passed it o'er,
When into Egypt from the patriarch's sight
    His favorite son they bore.

Perhaps the feet of Moses, burnt and bare,
  Crushed it beneath their tread;
Or Pharaoh's flashing wheels into the air
  Scattered it as they sped;

Or Mary, with the Christ of Nazareth
  Held close in her caress,
Whose pilgrimage of hope and love and faith
  Illumed the wilderness;

Or anchorites beneath Engaddi's palms
  Pacing the Dead Sea beach,
And singing slow their old Armenian psalms
  In half-articulate speech;

Or caravans, that from Hazzorn's gate
  With westward steps depart;
Or Mecca's pilgrims, confident of Fate,
  And resolute in heart;

These have passed over it, or may have passed!
  Now in this crystal tower
Imprisoned by some curious hand at last,
  It counts the passing hour.

And as I gaze, these narrow walls expand;—
  Before my dreamy eye
Stretches the desert with its shifting sand,
  Its unimpeded sky.

And borne aloft by the sustaining blast,
  This little golden thread
Dilates into a column high and vast,
  A form of fear and dread.

And onward, and across the setting sun,
  Across the boundless plain,
The column and its broader shadow run,
  Till thought pursues in vain.

The vision vanishes! These walls again
  Shut out the lurid sun,
Shut out the hot, immeasurable plain;
  The half-hour's sand is run!

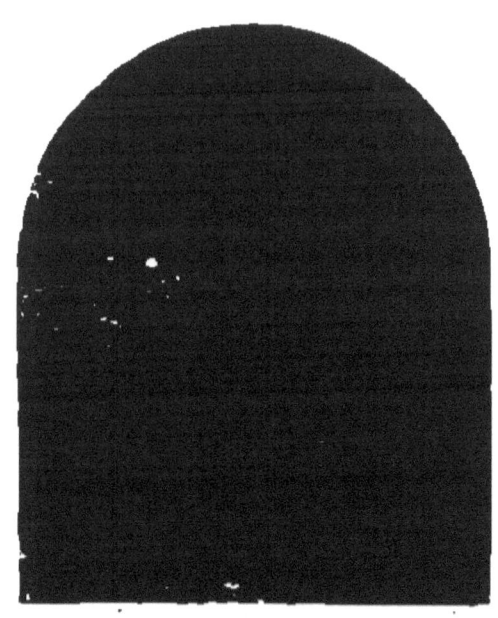

BIRDS OF PASSAGE.

Black shadows fall
From the lindens tall,
That lift aloft their massive wall
  Against the southern sky;

And from the realms
Of the shadowy elms
A tide-like darkness overwhelms
  The fields that round us lie.

But the night is fair,
And everywhere
A warm, soft vapor fills the air,
  And distant sounds seem near;

And above, in the light
Of the star-lit night,
Swift birds of passage wing their flight
  Through the dewy atmosphere.

I hear the beat
Of their pinions fleet,
As from the land of snow and sleet
  They seek a southern lea.

I hear the cry
Of their voices high
Falling dreamily through the sky,
  But their forms I cannot see.

O, say not so!
Those sounds that flow
In murmurs of delight and woe
  Come not from wings of birds.

They are the throngs
Of the poet's songs,
Murmurs of pleasures, and pains, and wrongs,
  The sound of winged words.

This is the cry
Of souls, that high
On toiling, beating pinions fly,
  Seeking a warmer clime.

From their distant flight
Through realms of light
It falls into our world of night,
  With the murmuring sound of rhyme.

THE OPEN WINDOW.

THE old house by the lindens
  Stood silent in the shade,
And on the gravelled pathway
  The light and shadow played.

I saw the nursery windows
  Wide open to the air;
But the faces of the children,
  They were no longer there.

The large Newfoundland house-dog
  Was standing by the door;
He looked for his little playmates,
  Who would return no more.

They walked not under the lindens,
  They played not in the hall;
But shadow, and silence, and sadness,
  Were hanging over all.

The birds sang in the branches,
  With sweet, familiar tone;
But the voices of the children
  Will be heard in dreams alone!

And the boy that walked beside me,
  He could not understand
Why closer in mine, ah! closer,
  I pressed his warm, soft hand!

PEGASUS IN POUND.

Once into a quiet village
   Without haste and without heed,
In the golden prime of morning,
   Strayed the poet's winged steed.

It was Autumn, and incessant
   Piped the quails from shocks and sheaves;
And, like living coals, the apples
   Burned among the withering leaves.

Loud the clamorous bell was ringing
   From its belfry gaunt and grim;
'Twas the daily call to labor,
   Not a triumph meant for him.

Not the less he saw the landscape,
   In its gleaming vapor veiled;
Not the less he breathed the odors
   That the dying leaves exhaled.

Thus, upon the village common,
   By the school-boys he was found;
And the wise men, in their wisdom,
   Put him straightway into pound.

Then the sombre village crier,
   Ringing loud his brazen bell,
Wandered down the street proclaiming
   There was an estray to sell.

And the curious country people,
   Rich and poor, and young and old,
Came in haste to see this wondrous
   Winged steed, with mane of gold.

Thus the day passed, and the evening
   Fell, with vapors cold and dim;
But it brought no food nor shelter,
   Brought no straw nor stall, for him.

PEGASUS IN POUND.

Patiently, and still expectant,
  Looked he through the wooden bars,
Saw the moon rise o'er the landscape,
  Saw the tranquil, patient stars;

Till at length the bell at midnight
  Sounded from its dark abode,
And, from out a neighbouring farm-yard,
  Loud the cock Alectryon crowed.

Then, with nostrils wide distended,
  Breaking from his iron chain,
And unfolding far his pinions,
  To those stars he soared again.

On the morrow, when the village
  Woke to all its toil and care,
Lo! the strange steed had departed,
  And they knew not when nor where.

But they found, upon the greensward
  Where his struggling hoofs had trod,
Pure and bright, a fountain flowing
  From the hoof-marks in the sod.

From that hour, the fount unfailing
  Gladdens the whole region round,
Strengthening all who drink its waters,
  While it soothes them with its sound.

GASPAR DECERRA.

By his evening fire the artist
  Pondered o'er his secret shame;
Baffled, weary, and disheartened,
  Still he mused, and dreamed of fame.

'Twas an image of the Virgin
  That had tasked his utmost skill;
But alas! his fair ideal
  Vanished and escaped him still.

From a distant Eastern island
    Had the precious wood been brought;
Day and night the anxious master
    At his toil untiring wrought;

Till, discouraged and desponding,
    Sat he now in shadows deep,
And the day's humiliation
    Found oblivion in sleep.

Then a voice cried, "Rise, O master!
    From the burning brand of oak
Shape the thought that stirs within thee!"
    And the startled artist woke,—

Woke, and from the smoking embers
    Seized and quenched the glowing wood:
And therefrom he carved an image,
    And he saw that it was good.

O thou sculptor, painter, poet!
    Take this lesson to thy heart:
That is best which lieth nearest;
    Shape from that thy work of art.

KING WITLAF'S DRINKING-HORN.

WITLAF, a king of the Saxons,
  Ere yet his last he breathed,
To the merry monks of Croyland
  His drinking-horn bequeathed,—

That, whenever they sat at their revels,
  And drank from the golden bowl,
They might remember the donor,
  And breathe a prayer for his soul.

So sat they once at Christmas,
  And bade the goblet pass;
In their bowls the red wine glistened
  Like dew-drops in the grass.

They drank to the soul of Witlaf,
  They drank to Christ the Lord,
And to each of the Twelve Apostles,
  Who had preached his holy word.

They drank to the Saints and Martyrs
  Of the dismal days of yore,
And as soon as the horn was empty
  They remembered one Saint more.

And the reader droned from the pulpit,
  Like the murmur of many bees,
The legend of good Saint Guthlac,
  And Saint Basil's homilies;

Till the great bells of the convent,
  From their prison in the tower,
Guthlac and Bartholomæus,
  Proclaimed the midnight hour.

And the Yule-log cracked in the chimney,
  And the Abbot bowed his head,
And the flamelets flapped and flickered,
  But the Abbot was stark and dead.

Yet still in his pallid fingers
  He clutched the golden bowl,
In which, like a pearl dissolving,
  Had sunk and dissolved his soul.

But not for this their revels
  The jovial monks forbore,
For they cried, "Fill high the goblet!
  We must drink to one Saint more!"

TEGNER'S DRAPA.

I heard a voice, that cried,
"Balder the Beautiful
Is dead, is dead!"
And through the misty air
Passed like the mournful cry
Of sunward sailing cranes.

I saw the pallid corpse
Of the dead sun

Borne through the Northern sky,
Blasts from Niffelheim
Lifted the sheeted mists
Around him as he passed.

And the voice for ever cried,
" Balder the Beautiful
Is dead, is dead!"
And died away
Through the dreary night,
In accents of despair.

Balder the Beautiful,
God of the summer sun,
Fairest of all the Gods!
Light from his forehead beamed,
Runes were upon his tongue,
As on the warrior's sword.

All things in earth and air
Bound were by magic spell
Never to do him harm;
Even the plants and stones;
All save the mistletoe,
The sacred mistletoe!

Hoeder, the blind old God,
Whose feet are shod with silence,
Pierced through that gentle breast
With his sharp spear, by fraud
Made of the mistletoe,
The accursed mistletoe!

They laid him in his ship,
With horse and harness,
As on a funeral pyre.
Odin placed
A ring upon his finger,
And whispered in his ear.

They launched the burning ship!
It floated far away
Over the misty sea,
Till like the sun it seemed,
Sinking beneath the waves,
Balder returned no more!

So perish the old Gods!
But out of the sea of Time
Rises a new land of song,
Fairer than the old,
Over its meadows green
Walk the young bards and sing.

Build it again,
O ye bards,
Fairer than before!
Ye fathers of the new race,
Feed upon morning dew,
Sing the new Song of Love!

The law of force is dead!
The law of love prevails!
Thor, the thunderer,
Shall rule the earth no more,
No more, with threats,
Challenge the meek Christ.

Sing no more,
O ye bards of the North,
Of Vikings and of Jarls!
Of the days of Eld
Preserve the freedom only,
Not the deeds of blood!

THE SINGERS.

God sent his Singers upon earth,
With songs of sadness and of mirth,
That they might touch the hearts of men,
And bring them back to heaven again.

The first, a youth, with soul of fire,
Held in his hand a golden lyre;
Through groves he wandered, and by streams,
Playing the music of our dreams.

The second, with a bearded face,
Stood singing in the market-place,
And stirred with accents deep and loud
The hearts of all the listening crowd.

A gray, old man, the third and last,
Sang in cathedrals dim and vast,
While the majestic organ rolled
Contrition from its mouths of gold.

And those who heard the Singers three
Disputed which the best might be;
For still their music seemed to start
Discordant echoes in each heart.

But the great Master said, " I see
No best in kind, but in degree;
I gave a various gift to each,
To charm, to strengthen, and to teach.

" These are the three great chords of might,
And he whose ear is tuned aright
Will hear no discord in the three,
But the most perfect harmony."

SUSPIRIA.

Take them, O Death! and bear away
   Whatever thou canst call thine own!
Thine image, stamped upon this clay,
   Doth give thee that, but that alone!

Take them, O Grave! and let them lie
   Folded upon thy narrow shelves,
As garments by the soul laid by,
   And precious only to ourselves!

Take them, O great Eternity!
   Our little life is but a gust,
That bends the branches of thy tree,
   And trails its blossoms in the dust.

HYMN

FOR MY BROTHER'S ORDINATION.

Christ to the young man said; " Yet one thing more ;
  If thou wouldst perfect be,
Sell all thou hast and give it to the poor,
  And come and follow me ! "

Within this temple Christ again, unseen,
  Those sacred words hath said,
And his invisible hands to-day have been
  Laid on a young man's head.

And evermore beside him on his way
  The unseen Christ shall move,
That he may lean upon his arm and say,
  " Dost thou, dear Lord, approve ? "

Beside him at the marriage feast shall be,
  To make the scene more fair ;
Beside him in the dark Gethsemane
  Of pain and midnight prayer.

O holy trust ! O endless sense of rest !
  Like the beloved John
To lay his head upon the Saviour's breast,
  And thus to journey on !

MISCELLANEOUS POEMS.

1841—1846—1858

THE VILLAGE BLACKSMITH.

Under a spreading chestnut tree
  The village smithy stands;
The smith, a mighty man is he,
  With large and sinewy hands;
And the muscles of his brawny arms
  Are strong as iron bands.

His hair is crisp, and black, and long,
  His face is like the tan;
His brow is wet with honest sweat,
  He earns whate'er he can,
And looks the whole world in the face,
  For he owes not any man.

Week in, week out, from morn till night,
  You can hear his bellows blow;
You can hear him swing his heavy sledge,
  With measured beat and slow,
Like a sexton ringing the village bell,
  When the evening sun is low.

And children coming home from school
  Look in at the open door;
They love to see the flaming forge,
  And hear the bellows roar,
And catch the burning sparks that fly
  Like chaff from a threshing floor.

He goes on Sunday to the church,
  And sits among his boys;
He hears the parson pray and preach.
  He hears his daughter's voice,
Singing in the village choir,
  And it makes his heart rejoice.

It sounds to him like her mother's voice,
  Singing in Paradise!

He needs must think of her once more,
　How in the grave she lies;
And with his hard, rough hand he wipes
　A tear out of his eyes.

Toiling,—rejoicing,—sorrowing,
　Onward through life he goes;
Each morning sees some task begin,
　Each evening sees it close;
Something attempted, something done,
　Has earned a night's repose.

Thanks, thanks to thee, my worthy friend,
　For the lesson thou hast taught!
Thus at the flaming forge of life
　Our fortunes must be wrought;
Thus on its sounding anvil shaped
　Each burning deed and thought!

THE RAINY DAY.

The day is cold, and dark, and dreary;
It rains, and the wind is never weary;
The vine still clings to the mouldering wall,
But at every gust the dead leaves fall,
　And the day is dark and dreary.

My life is cold, and dark, and dreary;
It rains, and the wind is never weary;
My thoughts still cling to the mouldering Past,
But the hopes of youth fall thick in the blast,
　And the days are dark and dreary.

Be still, sad heart! and cease repining;
Behind the clouds is the sun still shining;
Thy fate is the common fate of all,
Into each life some rain must fall,
　Some days must be dark and dreary.

ENDYMION.

THE rising moon has hid the stars;
Her level rays, like golden bars,
    Lie on the landscape green,
    With shadows brown between.

And silver white the river gleams,
As if Diana in her dreams,
    Had dropt her silver bow
    Upon the meadows low.

On such a tranquil night as this,
She woke Endymion with a kiss,
    When, sleeping in the grove,
    He dreamed not of her love.

Like Dian's kiss, unasked, unsought,
Love gives itself, but is not bought;
    Nor voice, nor sound betrays
    Its deep, impassioned gaze.

It comes,—the beautiful, the free,
The crown of all humanity,—
    In silence and alone
    To seek the elected one.

It lifts the boughs, whose shadows deep
Are Life's oblivion, the soul's sleep,
    And kisses the closed eyes
    Of him, who slumbering lies.

O weary hearts! O slumbering eyes!
O drooping souls, whose destinies
    Are fraught with fear and pain,
    Ye shall be loved again!

No one is so accursed by fate,
No one so utterly desolate,
    But some heart, though unknown,
    Responds unto his own.

Responds,—as if with unseen wings,
An angel touched its quivering strings;
    And whispers, in its song,
    "Where hast thou stayed so long!"

IT IS NOT ALWAYS MAY.

NO HAY PAJAROS EN LOS NIDOS ANTAÑO.—Spanish Proverb

The sun is bright,—the air is clear,
　The darling swallows soar and sing,
And from the stately elms I hear
　The blue-bird prophesying Spring.

So blue yon winding river flows,
　It seems an outlet from the sky,
Where, waiting till the west wind blows,
　The freighted clouds at anchor lie.

All things are new;—the buds, the leaves,
　That gild the elm-tree's nodding crest,
And even the nest beneath the eaves;—
　There are no birds in last year's nest!

All things rejoice in youth and love,
　The fulness of their first delight!
And learn from the soft heavens above
　The melting tenderness of night.

Maiden, that read'st this simple rhyme,
　Enjoy thy youth, it will not stay;
Enjoy the fragrance of thy prime,
　For O! it is not always May!

Enjoy the Spring of Love and Youth,
　To some good angel leave the rest;
For Time will teach thee soon the truth,
　There are no birds in last year's nest!

GOD'S-ACRE.

I LIKE that ancient Saxon phrase, which calls
   The burial-ground God's-Acre! It is just;
It consecrates each grave within its walls,
   And breathes a benison o'er the sleeping dust.

God's-Acre! Yes, that blessed name imparts
   Comfort to those, who in the grave have sown
The seed, that they had garnered in their hearts,
   Their bread of life, alas! no more their own.

Into its furrows shall we all be cast,
   In the sure faith, that we shall rise again
At the great harvest, when the archangel's blast
   Shall winnow, like a fan, the chaff and grain.

Then shall the good stand in immortal bloom,
    In the fair gardens of that second birth ;
And each bright blossom mingle its perfume
    With that of flowers which never bloomed on earth.

With thy rude ploughshare, Death, turn up the sod,
    And spread the furrow for the seed we sow ;
This is the field and Acre of our God,
    This is the place where human harvests grow !

THE GOBLET OF LIFE.

FILLED is Life's goblet to the brim ;
And though my eyes with tears are dim,
I see its sparkling bubbles swim,
And chaunt a melancholy hymn
    With solemn voice and slow.

No purple flowers,—no garlands green,
Conceal the goblet's shade or sheen,
Nor maddening draughts of Hippocrene,
Like gleams of sunshine, flash between
    Thick leaves of mistletoe.

This goblet, wrought with curious art,
Is filled with waters, that upstart,
When the deep fountains of the heart,
By strong convulsions rent apart,
    Are running all to waste.

And as it mantling passes round,
With fennel is it wreathed and crowned,
Whose seed and foliage sun-imbrowned
Are in its waters steeped and drowned,
    And give a bitter taste.

Above the lowly plants it towers,
The fennel, with its yellow flowers,
And in an earlier age than ours
Was gifted with the wondrous powers,
    Lost vision to restore.

It gave new strength and fearless mood ;
And gladiators, fierce and rude,
Mingled it in their daily food ;
And he who battled and subdued,
    A wreath of fennel wore.

Then in Life's goblet freely press
The leaves that give it bitterness,
Nor prize the coloured waters less.
For in thy darkness and distress
    New light and strength they give !

And he who has not learned to know
How false its sparkling bubbles show,
How bitter are the drops of woe,
With which its brim may overflow,
    He has not learned to live.

The prayer of Ajax was for light ;
Through all that dark and desperate fight,
The blackness of that noonday night,
He asked but the return of sight,
    To see his foeman's face.

Let our unceasing, earnest prayer
Be, too, for light,—for strength to bear
Our portion of the weight of care,
That crushes into dumb despair
    One half the human race.

O suffering, sad humanity !
O ye afflicted ones, who lie
Steeped to the lips in misery,
Longing, and yet afraid to die,
    Patient, though sorely tried !

I pledge you in this cup of grief,
Where floats the fennel's bitter leaf!
The Battle of our Life is brief,
The alarm,—the struggle,—the relief,—
  Then sleep we side by side.

BLIND BARTIMEUS.

Blind Bartimeus at the gates
Of Jericho in darkness waits;
He hears the crowd;—he hears a breath
Say, "It is Christ of Nazareth;"
And calls, in tones of agony,
Ἰησοῦ, ἐλέησόν με!

The thronging multitudes increase:
Blind Bartimeus, hold thy peace!
But still, above the noisy crowd,
The beggar's cry is shrill and loud;
Until they say, "He calleth thee!"
Θάρσει, ἔγειραι, φωνεῖ σε!

Then saith the Christ, as silent stands
The crowd, "What wilt thou at my hands?"
And he replies, "O give me light!
Rabbi, restore the blind man's sight!"
And Jesus answers, Ὕπαγε·
Ἡ πίστις σου σέσωκέ σε!

Ye that have eyes, yet cannot see,
In darkness and in misery,
Recall those mighty Voices Three,
Ἰησοῦ, ἐλέησόν με!
Θάρσει, ἔγειραι, ὕπαγε!
Ἡ πίστις σου σέσωκέ σε!

TO THE RIVER CHARLES.

River! that in silence windest
  Through the meadows, bright and free,
Till at length thy rest thou findest
  In the bosom of the sea!

Four long years of mingled feeling,
  Half in rest, and half in strife,
I have seen thy waters stealing
  Onward, like the stream of life.

Thou hast taught me, Silent River!
  Many a lesson, deep and long:
Thou hast been a generous giver:
  I can give thee but a song.

Oft in sadness and in illness,
  I have watched thy current glide,
Till the beauty of its stillness
  Overflowed me, like a tide.

And in better hours and brighter,
  When I saw thy waters gleam,
I have felt my heart beat lighter,
  And leap onward with thy stream.

Not for this alone I love thee,
  Nor because thy waves of blue
From celestial seas above thee
  Take their own celestial hue.

Where yon shadowy woodlands hide thee,
  And thy waters disappear,
Friends I love have dwelt beside thee,
  And have made thy margin dear.

More than this;—thy name reminds me
  Of three friends, all true and tried;
And that name, like magic, binds me
  Closer, closer to thy side.

Friends my soul with joy remembers!
  How like quivering flames they start,
When I fan the living embers
  On the hearth-stone of my heart!

'Tis for this, thou Silent River!
  That my spirit leans to thee;
Thou hast been a generous giver,
  Take this idle song from me.

EXCELSIOR.

The shades of night were falling fast,
As through an Alpine village passed
A youth, who bore, 'mid snow and ice,
A banner with the strange device,
        Excelsior!

His brow was sad; his eye beneath,
Flashed like a faulchion from its sheath,
And like a silver clarion rung
The accents of that unknown tongue,
        Excelsior!

In happy homes he saw the light
Of household fires gleam warm and bright;
Above, the spectral glaciers shone,
And from his lips escaped a groan,
        Excelsior!

"Try not the Pass!" the old man said;
"Dark lowers the tempest overhead,
The roaring torrent is deep and wide!"
And loud that clarion voice replied,
          Excelsior!

"O stay," the maiden said, "and rest
Thy weary head upon this breast!"
A tear stood in his bright blue eye,
But still he answered, with a sigh,
          Excelsior!

"Beware the pine-tree's withered branch!
Beware the awful avalanche!"
This was the peasant's last Good-night,
A voice replied, far up the height,
          Excelsior!

At break of day, as heavenward
The pious monks of Saint Bernard
Uttered the oft-repeated prayer,
A voice cried through the startled air,
          Excelsior!

A traveller, by the faithful hound,
Half-buried in the snow was found,
Still grasping in his hand of ice
That banner with the strange device
          Excelsior!

There in the twilight cold and gray,
Lifeless, but beautiful, he lay,
And from the sky, serene and far,
A voice fell, like a falling star,
          Excelsior!

MAIDENHOOD.

Maidens! with the meek, brown eyes,
In whose orbs a shadow lies,
Like the dusk in evening skies!

Thou whose locks outshine the sun,
Golden tresses, wreathed in one,
As the braided streamlets run!

Standing, with reluctant feet,
Where the brook and river meet,
Womanhood and childhood fleet!

Gazing, with a timid glance,
On the brooklet's swift advance,
On the river's broad expanse!

Deep and still, that gliding stream
Beautiful to thee must seem,
As the river of a dream.

Then why pause with indecision,
When bright angels in thy vision
Beckon thee to fields Elysian?

Seest thou shadows sailing by,
As the dove, with startled eye,
Sees the falcon's shadow fly?

Hearest thou voices on the shore,
That our ears perceive no more,
Deafened by the cataract's roar?

O, thou child of many prayers!
Life hath quicksands,—Life hath snares!
Care and age come unawares!

Like the swell of some sweet tune,
Morning rises into noon,
May glides onward into June.

Childhood is the bough, where slumbered
Birds and blossoms many-numbered;—
Age, that bough with snows encumbered.

Gather, then, each flower that grows,
When the young heart overflows,
To embalm that tent of snows.

Bear a lily in thy hand;
Gates of brass cannot withstand
One touch of that magic wand.

Bear through sorrow, wrong, and ruth,
In thy heart the dew of youth,
On thy lips the smile of truth.

O, that dew, like balm, shall steal
Into wounds, that cannot heal,
Even as sleep our eyes doth seal;

And that smile, like sunshine, dart
Into many a sunless heart,
For a smile of God thou art.

THE BELFRY OF BRUGES.

CARILLON.

In the ancient town of Bruges,
In the quaint old Flemish city,
As the evening shades descended,
Low and loud and sweetly blended,
Low at times and loud at times,
And changing like a poet's rhymes,
Rang the beautiful wild chimes
From the Belfry in the market
Of the ancient town of Bruges.

Then, with deep sonorous clangor
Calmly answering their sweet anger,
When the wrangling bells had ended,
Slowly struck the clock eleven,
And, from out the silent heaven,
Silence on the town descended.
Silence, silence everywhere,
On the earth and in the air,
Save that footsteps here and there
Of some burgher home returning,
By the street lamps faintly burning.
For a moment woke the echoes
Of the ancient town of Bruges.

But amid my broken slumbers
Still I heard those magic numbers,
As they loud proclaimed the flight
And stolen marches of the night;
Till their chimes in sweet collision
Mingled with each wandering vision,
Mingled with the fortune-telling
Gipsy-bands of dreams and fancies,
Which amid the waste expanses
Of the silent land of trances
Have their solitary dwelling.

All else seemed asleep in Bruges,
In the quaint old Flemish city.

And I thought how like these chimes
Are the poet's airy rhymes,
All his rhymes and roundelays,
His conceits, and songs, and ditties,
From the belfry of his brain,
Scattered downward, though in vain,
On the roofs and stones of cities!
For by night the drowsy ear
Under its curtains cannot hear,
And by day men go their ways,
Hearing the music as they pass,
But deeming it no more, alas!
Than the hollow sound of brass.

Yet perchance a sleepless wight,
Lodging at some humble inn
In the narrow lanes of life,
When the dusk and hush of night
Shut out the incessant din
Of daylight and its toil and strife,
May listen with a calm delight
To the poet's melodies,
Till he hears, or dreams he hears,
Intermingled with the song,
Thoughts that he has cherished long;
Hears amid the chime and singing
The bells of his own village ringing,
And wakes, and finds his slumberous eyes
Wet with most delicious tears.

Thus dreamed I, as by night I lay
In Bruges, at the Fleur-de-Blé,
Listening with a wild delight
To the chimes that, through the night
Rang their changes from the Belfry
Of that quaint old Flemish city.

THE BELFRY OF BRUGES.

In the market-place of Bruges stands the belfry old and brown;
Thrice consumed and thrice rebuilded, still it watches o'er the town.

As the summer morn was breaking, on that lofty tower I stood,
And the world threw off the darkness, like the weeds of widowhood.

Thick with towns and hamlets studded, and with streams and vapors gray,
Like a shield embossed with silver, round and vast the landscape lay.

At my feet the city slumbered.   From its chimneys, here and there,
Wreaths of snow-white smoke, ascending, vanished, ghost-like, into air.

Not a sound rose from the city at that early morning hour,
But I heard a heart of iron beating in the ancient tower.

From their nests beneath the rafters sang the swallows wild and high;
And the world, beneath me sleeping, seemed more distant than the sky.

Then most musical and solemn, bringing back the olden times,
With their strange, unearthly changes, rang the melancholy chimes,

Like the psalms from some old cloister, when the nuns sing in the choir;
And the great bell tolled among them, like the chanting of a friar.

Visions of the day departed, shadowy phantoms filled my brain;
They who live in history only seemed to walk the earth again;

All the Foresters of Flanders,[1]—mighty Baldwin Bras de Fer,
Lyderick du Bucq and Cressy, Philip, Guy de Dampierre.

I beheld the pageants splendid, that adorned those days of old;
Stately dames, like queens attended,[2] knights who bore the Fleece of Gold;[3]

Lombard and Venetian merchants with deep-laden argosies;
Ministers from twenty nations; more than royal pomp and ease.

I beheld proud Maximilian, kneeling humbly on the ground;
I beheld the gentle Mary,[4] hunting with her hawk and hound;

And her lighted bridal-chamber, where a duke slept with the queen,
And the armed guard around them, and the sword unsheathed between.

I beheld the Flemish weavers, with Namur and Juliers bold,
Marching homeward from the bloody battle of the Spurs of Gold;[5]

Saw the fight at Minnewater,[6] saw the White Hoods moving west,
Saw great Artevelde victorious scale the Golden Dragon's nest.[7]

And again the whiskered Spaniard all the land with terror smote;
And again the wild alarum sounded from the tocsin's throat;

Till the bell of Ghent responded o'er lagoon and dike of sand,
"I am Roland! I am Roland! there is victory in the land!"'

Then the sound of drums aroused me.   The awakened city's roar
Chased the phantoms I had summoned back into their graves once more.

Hours had passed away like minutes; and, before I was aware,
Lo! the shadow of the belfry crossed the sun-illumined square.

NOTES.

(1.) *All the Foresters of Flanders.*

The title of Foresters was given to the early governors of Flanders, appointed by the kings of France. Lyderick du Burg, in the days of Clotaire the Second, was the first of them; and Beauldin Bras-de-Fer, who stole away the fair Judith, daughter of Charles the Bald, from the French court, and married her in Bruges, was the last. After him the title of Forester was changed to that of Count. Philippe d'Alsace, Guy de Dampierre, and Louis de Crécy, coming later in the order of time, were therefore rather Counts than Foresters. Philippe went over to the Holy Land as a Crusader, and died of the plague at St. Jean d'Acre, shortly after the capture of the city by the Christians. Guy de Dampierre died in the prison of Compiègne. Louis de Crécy was son and successor of Robert de Béthune, who strangled his wife, Yolande de Bourgogne, with the bridle of his horse, for having poisoned, at the age of eleven years, Charles, his son by his first wife, Blanche d'Anjou.

(2.) *Fondly dames, like queens attended.*

When Philippe-le-Bel, king of France, visited Flanders with his queen, she was so astonished at the magnificence of the dames of Bruges, that she exclaimed,—"Je croyais être seule reine ici, mais il paraît que ceux de Flandre qui se trouvent dans nos prisons sont tous des princes, car leurs femmes sont habillées comme des princesses et des reines."

When the burgomasters of Ghent, Bruges, and Ypres went to Paris to pay homage to King John, in 1351, they were received with great pomp and distinction; but, being invited to a festival, they observed that their seats at table were not furnished with cushions; whereupon, to make known their displeasure at this want of regard to their dignity, they folded their richly embroidered cloaks and seated themselves upon them. On rising from the table, they left their cloaks behind them, and being informed of their apparent forgetfulness, Simon van Herisycke, burgomaster of Bruges, replied,—"We Flemings are not in the habit of carrying away our cushions after dinner."

(3.) *Knights who bore the Fleece of Gold.*

Philippe de Bourgogne, surnamed Le Bon, espoused Isabella of Portugal, on the 10th of January, 1430; and on the same day instituted the famous order of the Fleece of Gold.

(4.) *I beheld the gentle Mary.*

Marie de Valois, Duchess of Burgundy, was left by the death of her father Charles-le-Téméraire, at the age of twenty, the richest heiress of Europe. She came to Bruges, as Countess of Flanders, in 1477, and in the same year was married by proxy to the Archduke

Maximilian. According to the custom of the time the Duke of Bavaria, Maximilian's substitute, slept with the princess. They were both in complete dress, separated by a naked sword, and attended by four armed guards. Mary was adored by her subjects for her gentleness and her many other virtues.

Maximilian was son of the Emperor Frederick the Third, and is the same person mentioned afterwards in the poem of Nuremberg as the Kaiser Maximilian, and the hero of Pflinzing's poem of Teuerdank. Having been imprisoned by the revolted burghers of Bruges, they refused to release him, till he consented to kneel in the public square, and to swear on the Holy Evangelists and the body of St. Donatus, that he would not take vengeance upon them for their rebellion.

(5.) The bloody battle of the Spurs of Gold.

This battle, the most memorable in Flemish history, was fought under the walls of Courtray, on the 11th of July, 1302, between the French and the Flemings, the former commanded by Robert, Comte d'Artois, and the latter by Guillaume de Juliers, and Jean, Comte de Namur. The French army was completely routed, with a loss of twenty thousand infantry, and seven thousand cavalry ; among whom were sixty-three princes, dukes and counts, seven hundred lords-banneret, and eleven hundred noblemen. The flower of the French nobility perished on that day to which history has given the name of the Journée des Eperons d'Or, from the great number of golden spurs found on the field of battle. Seven hundred of them were hung up as a trophy in the church of Notre Dame de Courtray ; and, as the cavaliers of that day wore but a single spur each, these reckoned to God for the violent and bloody death of seven hundred of his creatures.

(6.) Saw the fight at Minnewater.

When the inhabitants of Bruges were digging a canal at Minnewater, to bring the waters of the Lys from Deynse to their city, they were attacked and routed by the citizens of Ghent, whose commerce would have been much injured by the canal. They were led by Jean Lyons, captain of a military company at Ghent, called the Chaperons Blancs. He had great sway over the turbulent populace, who in those prosperous times of the city, gained an easy livelihood by labouring two or three days in the week, and had the remaining four or five to devote to public affairs. The fight at Minnewater was followed by open rebellion against Louis de Maele, the Count of Flanders and Protector of Bruges. His superb Château of Wondelghem was pillaged and burnt ; and the insurgents forced the gates of Bruges, and entered in triumph, with Lyons mounted at their head. A few days afterwards he died suddenly, perhaps by poison.

Meanwhile the insurgents received a check at the village of Nevele ; and two hundred of them perished in the church, which was burned by the Count's orders. One of the chiefs, Jean de Lannoy, took refuge in the belfry. From the summit of the tower he held forth his purse filled with gold, and begged deliverance. It was in vain. His enemies cried from below to save himself as best he might ; and, half suffocated with smoke and flame, he threw himself from the tower and perished at their feet. Peace was soon afterwards established, and the Count retired to faithful Bruges.

(7.) The Golden Dragon's nest.

The Golden Dragon, taken from the church of St. Sophia, at Constantinople, in one of the Crusades, and placed on the belfry of Bruges, was afterwards transported to Ghent, by Philip van Artevelde, and still adorns the belfry of that city.

(8.) "There is victory in the land!"

The inscription on the alarm-bell at Ghent is, "Mynen naem is Roland ; als ikklep is er brand, and als ik luy is er victorie in het land." — My name is Roland ; when I toll there is fire, and when I ring there is victory in the land.

THE ARSENAL AT SPRINGFIELD.

This is the Arsenal. From floor to ceiling,
  Like a huge organ, rise the burnished arms;
But from their silent pipes no anthem pealing
  Startles the villages with strange alarms.

Ah! what a sound will rise, how wild and dreary,
  When the death-angel touches those swift keys!
What loud lament and dismal Miserere
  Will mingle with their awful symphonies!

I hear even now the infinite fierce chorus,
  The cries of agony, the endless groan,
Which, through the ages that have gone before us,
  In long reverberations reach our own.

On helm and harness rings the Saxon hammer,
  Through Cimbric forest roars the Norseman's song,
And loud, amid the universal clamor,
  O'er distant deserts sounds the Tartar gong.

I hear the Florentine, who from his palace
  Wheels out his battle-bell with dreadful din,
And Aztec priests upon their teocallis
  Beat the wild war-drums made of serpent's skin;

The tumult of each sacked and burning village;
  The shout that every prayer for mercy drowns;
The soldier's revels in the midst of pillage;
  The wail of famine in beleaguered towns;

The bursting shell, the gateway wrenched asunder,
  The rattling musketry, the clashing blade;
And ever and anon, in tones of thunder,
  The diapason of the cannonade.

Is it, O man, with such discordant noises,
    With such accursed instruments as these,
Thou drownest Nature's sweet and kindly voices,
    And jarrest the celestial harmonies?

Were half the power, that fills the world with terror,
    Were half the wealth, bestowed on camps and courts,
Given to redeem the human mind from error,
    There were no need for arsenals nor forts:

The warrior's name would be a name abhorred!
    And every nation, that should lift again
Its hand against a brother, on its forehead
    Would wear for evermore the curse of Cain!

Down the dark future, through long generations,
    The echoing sounds grow fainter and then cease;
And like a bell, with solemn, sweet vibrations,
    I hear once more the voice of Christ say, "Peace!"

Peace! and no longer from its brazen portals
    The blast of War's great organ shakes the skies!
But beautiful as songs of the immortals,
    The holy melodies of love arise.

A GLEAM OF SUNSHINE.

This is the place. Stand still, my steed,
  Let me review the scene,
And summon from the shadowy Past
  The forms that once have been.

The Past and Present here unite
  Beneath Time's flowing tide,
Like footprints hidden by a brook,
  But seen on either side.

Here runs the highway to the town;
  There the green lane descends,
Through which I walked to church with thee,
  O gentlest of my friends!

The shadow of the linden-trees
  Lay moving on the grass;
Between them and the moving boughs,
  A shadow, thou didst pass.

Thy dress was like the lilies,
  And thy heart as pure as they:
One of God's holy messengers
  Did walk with me that day.

I saw the branches of the trees
  Bend down thy touch to meet,
The clover-blossoms in the grass
  Rise up to kiss thy feet.

" Sleep, sleep to-day, tormenting cares,
  Of earth and folly born! "
Solemnly sang the village choir
  On that sweet Sabbath morn.

Through the closed blinds the golden sun
  Poured in a dusty beam,
Like the celestial ladder seen
  By Jacob in his dream.

And ever and anon, the wind,
  Sweet-scented with the hay,
Turned o'er the hymn-book's fluttering leaves
  That on the window lay.

Long was the good man's sermon,
  Yet it seemed not so to me;
For he spake of Ruth the beautiful,
  And still I thought of thee.

Long was the prayer he uttered,
  Yet it seemed not so to me;
For in my heart I prayed with him,
  And still I thought of thee.

But now, alas! the place seems changed;
  Thou art no longer here:
Part of the sunshine of the scene
  With thee did disappear.

Though thoughts, deep-rooted in my heart,
  Like pine-trees dark and high,
Subdue the light of noon, and breathe
  A low and ceaseless sigh;

This memory brightens o'er the past,
  As when the sun, concealed
Behind some cloud that near us hangs,
  Shines on a distant field.

THE OCCULTATION OF ORION.*

I saw, as in a dream sublime,
The balance in the hand of Time.
O'er East and West its beam impended;
And day, with all its hours of light,
Was slowly sinking out of sight,
While, opposite, the scale of night
Silently with the stars ascended.

* Astronomically speaking, this little is incorrect: as I apply to a constellation what can properly be applied to some of its stars only. But my observation is made from the hill of song, and not from that of science; and will, I trust, be found sufficiently accurate for the poetical purpose.

Like the astrologers of old,
In that bright vision I beheld
Greater and deeper mysteries.
I saw, with its celestial keys,
Its chords of air, its frets of fire,
The Samian's great Æolian lyre,
Rising through all its sevenfold bars,
From earth unto the fixèd stars.
And through the dewy atmosphere,
Not only could I see, but hear,
Its wondrous and harmonious strings,
In sweet vibration, sphere by sphere,
From Dian's circle light and near,
Onward to vaster and wider rings.
Where, chanting through his beard of snows,
Majestic, mournful, Saturn goes,
And down the sunless realms of space
Reverberates the thunder of his bass.
Beneath the sky's triumphal arch
This music sounded like a march,
And with its chorus seemed to be
Preluding some great tragedy.
Sirius was rising in the east:
And, slow ascending one by one,
The kindling constellations shone.
Begirt with many a blazing star,
Stood the great giant Algebar,
Orion, hunter of the beast!
His sword hung gleaming by his side,
And, on his arm, the lion's hide
Scattered across the midnight air
The golden radiance of its hair.

The moon was pallid, but not faint
And beautiful as some fair saint.
Serenely moving on her way
In hours of trial and dismay.
As if she feared the voice of God,
Unharmed with naked feet she trod

Upon the hot and burning stars,
As on the glowing coals and bars
That were to prove her strength, and try
Her holiness and her purity.

Thus moving on, with silent pace,
And triumph in her sweet, pale face,
She reached the station of Orion.
Aghast he stood in strange alarm!
And suddenly from his outstretched arm
Down fell the red skin of the lion
Into the river at his feet.
His mighty club no longer beat
The forehead of the bull; but he
Reeled as of yore beside the sea,
When, blinded by Œnopion,
He sought the blacksmith at his forge,
And, climbing up the mountain gorge,
Fixed his blank eyes upon the sun.

Then, through the silence overhead,
An angel with a trumpet said,
" Forevermore, forevermore,
The reign of violence is o'er! "
And like an instrument that flings
Its music on another's strings,
The trumpet of the angel cast
Upon the heavenly lyre its blast,
And on from sphere to sphere the words
Re-echoed down the burning chords,—
" Forevermore, forevermore,
The reign of violence is o'er! "

NUREMBERG.

In the valley of the Pegnitz, where across broad meadow-lands
Rise the blue Franconian Mountains, Nuremberg, the ancient, stands.

Quaint old town of toil and traffic, quaint old town of art and song,
Memories haunt thy pointed gables, like the rooks that round them throng;

Memories of the Middle Ages, when the emperors, rough and bold,
Had their dwelling in thy castle, time-defying, centuries old;

And thy brave and thrifty burghers boasted, in their uncouth rhyme,
That their great imperial city stretched its hand through every clime.[1]

In the court-yard of the castle, bound with many an iron band,
Stands the mighty linden planted by Queen Cunigunde's hand;

On the square the oriel window, where in old heroic days
Sat the poet Melchior singing Kaiser Maximilian's praise.[2]

Everywhere I see around me rise the wondrous world of Art:
Fountains wrought with richest sculpture standing in the common mart;

And above cathedral doorways saints and bishops carved in stone,
By a former age commissioned as apostles to our own.

In the church of sainted Sebald sleeps enshrined his holy dust,[3]
And in bronze the Twelve Apostles guard from age to age their trust;

In the church of sainted Lawrence stands a pix of sculpture rare,[4]
Like the foamy sheaf of fountains, rising through the painted air.

Here, when Art was still religion, with a simple, reverent heart,
Lived and laboured Albrecht Dürer, the Evangelist of Art;

Hence in silence and in sorrow, toiling still with busy hand,
Like an emigrant he wandered, seeking for the Better Land.

Emigravit is the inscription on the tomb-stone where he lies ;
Dead he is not,—but departed,—for the artist never dies.

Fairer seems the ancient city, and the sunshine seems more fair,
That he once has trod its pavement, that he once has breathed its air !

Through these streets so broad and stately, these obscure and dismal lanes,
Walked of yore the Mastersingers, chanting rude poetic strains.

From remote and sunless suburbs, came they to the friendly guild,
Building nests in Fame's great temple, as in spouts the swallows build.

As the weaver plied the shuttle, wove he too the mystic rhyme,
And the smith his iron measures hammered to the anvil's chime ;

Thanking God, whose boundless wisdom makes the flowers of poesy bloom
In the forge's dust and cinders, in the tissues of the loom.

Here Hans Sachs, the cobbler-poet, laureate of the gentle craft,
Wisest of the Twelve Wise Masters,[1] in huge folios sang and laughed.

But his house is now an ale-house, with a nicely sanded floor,
And a garland in the window, and his face above the door ;

Painted by some humble artist, as in Adam Puschman's song,[4]
As the " old man gray and dove-like, with his great beard white and long."

And at night the swart mechanic comes to drown his cark and care,
Quaffing ale from pewter tankards, in the master's antique chair.

Vanished is the ancient splendor, and before my dreamy eye
Wave these mingling shapes and figures, like a faded tapestry.

Not thy Councils, not thy Kaisers, win for thee the world's regard ;
But thy painter, Albrecht Dürer, and Hans Sachs, thy cobbler-bard.

Thus, O Nuremberg, a wanderer from a region far away,
As he paced thy streets and court-yards, sang in thought his careless lay:

Gathering from the pavement's crevice, as a floweret of the soil,
The nobility of labor,—the long pedigree of toil.

NOTES.

(1.) *That their great imperial city stretched its hand through every clime.*

An old popular proverb of the town runs thus:—

"*Nuremberg's Hand*   "*Nuremberg's hand
Geht durch alle Land*"   Goes through every land.*"

(2.) *Sat the poet Melchior singing Kaiser Maximilian's praise.*

Melchior Pfinzing was one of the most celebrated German poets of the sixteenth century. The hero of his *Teuerdank* was the reigning emperor, Maximilian; and the poem was to the Germans of that day what the *Orlando Furioso* was to the Italians. Maximilian is mentioned before, in the *Belfry of Bruges*. See page 291.

(3.) *In the church of sainted Sebald sleeps enshrined his holy dust.*

The tomb of Saint Sebald, in the church which bears his name, is one of the richest works of art in Nuremberg. It is of bronze, and was cast by Peter Vischer and his sons, who labored upon it thirteen years. It is adorned with nearly one hundred figures, among which those of the Twelve Apostles are conspicuous for size and beauty.

(4.) *In the church of sainted Lawrence stands a pix of sculpture rare.*

This pix, or tabernacle for the vessels of the sacrament, is by the hand of Adam Kraft. It is an exquisite piece of sculpture in white stone, and rises to the height of sixty-four feet. It stands in the choir, whose richly-painted windows cover it with varied colours.

(5.) *Wisest of the Twelve Wise Masters.*

The Twelve Wise Masters was the title of the original corporation of the Master-singers. Hans Sachs, the cobbler of Nuremberg, though not one of the original Twelve, was the most renowned of the Master-singers, as well as the most voluminous. He flourished in the sixteenth century; and left behind him thirty-four folio volumes of manuscript, containing two hundred and eight plays, one thousand and seven hundred comic tales, and between four and five thousand lyric poems.

(6.) *As in Adam Puschman's song.*

Adam Puschman, in his poem on the death of Hans Sachs, describes him as he appeared in a vision:—

"An old man,
Gray and white, and dove-like,
Who had, in sooth, a great beard,
And read in a fair, great book,
Beautiful with golden clasps."

THE NORMAN BARON.

Dans les moments de la vie où la réflexion devient plus calme et plus profonde, où l'intérêt et l'avarice parlent moins haut que la raison, dans les instants de chagrin domestique, de maladie, et de péril de mort, les nobles se repentirent de posséder des serfs, comme d'une chose peu agréable à Dieu, qui avait créé tous les hommes à son image. — THIERRY, Conquête de l'Angleterre.

Is his chamber, weak and dying,
Was the Norman baron lying;

Loud, without, the tempest thundered,
    And the castle-turret shook.

In this fight was Death the gainer,
Spite of vassal and retainer,
And the lands his sires had plundered,
    Written in the Doomsday Book.

By his bed a monk was seated,
Who in humble voice repeated
Many a prayer and pater-noster,
    From the missal on his knee :

And, amid the tempest pealing,
Sounds of bells came faintly stealing,
Bells, that, from the neighbouring kloster,
    Rang for the Nativity.

In the hall, the serf and vassal
Held, that night, their Christmas wassail ;
Many a carol, old and saintly,
    Sang the minstrels and the waits.

And so loud these Saxon gleemen
Sang to slaves the songs of freemen,
That the storm was heard but faintly,
    Knocking at the castle-gates.

Till at length the lays they chaunted
Reached the chamber terror-haunted,
Where the monk, with accents holy,
    Whispered at the baron's ear.

Tears upon his eyelids glistened,
As he paused awhile and listened,
And the dying baron slowly
    Turned his weary head to hear.

" Wassail for the kingly stranger
Born and cradled in a manger !
King, like David, priest, like Aaron,
    Christ is born to set us free ! "

And the lightning showed the sainted
Figures on the casement painted,
And exclaimed the shuddering baron,
        " Miserere, Domine !"

In that hour of deep contrition,
He beheld, with clearer vision,
Through all outward show and fashion,
        Justice, the Avenger, rise.

All the pomp of earth had vanished,
Falsehood and deceit were banished,
Reason spake more loud than passion,
        And the truth wore no disguise.

Every vassal of his banner,
Every serf born to his manor,
All those wronged and wretched creatures,
        By his hand were freed again.

And, as on the sacred missal
He recorded their dismissal,
Death relaxed his iron features,
        And the monk replied, " Amen !"

Many centuries have been numbered
Since in death the baron slumbered
By the convent's sculptured portal,
        Mingling with the common dust :

But the good deed, through the ages
Living in historic pages,
Brighter glows and gleams immortal,
        Unconsumed by moth or rust.

RAIN IN SUMMER.

How beautiful is the rain!
After the dust and heat,
In the broad and fiery street,
In the narrow lane,
How beautiful is the rain!

How it clatters along the roofs,
Like the tramp of hoofs!
How it gushes and struggles out
From the throat of the overflowing spout!
Across the window pane
It pours and pours;
And swift and wide,
With a muddy tide,
Like a river down the gutter roars
The rain, the welcome rain!

The sick man from his chamber
Looks at the twisted brooks;
He can feel the cool
Breath of each little pool;
His fevered brain
Grows calm again,
And he breathes a blessing on the rain.

From the neighbouring school
Come the boys,
With more than their wonted noise
And commotion;
And down the wet streets
Sail their mimic fleets,
Till the treacherous pool

Engulfs them in its whirling
And turbulent ocean.

In the country, on every side,
Where far and wide,
Like a Leopard's tawny and spotted hide,
Stretches the plain,
To the dry grass and the drier grain
How welcome is the rain!

In the furrowed land
The toilsome and patient oxen stand;
Lifting the yoke-encumbered head,
With their dilated nostrils spread,
They silently inhale
The clover-scented gale,
And the vapors that arise
From the well-watered and smoking soil.
For this rest in the furrow after toil
Their large and lustrous eyes
Seem to thank the Lord,
More than man's spoken word.

Near at hand,
From under the sheltering trees,
The farmer sees
His pastures, and his fields of grain,
As they bend their tops
To the numberless beating drops
Of the incessant rain.
He counts it as no sin
That he sees therein
Only his own thrift and gain.

These, and far more than these,
The Poet sees!
He can behold
Aquarius old
Walking the fenceless fields of air:

And from each ample fold
Of the clouds about him rolled
Scattering everywhere
The showery rain,   .
As the farmer scatters his grain.

He can behold
Things manifold
That have not yet been wholly told,
Have not been wholly sung nor said.
For his thought, that never stops,
Follows the water-drops
Down to the graves of the dead,
Down through chasms and gulfs profound,
To the dreary fountain-head
Of lakes and rivers under ground;
And sees them, when the rain is done,
On the bridge of colors seven
Climbing up once more to heaven,
Opposite the setting sun.

Thus the Seer,
With vision clear,
Sees forms appear and disappear,
In the perpetual round of strange
Mysterious change,
From birth to death, from death to birth.
From earth to heaven, from heaven to earth;
Till glimpses more sublime
Of things, unseen before,
Unto his wondering eyes reveal
The Universe, as an immeasurable wheel
Turning for evermore
In the rapid and rushing river of Time.

TO THE DRIVING CLOUD

Gloomy and dark art thou, O chief of the mighty Omawhaws;
Gloomy and dark, as the driving cloud, whose name thou hast taken!
Wrapt in thy scarlet blanket, I see thee stalk through the city's
Narrow and populous streets, as once by the margin of rivers
Stalked those birds unknown, that have left us only their footprints.
What, in a few short years, will remain of thy race but the footprints?
How canst thou walk in these streets, who hast trod the green turf of the
    prairies?

How canst thou breathe in this, who hast breathed the sweet air of the
     mountains?
Ah! 'tis in vain that with lordly looks of disdain thou dost challenge
Looks of dislike in return, and question these walls and these pavements,
Claiming the soil for thy hunting-grounds, while down-trodden millions
Starve in the garrets of Europe, and cry from its caverns that they, too,
Have been created heirs of the earth, and claim its division!

Back, then, back to thy woods in the regions west of the Wabash!
There as a monarch thou reignest.   In autumn the leaves of the maple
Pave the floors of thy palace-halls with gold, and in summer
Pine-trees waft through its chambers the odorous breath of their branches.
There thou art strong and great, a hero, a tamer of horses!
There thou chasest the stately stag on the banks of the Elk-horn,
Or, by the roar of the Running-Water, or where the Omawhaw
Calls thee, and leaps through the wild ravine like a brave of the Blackfeet!
Hark! what murmurs arise from the heart of those mountainous deserts?
Is it the cry of the Foxes and Crows, or the mighty Behemoth,
Who, unharmed, on his tusks once caught the bolts of the thunder,
And now lurks in his lair to destroy the race of the red man?
Far more fatal to thee and thy race than the Crows and the Foxes,
Far more fatal to thee and thy race than the tread of Behemoth,
Lo! the big thunder-canoe, that steadily breasts the Missouri's
Merciless current! and yonder, afar on the prairies, the camp-fires
Gleam through the night; and the cloud of dust in the gray of the daybreak
Marks not the buffalo's track, nor the Mandan's dexterous horse-race;
It is a caravan, whitening the desert where dwell the Camanches!
Ha! how the breath of these Saxons and Celts, like the blast of the east-wind,
Drifts evermore to the west the scanty smokes of thy wigwams!

TO A CHILD.

Dear child! how radiant on thy mother's knee,
With merry-making eyes and jocund smiles,
Thou gazest at the painted tiles,
Whose figures grace,
With many a grotesque form and face,
The ancient chimney of thy nursery!
The lady with the gay macaw,
The dancing girl, the grave bashaw
With bearded lip and chin;
And, leaning idly o'er his gate,
Beneath the imperial fan of state,
The Chinese mandarin.

With what a look of proud command
Thou shakest in thy little hand
The coral rattle with its silver bells,
Making a merry tune!
Thousands of years in Indian seas
That coral grew, by slow degrees,
Until some deadly and wild monsoon
Dashed it on Coromandel's sand!
Those silver bells
Reposed of yore,
As shapeless ore,
Far down in the deep-sunken wells

Of darksome mines,
In some obscure and sunless place,
Beneath huge Chimborazo's base,
Or Potosi's o'erhanging pines!

And thus for thee, O little child,
Through many a danger and escape,
The tall ships passed the stormy cape;
For thee in foreign lands remote,
Beneath the burning, tropic skies,
The Indian peasant, chasing the wild goat,
Himself as swift and wild,
In falling, clutched the frail arbute,
The fibres of whose shallow root,
Uplifted from the soil, betrayed
The silver veins beneath it laid,
The buried treasures of dead centuries.

But, lo! thy door is left ajar!
Thou hearest footsteps from afar!
And, at the sound,
Thou turnest round
With quick and questioning eyes,
Like one, who, in a foreign land,
Beholds on every hand
Some source of wonder and surprise!
And, restlessly, impatiently,
Thou strivest, strugglest, to be free.
The four walls of thy nursery
Are now like prison walls to thee,
No more thy mother's smiles,
No more the painted tiles,
Delight thee, nor the playthings on the floor,
That won thy little, beating heart before:
Thou strugglest for the open door.

Through these once solitary halls
Thy pattering footstep falls,

The sound of thy merry voice
Makes the old walls
Jubilant, and they rejoice
With the joy of thy young heart,
O'er the light of whose gladness
No shadows of sadness
From the sombre background of memory start.

Once, ah, once, within these walls,
One whom memory oft recalls,
The Father of his Country dwelt.
And yonder meadows broad and damp
The fires of the besieging camp
Encircled with a burning belt.
Up and down these echoing stairs,
Heavy with the weight of cares,
Sounded his majestic tread;
Yes, within this very room
Sat he in those hours of gloom,
Weary both in heart and head.

But what are these grave thoughts to thee?
Out, out! into the open air!
Thy only dream is liberty,
Thou carest little how or where.
I see thee eager at thy play,
Now shouting to the apples on the tree,
With cheeks as round and red as they;
And now among the yellow stalks,
Among the flowering shrubs and plants,
As restless as the bee.
Along the garden walks,
The tracks of thy small carriage-wheels I trace
And see at every turn how they efface
Whole villages of sand-roofed tents,
That rise like golden domes
Above the cavernous and secret homes
Of wandering and nomadic tribes of ants.
Ah, cruel little Tamerlane,
Who with thy dreadful reign,

Dost persecute and overwhelm
These hapless Troglodytes of thy realm!

What! tired already! with those suppliant looks,
And voice more beautiful than a poet's books,
Or murmuring sound of water as it flows,
Thou comest back to parley with repose!
This rustic seat in the old apple-tree,
With its o'erhanging golden canopy
Of leaves illuminate with autumnal hues,
And shining with the argent light of dews,
Shall for a season be our place of rest.
Beneath us, like an oriole's pendent nest,
From which the laughing birds have taken wing,
By thee abandoned, hangs thy vacant swing.
Dream-like the waters of the rivers gleam;
A sailless vessel drops adown the stream,
And like it, to a sea as wide and deep,
Thou driftest gently down the tides of sleep.

O child! O new-born denizen
Of life's great city! on thy head
The glory of the morn is shed,
Like a celestial benison!
Here at the portal thou dost stand,
And with thy little hand
Thou openest the mysterious gate
Into the future's undiscovered land.
I see its valves expand,
As at the touch of Fate!
Into those realms of love and hate,
Into that darkness blank and drear,
By some prophetic feeling taught,
I launch the bold, adventurous thought,
Freighted with hope and fear;
As upon subterranean streams,
In caverns unexplored and dark,
Men sometimes launch a fragile bark,
Laden with flickering fire,
And watch its swift-receding beams,

Until at length they disappear,
And in the distant dark expire.

By what astrology of fear or hope
Dare I to cast thy horoscope !
Like the new moon thy life appears ;
A little strip of silver light,
And widening outward into night
The shadowy disk of future years ;
And yet upon its outer rim,
A luminous circle, faint and dim,
And scarcely visible to us here,
Rounds and completes the perfect sphere,
A prophecy and intimation,
A pale and feeble adumbration,
Of the great world of light, that lies
Behind all human destinies.
Ah ! if thy fate, with anguish fraught,
Should be to wet the dusty soil
With the hot tears and sweat of toil,—
To struggle with imperious thought,
Until the overburdened brain,
Weary with labour, faint with pain,
Like a jarred pendulum, retain
Only its motion, not its power,—
Remember, in that perilous hour.
When most afflicted and oppressed,
From labor there shall come forth rest.

And if a more auspicious fate
On thy advancing steps await,
Still let it ever be thy pride
To linger by the laborer's side ;
With words of sympathy or song
To cheer the dreary march along
Of the great army of the poor,
O'er desert sand, o'er dangerous moor.
Nor to thyself the task shall be
Without reward ; for thou shalt learn

The wisdom early to discern
True beauty in utility :
As great Pythagoras of yore,
Standing beside the blacksmith's door,
And hearing the hammers, as they smote
The anvils with a different note,
Stole from the varying tones, that hung
Vibrant on every iron tongue.
The secret of the sounding wire,
And formed the seven-chorded lyre.

Enough ! I will not play the Seer ;
I will no longer strive to ape
The mystic volume, where appear
The herald Hope, forerunning Fear,
And Fear, the pursuivant of Hope.
Thy destiny remains untold :
For, like Acestes' shaft of old,
The swift thought kindles as it flies,
And burns to ashes in the skies.

THE BRIDGE.

I stood on the bridge at midnight,
  As the clocks were striking the hour,
And the moon rose o'er the city,
  Behind the dark church-tower.

I saw her bright reflection
  In the waters under me,
Like a golden goblet falling
  And sinking into the sea.

And far in the hazy distance
  Of that lovely night in June,
The blaze of the flaming furnace
  Gleamed redder than the moon.

Among the long, black rafters
  The wavering shadows lay,
And the current that came from the ocean
  Seemed to lift and bear them away;

As, sweeping and eddying through them,
  Rose the belated tide,
And, streaming into the moonlight,
  The sea-weed floated wide.

And like those waters rushing
  Among the wooden piers,
A flood of thoughts came o'er me
  That filled my eyes with tears.

How often, O, how often,
  In the days that had gone by,
I had stood on that bridge at midnight
  And gazed on that wave and sky!

How often, O, how often,
  I had wished that the ebbing tide
Would bear me away on its bosom
  O'er the ocean wild and wide!

For my heart was hot and restless,
  And my life was full of care,
And the burden laid upon me
  Seemed greater than I could bear.

But now it has fallen from me,
  It is buried in the sea;
And only the sorrow of others
  Throws its shadow over me.

Yet whenever I cross the river
  On its bridge with wooden piers,
Like the odor of brine from the ocean
  Comes the thought of other years.

And I think how many thousands
  Of care-encumbered men,
Each bearing his burden of sorrow,
  Have crossed the bridge since then.

I see the long procession
  Still passing to and fro,
The young heart hot and restless,
  And the old subdued and slow !

And forever and forever,
  As long as the river flows,
As long as the heart has passions,
  As long as life has woes;

The moon and its broken reflection
  And its shadows shall appear,
As the symbol of love in heaven,
  And its wavering image here.

CURFEW.

I.

SOLEMNLY, mournfully,
  Dealing its dole,
The Curfew Bell
  Is beginning to toll.

Cover the embers,
  And put out the light;
Toil comes with the morning.
  And rest with the night.

Dark grow the windows,
  And quenched is the fire;
Sound fades into silence,—
  All footsteps retire.

No voice in the chambers,
  No sound in the hall!
Sleep and oblivion
  Reign over all!

II.

The book is completed,
  And closed, like the day;
And the hand that has written it
  Lays it away.

Dim grow its fancies,
  Forgotten they lie;
Like coals in the ashes,
  They darken and die.

Song sinks into silence,
  The story is told,
The windows are darkened,
  The hearth-stone is cold.

Darker and darker
  The black shadows fall;
Sleep and oblivion
  Reign over all.

BIRDS OF PASSAGE.

THE ROPE WALK

THE ROPE WALK.

In that building long and low,
With its windows all a row,
  Like the port-holes of a hulk,
Human spiders spin and spin,
Backward down their threads so thin,
  Dropping, each, a hempen bulk.

At the end an open door;
Squares of sunshine on the floor
  Light the long and dusky lane;
And the whirling of a wheel,
Dull and drowsy, makes me feel
  All its spokes are in my brain.

As the spinners to the end
Downward go and re-ascend,
  Gleam the long threads in the sun;
While within this brain of mine
Cobwebs brighter and more fine
  By the busy wheel are spun.

Two fair maidens in a swing,
Like white doves upon the wing,
  First before my vision pass;
Laughing, as their gentle hands
Closely clasp the twisted strands,
  At their shadow on the grass.

Then a booth of mountebanks,
With its smell of tan and planks,
  And a girl poised high in air
On a cord, in spangled dress,
With a faded loveliness,
  And a weary look of care.

Then a homestead among farms,
And a woman with bare arms,
  Drawing water from a well;
As the bucket mounts apace,
With it mounts her own fair face,
  As at some magician's spell.

Then an old man in a tower
Ringing loud the noontide hour,
  While the rope coils round and round,
Like a serpent, at his feet,
And again in swift retreat
  Almost lifts him from the ground.

Then within a prison-yard,
Faces fixed, and stern, and hard,
  Laughter and indecent mirth;
Ah! it is the gallows-tree!
Breath of Christian charity,
  Blow, and sweep it from the earth!

Then a schoolboy, with his kite,
Gleaming in a sky of light,
  And an eager, upward look;
Steeds pursued through lane and field:
Fowlers with their snares concealed,
  And an angler by a brook.

Ships rejoicing in the breeze,
Wrecks that float o'er unknown seas,
  Anchors dragged through faithless sand;
Sea-fog drifting overhead,
And with lessening line and lead
  Sailors feeling for the land.

All these scenes do I behold,
These and many left untold,
  In that building long and low;
While the wheels go round and round
With a drowsy, dreamy sound,
  And the spinners backward go.

THE WARDEN OF THE CINQUE PORTS.

A mist was driving down the British Channel,
   The day was just begun,
And through the window-panes, on floor and panel,
   Streamed the red autumn sun.

It glanced on flowing flag and rippling pennon,
   And the white sails of ships;
And, from the frowning rampart, the black cannon
   Hailed it with feverish lips.

Sandwich and Romney, Hastings, Hythe and Dover,
  Were all alert that day,
To see the French war-steamers speeding over,
  When the fog cleared away.

Sullen and silent, and like couchant lions,
  Their cannon through the night,
Holding their breath, had watched in grim defiance
  The sea-coast opposite.

And now they roared at drum-beat from their stations
  On every citadel;
Each answering each with morning salutations
  That all was well.

And down the coast, all taking up the burden,
  Replied the distant forts,
As if to summon from his sleep the Warden
  And Lord of the Cinque Ports.

Him shall no sunshine from the fields of azure,
  No drum-beat from the wall,
No morning-gun from the black fort's embrasure
  Awaken with their call.

No more surveying with an eye impartial
  The long line of the coast,
Shall the gaunt figure of the old Field-Marshal
  Be seen upon his post.

For in the night, unseen, a single warrior,
  In sombre harness mailed,
Dreaded of man, and surnamed the Destroyer,
  The rampart wall has scaled.

He passed into the chamber of the sleeper,
    The dark and silent room;
And as he entered, darker grew and deeper
    The silence and the gloom.

He did not pause to parley or dissemble,
    But smote the Warden hoar;
Ah! what a blow! that made all England tremble,
    And groan from shore to shore.

Meanwhile, without the surly cannon waited,
    The sun rose bright o'erhead;
Nothing in Nature's aspect intimated
    That a great man was dead!

— — ———

THE TWO ANGELS.

THE TWO ANGELS.

Two Angels, one of Life, and one of Death,
    Passed o'er the village as the morning broke;
The dawn was on their faces; and beneath,
    The sombre houses capped with plumes of smoke.

Their attitude and aspect were the same:
    Alike their features and their robes of white;
And one was crowned with amaranth, as with flame,
    And one with asphodels, like flakes of light.

I saw them pause on their celestial way:—
    Then said I, with deep fear and doubt oppressed,
" Beat not so loud, my heart, lest thou betray
    The place where thy beloved are at rest!"

And he who wore the crown of asphodels,
    Descending at my door, began to knock:
And my soul sank within me, as in wells
    The waters sink before an earthquake's shock.

I recognised the nameless agony—
    The terror, and the tremor, and the pain—
That oft before had filled and haunted me,
    And now returned with threefold strength again.

The door I opened to my heavenly guest,
    And listened, for I thought I heard God's voice;
And, knowing whatsoe'er He sent was best,
    Dared neither to lament nor to rejoice.

Then with a smile that filled the house with light—
   " My errand is not Death, but Life," he said ;
And, ere I answered, passing out of sight,
   On his celestial embassy he sped.

'Twas at thy door, O friend, and not at mine,
   The angel with the amaranthine wreath,
Pausing, descended ; and, with voice divine,
   Whispered a word that had a sound like Death.

Then fell upon the house a sudden gloom—
   A shadow on those features fair and thin ;
And softly, from that hushed and darkened room,
   Two angels issued, where but one went in.

All is of God !   If He but wave his hand,
   The mists collect, the rains fall thick and loud ;
Till, with a smile of light on sea and land,
   Lo ! He looks back from the departing cloud.

Angels of Life and Death alike are His ;
   Without His leave they pass no threshold o'er ;
Who, then, would wish or dare, believing this,
   Against His messengers to shut the door ?

<hr/>

Inspired by the birth of a child to the writer, and the death of Mrs. Maria
Lowell, the wife of another American poet, on the same day, at Cambridge, U.S.

PROMETHEUS,

OR THE POET'S FORETHOUGHT.

Of Prometheus, how undaunted
  On Olympus' shining bastions
His audacious foot he planted,
Myths are told and songs are chaunted,
  Full of promptings and suggestions.

Beautiful is the tradition
  Of that flight through heavenly portals,
The old classic superstition
Of the theft and the transmission
  Of the fire of the Immortals!

First the deed of noble daring,
  Born of heavenward aspiration,
Then the fire with mortals sharing,
Then the vulture,—the despairing
  Cry of pain on crags Caucasian.

All is but a symbol painted
  Of the Poet, Prophet, Seer;
Only those are crowned and sainted
Who with grief have been acquainted,
  Making nations nobler, freer.

In their feverish exultations,
  In their triumph and their yearning,
In their passionate pulsations,
In their words among the nations,
  The Promethean fire is burning.

Shall it, then, be unavailing,
  All this toil for human culture?
Through the cloud-rack, dark and trailing,
Must they see above them sailing
  O'er life's barren crags the vulture?

Such a fate as this was Dante's,
  By defeat and exile maddened;
Thus were Milton and Cervantes,
Nature's priests and Corybantes,
  By affliction touched and saddened.

But the glories so transcendent
  That around their memories cluster,
And, on all their steps attendant,
Make their darkened lives resplendent
  With such gleams of inward lustre!

All the melodies mysterious,
  Through the dreary darkness chaunted;
Thoughts in attitudes imperious,
Voices soft, and deep, and serious,
  Words that whispered, songs that haunted!

All the soul in rapt suspension,
  All the quivering, palpitating
Chords of life in utmost tension,
With the fervor of invention,
  With the rapture of creating!

Ah, Prometheus! heaven-scaling!
    In such hours of exultation
Even the faintest heart, unquailing,
Might behold the vulture sailing
    Round the cloudy crags Caucasian!

Though to all there is not given
    Strength for such sublime endeavor,
Thus to scale the walls of heaven,
And to leaven with fiery leaven
    All the hearts of men for ever;

Yet all bards, whose hearts unblighted
    Honor and believe the presage,
Hold aloft their torches lighted,
Gleaming through the realms benighted,
    As they onward bear the message!

THE LADDER OF ST. AUGUSTINE.

Saint Augustine! well hast thou said,
    That of our vices we can frame
A ladder,* if we will but tread
    Beneath our feet each deed of shame!

All common things, each day's events,
    That with the hour begin and end,
Our pleasures and our discontents,
    Are rounds by which we may ascend.

* The words of St. Augustine are, " De vitiis nostris scalam nobis facimus, si vitia
ipsa calcamus."—Sermon III. De Ascensione

The low desire, the base design,
  That makes another's virtue less;
The revel of the treacherous wine,
  And all occasions of excess;

The longing for ignoble things;
  The strife for triumph more than truth;
The hardening of the heart, that brings
  Irreverence for the dreams of youth;

All thoughts of ill; all evil deeds,
  That have their root in thoughts of ill;
Whatever hinders or impedes
  The action of the nobler will;—

All these must first be trampled down
  Beneath our feet, if we would gain
In the bright fields of fair renown
  The right of eminent domain.

We have not wings, we cannot soar;
  But we have feet to scale and climb
By slow degrees, by more and more,
  The cloudy summits of our time.

The mighty pyramids of stone
  That wedge-like cleave the desert airs,
When nearer seen, and better known,
  Are but gigantic flights of stairs.

The distant mountains, that uprear
  Their solid bastions to the skies,
Are crossed by pathways, that appear
  As we to higher levels rise.

The heights by great men reached and kept
  Were not attained by sudden flight,
But they, while their companions slept,
  Were toiling upward in the night.

Standing on what too long we bore
  With shoulders bent and downcast eyes,
We may discern—unseen before—
  A path to higher destinies.

Nor deem the irrevocable Past
  As wholly wasted, wholly vain,
If, rising on its wrecks, at last
  To something nobler we attain.

—

THE PHANTOM SHIP. *

In Mather's Magnalia Christi,
  Of the old colonial time,
May be found in prose the legend
  That is here set down in rhyme.

A ship sailed from New Haven,
  And the keen and frosty airs,
That filled her sails at parting,
  Were heavy with good men's prayers.

" O Lord! if it be thy pleasure "—
  Thus prayed the old divine—
" To bury our friends in the ocean,
  Take them, for they are thine! "

---

* A detailed account of this "apparition of a Ship in the Air" is given by Cotton
Mather in his Magnalia Christi, Book I. Ch. VI. It is contained in a letter from the
Rev. James Pierpont, Pastor of New Haven. To this account Mather adds these
words:—

" Reader, there being yet living so many credible gentlemen, that were eye-
witnesses of this wonderful thing, I venture to publish it for a thing as undoubted
as 'tis wonderful."

But Master Lamberton muttered,
  And under his breath said he,
" This ship is so crank and walty,
  I fear our grave she will be ! "

And the ships that came from England
  When the winter months were gone,
Brought no tidings of this vessel,
  Nor of Master Lamberton.

This put the people to praying
  That the Lord would let them hear
What in his greater wisdom
  He had done with friends so dear.

And at last their prayers were answered :—
  It was in the month of June,
An hour before the sunset
  Of a windy afternoon,

When, steadily steering landward,
  A ship was seen below,
And they knew it was Lamberton, Master,
  Who sailed so long ago.

On she came, with a cloud of canvas,
  Right against the wind that blew,
Until the eye could distinguish
  The faces of the crew.

Then fell her straining topmasts,
  Hanging tangled in the shrouds ;
And her sails were loosened and lifted,
  And blown away like clouds.

And the masts, with all their rigging,
  Fell slowly, one by one ;
And the hulk dilated and vanished,
  As a sea-mist in the sun !

And the people who saw this marvel
  Each said unto his friend,
That this was the mould of their vessel,
  And thus her tragic end.

And the pastor of the village
  Gave thanks to God in prayer,
That, to quiet their troubled spirits,
  He had sent this Ship of Air.

HAUNTED HOUSES.

ALL houses wherein men have lived and died
  Are haunted houses. Through the open doors
The harmless phantoms on their errands glide,
  With feet that make no sound upon the floors.

We meet them at the door-way, on the stair,
  Along the passages they come and go,
Impalpable impressions on the air,
  A sense of something moving to and fro.

There are more guests at table than the hosts
  Invited; the illuminated hall
Is thronged with quiet, inoffensive ghosts,
  As silent as the pictures on the wall.

The stranger at my fireside cannot see
  The forms I see, nor hear the sounds I hear;
He but perceives what is; while unto me
  All that has been is visible and clear.

We have no title-deeds to house or lands ;
  Owners and occupants of earlier dates
From graves forgotten stretch their dusty hands,
  And hold in mortmain still their old estates.

The spirit-world around this world of sense
  Floats like an atmosphere, and everywhere
Wafts through these earthly mists and vapours dense
  A vital breath of more ethereal air.

Our little lives are kept in equipoise
  By opposite attractions and desires !
The struggle of the instinct that enjoys,
  And the more noble instinct that aspires.

These perturbations, this perpetual jar
  Of earthly wants and aspirations high,
Come from the influence of an unseen star,
  An undiscovered planet in our sky.

And as the moon from some dark gate of cloud
  Throws o'er the sea a floating bridge of light,
Across whose trembling planks our fancies crowd
  Into the realm of mystery and night,—

So from the world of spirits there descends
  A bridge of light, connecting it with this,
O'er whose unsteady floor, that sways and bends,
  Wander our thoughts above the dark abyss.

DAYLIGHT AND MOONLIGHT.

In broad daylight, and at noon,
Yesterday I saw the moon
Sailing high, but faint and white,
As a schoolboy's paper kite.

In broad daylight, yesterday,
I read a Poet's mystic lay:
And it seemed to me at most
As a phantom, or a ghost.

But at length the feverish day
Like a passion died away,
And the night, serene and still,
Fell on village, vale, and hill.

Then the moon, in all her pride,
Like a spirit glorified,
Filled and overflowed the night
With revelations of her light.

And the Poet's song again
Passed like music through my brain;
Night interpreted to me
All its grace and mystery.

IN THE CHURCHYARD AT CAMBRIDGE.

In the village churchyard she lies,
Dust is in her beautiful eyes,
    No more she breathes, nor feels, nor stirs ;
At her foot and at her head
Lies a slave to attend the dead,
    But their dust is white as hers.

Was she a lady of high degree,
So much in love with vanity
    And foolish pomp of this world of ours?
Or was it Christian charity,
And lowliness and humility,
    The richest and rarest of all dowers?

Who shall tell us? No one speaks ;
No color shoots into those cheeks,
    Either of anger or of pride,
At the rude question we have asked ;
Nor will the mystery be unmasked
    By those who are sleeping at her side.

Hereafter?—And do you think to look
On the terrible pages of that Book
    To find her failings, faults, and errors?
Ah, you will then have other cares,
In your own short-comings and despairs,
    In your own secret sins and terrors!

THE EMPEROR'S BIRD'S NEST.

Once the Emperor Charles of Spain,
  With his swarthy, grave commanders,
I forget in what campaign,
Long besieged, in mud and rain,
  Some old frontier town of Flanders.

Up and down the dreary camp,
  In great boots of Spanish leather,
Striding with a measured tramp,
These Hidalgos, dull and damp,
  Cursed the Frenchmen, cursed the weather.

Thus as to and fro they went,
  Over upland and through hollow,
Giving their impatience vent,
Perched upon the Emperor's tent
  In her nest they spied a swallow.

Yes, it was a swallow's nest,
  Built of clay and hair of horses,
Mane, or tail, or dragoon's crest,
Found on hedge-rows east and west,
  After skirmish of the forces.

Then an old Hidalgo said,
  As he twirled his gray mustachio,
"Sure this swallow overhead
Thinks the Emperor's tent a shed,
  And the Emperor but a Macho!" *

* Macho, in Spanish, signifies a mule. Golondrina is the feminine form of Golondrino, a swallow, and also a cant name for a deserter.

Hearing his imperial name
  Coupled with those words of malice,
Half in anger, half in shame,
Forth the great campaigner came
  Slowly from his canvas palace.

"Let no hand the bird molest,"
  Said he solemnly, "nor hurt her!"
Adding then, by way of jest,
"Golondrina is my guest,
  'Tis the wife of some deserter!"

Swift as bowstring speeds a shaft,
  Through the camp was spread the rumor,
And the soldiers, as they quaffed
Flemish beer at dinner, laughed
  At the Emperor's pleasant humor.

So unharmed and unafraid
  Sat the swallow still and brooded,
Till the constant cannonade
Through the walls a breach had made,
  And the siege was thus concluded.

Then the army, elsewhere bent,
  Struck its tents as if disbanding.
Only not the Emperor's tent,
For he ordered, ere he went,
  Very curtly, "Leave it standing!"

So it stood there all alone,
  Loosely flapping, torn and tattered,
Till the brood was fledged and flown,
Singing o'er those walls of stone
  Which the cannon-shot had shattered.

THE GOLDEN MILE-STONE.

LEAFLESS are the trees; their purple branches
Spread themselves abroad, like reefs of coral,
    Rising silent
In the Red Sea of the Winter sunset.

From the hundred chimneys of the village,
Like the Afreet in the Arabian story,
    Smoky columns
Tower aloft into the air of amber.

          v v

At the window winks the flickering fire-light;
Here and there the lamps of evening glimmer,
   Social watch-fires
Answering one another through the darkness.

On the hearth the lighted logs are glowing,
And like Ariel in the cloven pine-tree
   For its freedom
Groans and sighs the air imprisoned in them.

By the fireside there are old men seated,
Seeing ruined cities in the ashes,
   Asking sadly
Of the Past what it can ne'er restore them.

By the fireside there are youthful dreamers,
Building castles fair, with stately stairways,
   Asking blindly
Of the Future what it cannot give them.

By the fireside tragedies are acted
In whose scenes appear two actors only,
   Wife and husband,
And above them God the sole spectator.

By the fireside there are peace and comfort,
Wives and children, with fair, thoughtful faces,
   Waiting, watching
For a well-known footstep in the passage.

Each man's chimney is his Golden Mile-stone;
Is the central point, from which he measures
   Every distance
Through the gateways of the world around him.

In his farthest wanderings still he sees it;
Hears the talking flame, the answering night-wind,
   As he heard them
When he sat with those who were, but are not.

Happy he whom neither wealth nor fashion,
Nor the march of the encroaching city,
        Drives an exile
From the hearth of his ancestral homestead.

We may build more splendid habitations,
Fill our rooms with paintings and with sculptures,
        But we cannot
Buy with gold the old associations!

THE JEWISH CEMETERY AT NEWPORT.

How strange it seems! These Hebrews in their graves,
  Close by the street of this fair seaport town,
Silent beside the never-silent waves,
  At rest in all this moving up and down!

The trees are white with dust, that o'er their sleep
  Wave their broad curtains in the south wind's breath,
While underneath such leafy tents they keep
  The long, mysterious Exodus of Death.

And these sepulchral stones, so old and brown,
  That pave with level flags their burial-place,
Seem like the tablets of the Law, thrown down
  And broken by Moses at the mountain's base.

The very names recorded here are strange,
    Of foreign accent, and of different climes ;
Alvares and Rivera interchange
    With Abraham and Jacob of old times.

" Blessed be God ! for He created Death ! "
    The mourners said, " and Death is rest and peace ; "
Then added, in the certainty of faith,
    " And giveth Life that never more shall cease."

Closed are the portals of their Synagogue,
    No Psalms of David now the silence break,
No Rabbi reads the ancient Decalogue
    In the grand dialect the Prophets spake.

Gone are the living, but the dead remain,
    And not neglected ; for a hand unseen,
Scattering its bounty, like a summer rain,
    Still keeps their graves and their remembrance green.

How came they here ?   What burst of Christian hate,
    What persecution, merciless and blind,
Drove o'er the sea—that desert desolate—
    These Ishmaels and Hagars of mankind ?

They lived in narrow streets and lanes obscure,
    Ghetto and Judenstrass, in mirk and mire ;
Taught in the school of patience to endure
    The life of anguish and the death of fire.

All their lives long, with the unleavened bread
    And bitter herbs of exile and its fears,
The wasting famine of the heart they fed,
    And slaked its thirst with marah of their tears.

Anathema maranatha! was the cry
  That rang from town to town, from street to street;
At every gate the accursed Mordecai
  Was mocked and jeered, and spurned by Christian feet.

Pride and humiliation hand in hand
  Walked with them through the world where'er they went;
Trampled and beaten were they as the sand,
  And yet unshaken as the continent.

For in the background figures vague and vast
  Of patriarchs and of prophets rose sublime,
And all the great traditions of the Past
  They saw reflected in the coming time.

And thus for ever with reverted look
  The mystic volume of the world they read,
Spelling it backward, like a Hebrew book,
  Till life became a Legend of the Dead.

But ah! what once has been shall be no more.
  The groaning earth in travail and in pain
Brings forth its races, but does not restore,
  And the dead nations never rise again.

OLIVER BASSELIN.*

In the Valley of the Vire
   Still is seen an ancient mill,
With its gables quaint and queer,
   And beneath the window-sill,
         On the stone,
         These words alone:
"Oliver Basselin lived here."

Far above it, on the steep,
   Ruined stands the old Château:
Nothing but the donjon-keep
   Left for shelter or for show.
         Its vacant eyes
         Stare at the skies,
Stare at the valley green and deep.

Once a convent, old and brown,
   Looked, but ah! it looks no more,
From the neighboring hillside down
   On the rushing and the roar
         Of the stream
         Whose sunny gleam
Cheers the little Norman town.

In that darksome mill of stone,
   To the water's dash and din,
Careless, humble, and unknown,
   Sang the poet Basselin
         Songs that fill
         That ancient mill
With a splendor of its own.

* Oliver Basselin, the "Père joyeux du Vaudeville," flourished in the fifteenth
century, and gave to his convivial songs the name of his native valleys, in which
he sang them, Vaux-de-Vire. This name was afterwards corrupted into the
modern Vaudeville.

Never feeling of unrest
  Broke the pleasant dream he dreamed;
Only made to be his nest,
  All the lovely valley seemed;
      No desire
      Of soaring higher
Stirred or fluttered in his breast.

True, his songs were not divine;
  Were not songs of that high art,
Which, as winds do in the pine,
  Find an answer in each heart;
      But the mirth
      Of this green earth
Laughed and revelled in his line.

From the alehouse and the inn,
  Opening on the narrow street,
Came the loud, convivial din,
  Singing and applause of feet,
      The laughing lays
      That in those days
Sang the poet Basselin.

In the castle, cased in steel,
  Knights, who fought at Agincourt,
Watched and waited, spur on heel;
  But the poet sang for sport
      Songs that rang
      Another clang,
Songs that lowlier hearts could feel.

In the convent, clad in gray,
  Sat the monks in lonely cells,
Paced the cloisters, knelt to pray,
  And the poet heard their bells;

But his rhymes
Found other chimes,
Nearer to the earth than they.

Gone are all the barons bold,
  Gone are all the knights and squires.
Gone the abbot stern and cold,
  And the brotherhood of friars;
    Not a name
    Remains to fame,
From those mouldering days of old!

But the poet's memory here
  Of the landscape makes a part;
Like the river, swift and clear,
  Flows his song through many a heart;
    Haunting still
    That ancient mill,
In the Valley of the Vire.

THE DISCOVERER OF THE NORTH CAPE.

A LEAF FROM KING ALFRED'S OROSIUS.

OTHERE, the old sea-captain,
  Who dwelt in Helgoland,
To King Alfred, the Lover of Truth,
Brought a snow-white walrus-tooth,
  Which he held in his brown right hand.

z 2

His figure was tall and stately,
  Like a boy's his eye appeared;
His hair was yellow as hay,
But threads of a silvery gray
  Gleamed in his tawny beard.

Hearty and hale was Othere,
  His cheek had the colour of oak;
With a kind of laugh in his speech,
Like the sea-tide on a beach,
  As unto the King he spoke.

And Alfred, King of the Saxons,
  Had a book upon his knees,
And wrote down the wondrous tale
Of him who was first to sail
  Into the Arctic seas.

"So far I live to the northward,
  No man lives north of me;
To the east are wild mountain-chains,
And beyond them meres and plains;
  To the westward all is sea.

"So far I live to the northward,
  From the harbour of Skeringes-hale,
If you only sailed by day,
With a fair wind all the way,
  More than a month would you sail.

"I own six hundred reindeer,
  With sheep and swine beside;
I have tribute from the Finns,
Whalebone and reindeer-skins,
  And ropes of walrus-hide.

"I ploughed the land with horses,
  But my heart was ill at ease,
For the old seafaring men
Came to me now and then,
  With their sagas of the seas:—

"Of Iceland and of Greenland,
  And the stormy Hebrides,
And the undiscovered deep;—
I could not eat nor sleep
  For thinking of those seas.

"To the northward stretched the desert,
  How far I fain would know;
So at last I sallied forth,
And three days sailed due north,
  As far as the whale-ships go.

"To the west of me was the ocean,
  To the right the desolate shore,
But I did not slacken sail
For the walrus or the whale,
  Till after three days more.

"The days grew longer and longer,
  Till they became as one,
And southward through the haze
I saw the sullen blaze
  Of the red midnight sun.

"And then uprose before me,
  Upon the water's edge,
The huge and haggard shape
Of that unknown North Cape,
  Whose form is like a wedge.

" The sea was rough and stormy,
    The tempest howled and wailed,
And the sea-fog, like a ghost,
Haunted that dreary coast,
    But onward still I sailed.

" Four days I steered to eastward,
    Four days without a night:
Round in a fiery ring
Went the great sun, O King,
    With red and lurid light."

Here Alfred, King of the Saxons,
    Ceased writing for a while;
And raised his eyes from his book,
With a strange and puzzled look,
    And an incredulous smile.

But Othere, the old sea-captain,
    He neither paused nor stirred,
Till the King listened, and then
Once more took up his pen,
    And wrote down every word.

" And now the land," said Othere,
    " Bent southward suddenly,
And I followed the curving shore
And ever southward bore
    Into a nameless sea.

" And there we hunted the walrus,
    The narwhale, and the seal;
Ha! 'twas a noble game!
And like the lightning's flame
    Flew our harpoons of steel.

" There were six of us altogether,
  Norsemen of Helgoland :
In two days and no more
We killed of them threescore,
  And dragged them to the strand ! "

Here Alfred the Truth-Teller
  Suddenly closed his book,
And lifted his blue eyes,
With doubt and strange surmise
  Depicted in their look.

And Othere the old sea-captain
  Stared at him wild and weird,
Then smiled, till his shining teeth
Gleamed white from underneath
  His tawny, quivering beard.

And to the King of the Saxons,
  In witness of the truth,
Raising his noble head,
He stretched his brown hand, and said,
  " Behold this walrus-tooth ! "

"VICTOR GALBRAITH."

Under the walls of Monterey
At daybreak the bugles began to play,
    Victor Galbraith !
In the mist of the morning damp and gray,
These were the words they seemed to say,
    " Come forth to thy death,
    Victor Galbraith ! "

Forth he came, with a martial tread ;
Firm was his step, erect his head ;
    Victor Galbraith,
He who so well the bugle played,
Could not mistake the words it said :
    " Come forth to thy death,
    Victor Galbraith ! "

He looked at the earth, he looked at the sky,
He looked at the files of musketry,
    Victor Galbraith !
And he said, with a steady voice and eye,
" Take good aim : I am ready to die ! "
    Thus challenges death
    Victor Galbraith.

* This poem is founded on fact. Victor Galbraith was a bugler in a company of volunteer cavalry ; and was shot in Mexico for some breach of discipline. It is a common superstition among soldiers, that no balls will kill them unless their names are written on them. The old proverb says, " Every bullet has its billet."

Twelve fiery tongues flashed straight and red,
Six leaden balls on their errand sped:
     Victor Galbraith
Falls to the ground, but he is not dead:
His name was not stamped on those balls of lead,
     And they only scath
     Victor Galbraith.

Three balls are in his breast and brain,
But he rises out of the dust again,
     Victor Galbraith!
The water he drinks has a bloody stain;
"O kill me, and put me out of my pain!"
     In his agony prayeth
     Victor Galbraith.

Forth dart once more those tongues of flame,
And the bugler has died a death of shame,
     Victor Galbraith!
His soul has gone back to whence it came,
And no one answers to the name,
     When the Sergeant saith,
     "Victor Galbraith!"

Under the walls of Monterey
By night a bugle is heard to play.
     Victor Galbraith!
Through the mist of the valley damp and gray
The sentinels hear the sound, and say,
     "That is the wraith
     Of Victor Galbraith!"

CHILDREN.

Come to me, O ye children!
  For I hear you at your play,
And the questions that perplexed me
  Have vanished quite away.

Ye open the eastern windows,
  That look towards the sun,
Where thoughts are singing swallows,
  And the brooks of morning run.

In your hearts are the birds and the sunshine,
  In your thoughts the brooklet's flow;
But in mine is the wind of Autumn
  And the first fall of the snow.

Ah! what would the world be to us
  If the children were no more?
We should dread the desert behind us
  Worse than the dark before.

What the leaves are to the forest,
  With light and air for food,
Ere their sweet and tender juices
  Have been hardened into wood,—

That to the world are children:
  Through them it feels the glow
Of a brighter and sunnier climate
  Than reaches the trunks below.

Come to me, O ye children!
  And whisper in my ear
What the birds and the winds are singing
  In your sunny atmosphere.

For what are all our contrivings,
  And the wisdom of our books,
When compared with your caresses,
  And the gladness of your looks?

Ye are better than all the ballads
  That ever were sung or said;
For ye are living poems,
  And all the rest are dead.

MY LOST YOUTH.

Often I think of the beautiful town
  That is seated by the sea;
Often in thought go up and down
The pleasant streets of that dear old town,
  And my youth comes back to me.
    And a verse of a Lapland song
    Is haunting my memory still:
    " A boy's will is the wind's will,
And the thoughts of youth are long, long thoughts."

I can see the shadowy lines of its trees,
  And catch, in sudden gleams,
The sheen of the far-surrounding seas,
And islands that were the Hesperides
  Of all my boyish dreams.
    And the burden of that old song,
    It murmurs and whispers still:
    " A boy's will is the wind's will,
And the thoughts of youth are long, long thoughts."

I remember the black wharves and the slips,
  And the sea-tides tossing free;
And Spanish sailors with bearded lips,
And the beauty and mystery of the ships,
  And the magic of the sea.
    And the voice of that wayward song
    Is singing and saying still:
    " A boy's will is the wind's will,
And the thoughts of youth are long, long thoughts."

I remember the bulwarks by the shore,
    And the fort upon the hill;
The sunrise gun, with its hollow roar,
The drum-beat repeated o'er and o'er,
    And the bugle wild and shrill.
        And the music of that old song
        Throbs in my memory still:
    "A boy's will is the wind's will,
And the thoughts of youth are long, long thoughts."

I remember the sea-fight far away,*
    How it thundered o'er the tide!
And the dead captains, as they lay
In their graves, o'erlooking the tranquil bay,
    Where they in battle died.
        And the sound of that mournful song
        Goes through me with a thrill:
    "A boy's will is the wind's will,
And the thoughts of youth are long, long thoughts."

I can see the breezy dome of groves,
    The shadows of Deering's Woods;
And the friendships old and the early loves
Come back with a sabbath sound, as of doves
    In quiet neighborhoods.
        And the verse of that sweet old song,
        It flutters and murmurs still:
    "A boy's will is the wind's will,
And the thoughts of youth are long, long thoughts."

I remember the gleams and glooms that dart
    Across the schoolboy's brain;
The song and the silence in the heart,
That in part are prophecies, and in part
    Are longings wild and vain.

* This was the engagement between the Enterprise and Boxer, off the harbour of Portland, in which both captains were slain. They were buried side by side, in the cemetery on Mountjoy.

And the voice of that fitful song
  Sings on, and is never still:
" A boy's will is the wind's will,
And the thoughts of youth are long, long thoughts."

There are things of which I may not speak;
  There are dreams that cannot die!
There are thoughts that make the strong heart weak,
And bring a pallor into the cheek,
  And a mist before the eye.
    And the words of that fatal song
    Come over me like a chill:
  " A boy's will is the wind's will,
And the thoughts of youth are long, long thoughts."

Strange to me now are the forms I meet
  When I visit the dear old town;
But the native air is pure and sweet,
And the trees that o'ershadow each well-known street,
  As they balance up and down,
    Are singing the beautiful song,
    Are sighing and whispering still:
  " A boy's will is the wind's will,
And the thoughts of youth are long, long thoughts."

And Deering's Woods are fresh and fair,
  And with joy that is almost pain
My heart goes back to wander there,
And among the dreams of the days that were
  I find my lost youth again.
    And the strange and beautiful song,
    The groves are repeating it still:
  " A boy's will is the wind's will,
And the thoughts of youth are long, long thoughts."

SANTA FILOMENA.*

Whene'er a noble deed is wrought,
Whene'er is spoken a noble thought,
    Our hearts, in glad surprise,
    To higher levels rise.

The tidal wave of deeper souls
Into our inmost being rolls,
    And lifts us unawares
    Out of all meaner cares.

Honor to those whose words or deeds
Thus help us in our daily needs,
    And by their overflow
    Raise us from what is low!

Thus thought I, as by night I read
Of the great army of the dead,
    The trenches cold and damp,
    The starved and frozen camp,—

The wounded from the battle-plain,
In dreary hospitals of pain,
    The cheerless corridors,
    The cold and stony floors.

* "At Pisa the church of San Francesco contains a chapel dedicated lately to Santa Filomena; over the altar is a picture, by Sabatelli, representing the Saint as a beautiful, nymph-like figure, floating down from heaven, attended by two angels bearing the lily, palm, and javelin, and beneath, in the foreground, the sick and wounded, who are healed by her intercession."—Mrs. Jameson, Sacred and Legendary Art, II 298

Lo! in that house of misery
A lady with a lamp I see
   Pass through the glimmering gloom,
   And flit from room to room.

And slow, as in a dream of bliss,
The speechless sufferer turns to kiss
   Her shadow, as it falls
   Upon the darkening walls.

As if a door in heaven should be
Opened and then closed suddenly,
   The vision came and went,
   The light shone and was spent.

On England's annals, through the long
Hereafter of her speech and song,
   That light its rays shall cast
   From portals of the past.

A Lady with a Lamp shall stand
In the great history of the land,
   A noble type of good,
   Heroic womanhood.

Nor even shall be wanting here
The palm, the lily, and the spear.
   The symbols that of yore
   Saint Filomena bore.

SANDALPHON.

HAVE you read in the Talmud of old,
In the Legends the Rabbins have told
  Of the limitless realms of the air,—
Have you read it,—the marvellous story
Of Sandalphon, the Angel of Glory,
  Sandalphon, the Angel of Prayer?

How, erect, at the outermost gates
Of the City Celestial he waits,
  With his feet on the ladder of light,
That, crowded with angels unnumbered,
By Jacob was seen, as he slumbered
  Alone in the desert at night?

The Angels of Wind and of Fire
Chaunt only one hymn, and expire
  With the song's irresistible stress;
Expire in their rapture and wonder,
As harp-strings are broken asunder
  By music they throb to express.

But serene in the rapturous throng,
Unmoved by the rush of the song,
  With eyes unimpassioned and slow,
Among the dead angels, the deathless
Sandalphon stands listening breathless
  To sounds that ascend from below;—

From the spirits on earth that adore,
From the souls that entreat and implore
  In the fervor and passion of prayer;
From the hearts that are broken with losses,
And weary with dragging the crosses
  Too heavy for mortals to bear.

And he gathers the prayers as he stands,
And they change into flowers in his hands,
  Into garlands of purple and red;
And beneath the great arch of the portal,
Through the streets of the City Immortal
  Is wafted the fragrance they shed.

It is but a legend, I know,
A fable, a phantom, a show,

Of the ancient Rabbinical lore ;
Yet tho old mediæval tradition,
The beautiful, strange superstition,
    But haunts me and holds me the more.

When I look from my window at night,
And the welkin above is all white,
    All throbbing and panting with stars,
Among them majestic is standing
Sandalphon, the angel, expanding
    His pinions in nebulous bars.

And the legend, I feel, is a part
Of the hunger and thirst of the heart,
    The frenzy and fire of the brain,
That grasps at the fruitage forbidden,
The golden pomegranates of Eden,
    To quiet its fever and pain.

DAYBREAK.

A wind came up out of the sea,
And said, " O mists, make room for me."

It hailed the ships, and cried, " Sail on,
Ye mariners, the night is gone."

And hurried landward far away,
Crying, " Awake ! it is the day."

It said unto the forest, " Shout !
Hang all your leafy banners out!"

It touched the wood-bird's folded wing,
And said, " O bird, awake and sing."

And o'er the farms, " O chanticleer,
Your clarion blow ; the day is near."

It whispered to the fields of corn,
" Bow down, and hail the coming morn."

It shouted through the belfry-tower,
" Awake, O bell ! proclaim the hour."

It crossed the churchyard with a sigh,
And said, " Not yet ! in quiet lie."

THE COURTSHIP OF MILES STANDISH.

I.

MILES STANDISH.

In the Old Colony days, in Plymouth the land of the Pilgrims,
To and fro in a room of his simple and primitive dwelling,
Clad in doublet and hose, and boots of Cordovan leather,
Strode with a martial air, Miles Standish the Puritan Captain.

Buried in thought he seemed, with his hands behind him, and pausing
Ever and anon to behold his glittering weapons of warfare,
Hanging in shining array along the walls of the chamber,—
Cutlass and corslet of steel, and his trusty sword of Damascus,
Curved at the point and inscribed with its mystical Arabic sentence,
While underneath, in a corner, were fowling-piece, musket, and matchlock.
Short of stature he was, but strongly built and athletic,
Broad in the shoulders, deep-chested, with muscles and sinews of iron ;
Brown as a nut was his face, but his russet beard was already
Flaked with patches of snow, as hedges sometimes in November.
Near him was seated John Alden, his friend, and household companion,
Writing with diligent speed at a table of pine by the window ;
Fair-haired, azure-eyed, with delicate Saxon complexion,
Having the dew of his youth, and the beauty thereof, as the captives
Whom Saint Gregory saw, and exclaimed, " Not Angles but Angels."
Youngest of all was he of the men who came in the May Flower.

Suddenly breaking the silence, the diligent scribe interrupting,
Spake, in the pride of his heart, Miles Standish the Captain of Plymouth.
" Look at those arms," he said, " the warlike weapons that hang here
Burnished and bright and clean, as if for parade or inspection !
This is the sword of Damascus I fought with in Flanders ; this breastplate,
Well I remember the day ! once saved my life in a skirmish ;
Here in front you can see the very dent of the bullet
Fired point-blank at my heart by a Spanish arcabucero.
Had it not been of sheer steel, the forgotten bones of Miles Standish
Would at this moment be mould, in their grave in the Flemish morasses."
Thereupon answered John Alden, but looked not up from his writing :
" Truly the breath of the Lord hath slackened the speed of the bullet ;
He in his mercy preserved you, to be our shield and our weapon !"
Still the Captain continued, unheeding the words of the stripling :
" See, how bright they are burnished, as if in an arsenal hanging ;
That is because I have done it myself, and not left it to others.
Serve yourself, would you be well served, is an excellent adage ;
So I take care of my arms, as you of your pens and your inkhorn.
Then, too, there are my soldiers, my great, invincible army,
Twelve men, all equipped, having each his rest and his matchlock,
Eighteen shillings a month, together with diet and pillage,
And, like Cæsar, I know the name of each of my soldiers !"
This he said with a smile, that danced in his eyes, as the sun-beams

Dance on the waves of the sea, and vanish again in a moment.
Alden laughed as he wrote, and still the Captain continued:
"Look! you can see from this window my brazen howitzer planted
High on the roof of the church, a preacher who speaks to the purpose,
Steady, straightforward, and strong, with irresistible logic,
Orthodox, flashing conviction right into the hearts of the heathen.
Now we are ready, I think, for any assault of the Indians;
Let them come, if they like, and the sooner they try it the better, —
Let them come if they like, be it sagamore, sachem, or pow-wow,
Aspinet, Samoset, Corbitant, Squanto, or Tokamahamon!"

Long at the window he stood, and wistfully gazed on the landscape,
Washed with a cold gray mist, the vapory breath of the east wind,
Forest and meadow and hill, and the steel-blue rim of the ocean,
Lying silent and sad, in the afternoon shadows and sunshine.
Over his countenance flitted a shadow like those on the landscape,
Gloom intermingled with light; and his voice was subdued with emotion,
Tenderness, pity, regret, as after a pause he proceeded:
" Yonder there, on the hill by the sea, lies buried Rose Standish;
Beautiful rose of love, that bloomed for me by the wayside!
She was the first to die of all who came in the May Flower!
Green above her is growing the field of wheat we have sown there,
Better to hide from the Indian scouts the graves of our people,
Lest they should count them and see how many already have perished!"
Sadly his face he averted, and strode up and down, and was thoughtful.

Fixed to the opposite wall was a shelf of books, and among them
Prominent three, distinguished alike for bulk and for binding:

Bariffe's Artillery Guide, and the Commentaries of Cæsar,
Out of the Latin translated by Arthur Goldinge of London,
And, as if guarded by these, between them was standing the Bible.
Musing a moment before them, Miles Standish paused, as if doubtful
Which of the three he should choose for his consolation and comfort,
Whether the wars of the Hebrews, the famous campaigns of the Romans,
Or the Artillery practice, designed for belligerent Christians.
Finally down from its shelf he dragged the ponderous Roman,
Seated himself at the window, and opened the book, and in silence
Turned o'er the well-worn leaves, where thumb-marks thick on the margin,
Like the trample of feet, proclaimed the battle was hottest.
Nothing was heard in the room but the hurrying pen of the stripling.

Busily writing epistles important, to go by the May Flower,
Ready to sail on the morrow, or next day at latest, God willing!
Homeward bound with the tidings of all that terrible winter,
Letters written by Alden, and full of the name of Priscilla,
Full of the name and the fame of the Puritan maiden Priscilla!

II.

LOVE AND FRIENDSHIP.

Nothing was heard in the room but the hurrying pen of the stripling,
Or an occasional sigh from the laboring heart of the Captain,
Reading the marvellous words and achievements of Julius Cæsar.
After a while he exclaimed, as he smote with his hand, palm downwards,
Heavily on the page: " A wonderful man was this Cæsar!
You are a writer, and I am a fighter, but here is a fellow
Who could both write and fight, and in both was equally skilful!"
Straightway answered and spake John Alden, the comely, the youthful:
" Yes, he was equally skilled, as you say, with his pen and his weapons.
Somewhere I have read, but where I forget, he could dictate
Seven letters at once, at the same time writing his memoirs."
" Truly," continued the Captain, not heeding or hearing the other.
" Truly a wonderful man was Caius Julius Cæsar!
Better be first, he said, in a little Iberian village,
Than be second in Rome, and I think he was right when he said it.
Twice was he married before he was twenty, and many times after;
Battles five hundred he fought, and a thousand cities he conquered;
He, too, fought in Flanders, as he himself has recorded;
Finally he was stabbed by his friend, the orator Brutus!
Now, do you know what he did on a certain occasion in Flanders,
When the rear-guard of his army retreated, the front giving way too,
And the immortal Twelfth Legion was crowded so closely together
There was no room for their swords? Why, he seized a shield from a soldier,
Put himself straight at the head of his troops, and commanded the captains,
Calling on each by his name, to order forward the ensigns;

Then to widen the ranks, and give more room for their weapons ;
So he won the day, the battle of Something-or-other.
That's what I always say; if you wish a thing to be well done,
You must do it yourself, you must not leave it to others ! "

All was silent again ; the Captain continued his reading.
Nothing was heard in the room but the hurrying pen of the stripling
Writing epistles important to go next day by the May Flower,
Filled with the name and the fame of the Puritan maiden Priscilla ;
Every sentence began or closed with the name of Priscilla,
Till the treacherous pen, to which he confided the secret,
Strove to betray it by singing and shouting the name of Priscilla !
Finally closing his book, with a bang of the ponderous cover,
Sudden and loud as the sound of a soldier grounding his musket,
Thus to the young man spake Miles Standish the Captain of Plymouth :
" When you have finished your work, I have something important to tell you.
Be not however in haste ; I can wait ; I shall not be impatient ! "
Straightway Alden replied, as he folded the last of his letters,
Pushing his papers aside, and giving respectful attention :
" Speak ; for whenever you speak, I am always ready to listen,
Always ready to hear whatever pertains to Miles Standish."
Thereupon answered the Captain, embarrassed, and culling his phrases :
" 'Tis not good for a man to be alone, say the Scriptures.
This I have said before, and again and again I repeat it :
Every hour in the day, I think it, and feel it, and say it.
Since Rose Standish died, my life has been weary and dreary ;
Sick at heart have I been, beyond the healing of friendship.
Oft in my lonely hours have I thought of the maiden Priscilla.
She is alone in the world ; her father and mother and brother
Died in the winter together ; I saw her going and coming,
Now to the grave of the dead, and now to the bed of the dying,
Patient, courageous and strong, and said to myself, that if ever
There were angels on earth, as there are angels in heaven,
Two have I seen and known ; and the angel whose name is Priscilla
Holds in my desolate life the place which the other abandoned.
Long have I cherished the thought, but never have dared to reveal it,
Being a coward in this, though valiant enough for the most part.
Go to the damsel Priscilla, the loveliest maiden of Plymouth,
Say that a blunt old Captain, a man not of words but of actions,
Offers his hand and his heart, the hand and heart of a soldier.

Not in these words, you know, but this in short is my meaning ;
I am a maker of war, and not a maker of phrases.
You, who are loved as a scholar, can say it in elegant language,
Such as you read in your books of the pleadings and wooings of lovers,
Such as you think best adapted to win the heart of a maiden."

When he had spoken, John Alden, the fair-haired, taciturn stripling,
All aghast at his words, surprised, embarrassed, bewildered,
Trying to mask his dismay by treating the subject with lightness,
Trying to smile, and yet feeling his heart stand still in his bosom,
Just as a timepiece stops in a house that is stricken by lightning.
Thus made answer and spake, or rather stammered than answered:
"Such a message as that, I am sure I should mangle and mar it;
If you would have it well done,—I am only repeating your maxim,—
You must do it yourself, you must not leave it to others!"
But with the air of a man whom nothing can turn from his purpose,
Gravely shaking his head, made answer the Captain of Plymouth:
"Truly the maxim is good, and I do not mean to gainsay it;
But we must use it discreetly, and not waste powder for nothing.
Now, as I said before, I was never a maker of phrases.
I can march up to a fortress and summon the place to surrender,
But march up to a woman with such a proposal, I dare not.
I'm not afraid of bullets, nor shot from the mouth of a cannon,
But of a thundering 'No!' point-blank from the mouth of a woman,—
That, I confess, I'm afraid of, nor am I ashamed to confess it!
So you must grant my request, for you are an elegant scholar,
Having the graces of speech, and skill in the turning of phrases."
Taking the hand of his friend, who still was reluctant and doubtful,
Holding it long in his own, and pressing it kindly, he added:
"Though I have spoken thus lightly, yet deep is the feeling that prompts me;
Surely you cannot refuse what I ask in the name of our friendship!"
Then made answer John Alden: "The name of friendship is sacred:
What you demand in that name, I have not the power to deny you!"
So the strong will prevailed, subduing and moulding the gentler;
Friendship prevailed over love, and Alden went on his errand.

III.

THE LOVER'S ERRAND.

So the strong will prevailed, and Alden went on his errand,
Out of the street of the village, and into the paths of the forest,
Into the tranquil woods, where blue-birds and robins were building
Towns in the populous trees, with hanging gardens of verdure,
Peaceful, aërial cities of joy and affection and freedom.
All around him was calm, but within him commotion and conflict,
Love contending with friendship, and self with each generous impulse.
To and fro in his breast his thoughts were heaving and dashing,
As in a foundering ship, with every roll of the vessel,
Washes the bitter sea, the merciless surge of the ocean !
" Must I relinquish it all," he cried with a wild lamentation,
" Must I relinquish it all, the joy, the hope, the illusion ?
Was it for this I have loved, and waited, and worshipped in silence ?
Was it for this I have followed the flying feet and the shadow
Over the wintry sea, to the desolate shores of New England ?
Truly the heart is deceitful, and out of its depths of corruption
Rise, like an exhalation, the misty phantoms of passion :
Angels of light they seem, but are only delusions of Satan.
All is clear to me now ; I feel it, I see it distinctly !
This is the hand of the Lord ; it is laid upon me in anger,
For I have followed too much the heart's desires and devices,
Worshipping Astaroth blindly, and impious idols of Baal.
This is the cross I must bear ; the sin and the swift retribution."

So through the Plymouth woods John Alden went on his errand ;
Crossing the brook at the ford, where it brawled over pebble and shallow,
Gathering still, as he went, the May-flowers blooming around him,
Fragrant, filling the air with a strange and wonderful sweetness,
Children lost in the woods, and covered with leaves in their slumber.
" Puritan flowers," he said, " and the type of Puritan maidens,
Modest and simple and sweet, the very type of Priscilla !

So I will take them to her; to Priscilla the May-flower of Plymouth,
Modest and simple and sweet, as a parting gift will I take them:
Breathing their silent farewells, as they fade and wither and perish,
Soon to be thrown away as is the heart of the giver."
So through the Plymouth woods John Alden went on his errand;
Came to an open space, and saw the disk of the ocean,
Sailless, sombre and cold with the comfortless breath of the east wind:
Saw the new-built house, and people at work in a meadow;
Heard, as he drew near the door, the musical voice of Priscilla
Singing the hundredth Psalm, the grand old Puritan anthem,
Music that Luther sang to the sacred words of the Psalmist,
Full of the breath of the Lord, consoling and comforting many.

Then, as he opened the door, he beheld the form of the maiden
Seated beside her wheel, and the carded wool like a snow-drift
Piled at her knee, her white hands feeling the ravenous spindle,
While with her foot on the treadle she guided the wheel in its motion.
Open wide on her lap lay the well-worn psalm-book of Ainsworth,
Printed in Amsterdam, the words and the music together,
Rough-hewn, angular notes, like stones in the wall of a churchyard,
Darkened and overhung by the running vine of the verses.
Such was the book from whose pages she sang the old Puritan anthem,
She, the Puritan girl, in the solitude of the forest,
Making the humble house and the modest apparel of home-spun
Beautiful with her beauty, and rich with the wealth of her being!

Over him rushed, like a wind that is keen and cold and relentless,
Thoughts of what might have been, and the weight and woe of his errand ;
All the dreams that had faded, and all the hopes that had vanished,
All his life henceforth a dreary and tenantless mansion,
Haunted by vain regrets, and pallid, sorrowful faces.

3 D

Still he said to himself, and almost fiercely he said it,
" Let not him that putteth his hand to the plough look backwards ;
Though the ploughshare cut through the flowers of life to its fountains,
Though it pass o'er the graves of the dead and the hearths of the living,
It is the will of the Lord ; and his mercy endureth for ever ! "

So he entered the house ; and the hum of the wheel and the singing
Suddenly ceased ; for Priscilla, aroused by his step on the threshold,
Rose as he entered, and gave him her hand, in signal of welcome,
Saying, " I knew it was you, when I heard your step in the passage ;
For I was thinking of you, as I sat there singing and spinning."
Awkward and dumb with delight, that a thought of him had been mingled
Thus in the sacred psalm, that came from the heart of the maiden,
Silent before her he stood, and gave her the flowers for an answer,
Finding no words for his thought.   He remembered that day in the winter,
After the first great snow, when he broke a path from the village,
Reeling and plunging along through the drifts that encumbered the doorway,
Stamping the snow from his feet as he entered the house, and Priscilla
Laughed at his snowy locks, and gave him a seat by the fireside,
Grateful and pleased to know he had thought of her in the snow-storm.
Had he but spoken then ! perhaps not in vain had he spoken ;
Now it was all too late ; the golden moment had vanished !
So he stood there abashed, and gave her the flowers for an answer.

Then they sat down and talked of the birds and the beautiful Spring-time,
Talked of their friends at home, and the May Flower that sailed on the
    morrow.
" I have been thinking all day," said gently the Puritan maiden,
" Dreaming all night, and thinking all day, of the hedge-rows of England,—
They are in blossom now, and the country is all like a garden ;
Thinking of lanes and fields, and the song of the lark and the linnet,
Seeing the village street, and familiar faces of neighbors
Going about as of old, and stopping to gossip together,
And, at the end of the street, the village church, with the ivy
Climbing the old gray tower, and the quiet graves in the churchyard.
Kind are the people I live with, and dear to me my religion ;
Still my heart is so sad, that I wish myself back in Old England.
You will say it is wrong, but I cannot help it : I almost
Wish myself back in Old England, I feel so lonely and wretched."

Thereupon answered the youth:—" Indeed I do not condemn you;
Stouter hearts than a woman's have quailed in this terrible winter.
Yours is tender and trusting, and needs a stronger to lean on;
So I have come to you now, with an offer and proffer of marriage
Made by a good man and true, Miles Standish the Captain of Plymouth!"

Thus he delivered his message, the dexterous writer of letters,—
Did not embellish the theme, nor array it in beautiful phrases,
But came straight to the point, and blurted it out like a schoolboy;
Even the Captain himself could hardly have said it more bluntly.
Mute with amazement and sorrow, Priscilla the Puritan maiden
Looked into Alden's face, her eyes dilated with wonder,
Feeling his words like a blow, that stunned her and rendered her speechless;
Till at length she exclaimed, interrupting the ominous silence:
" If the great Captain of Plymouth is so very eager to wed me,
Why does he not come himself, and take the trouble to woo me?
If I am not worth the wooing, I surely am not worth the winning!"
Then John Alden began explaining and smoothing the matter,
Making it worse as he went, by saying the Captain was busy,—
Had no time for such things;—such things! the words grating harshly

Fell on the ear of Priscilla; and swift as a flash she made answer:
" Has he no time for such things, as you call it, before he is married,
Would he be likely to find it, or make it, after the wedding?
That is the way with you men; you don't understand us, you cannot.
When you have made up your minds, after thinking of this one and that one,
Choosing, selecting, rejecting, comparing one with another.

Then you make known your desire, with abrupt and sudden avowal,
And are offended and hurt, and indignant perhaps, that a woman
Does not respond at once to a love that she never suspected,
Does not attain at a bound the height to which you have been climbing.
This is not right nor just: for surely a woman's affection
Is not a thing to be asked for, and had for only the asking.
When one is truly in love, one not only says it, but shows it.
Had he but waited awhile, had he only showed that he loved me,
Even this Captain of yours—who knows?—at last might have won me,
Old and rough as he is; but now it never can happen."

Still John Alden went on, unheeding the words of Priscilla,
Urging the suit of his friend, explaining, persuading, expanding;
Spoke of his courage and skill, and of all his battles in Flanders,
How with the people of God he had chosen to suffer affliction,
How, in return for his zeal, they had made him Captain of Plymouth:
He was a gentleman born, could trace his pedigree plainly
Back to Hugh Standish of Duxbury Hall, in Lancashire, England,
Who was the son of Ralph, and the grandson of Thurston de Standish;
Heir unto vast estates, of which he was basely defrauded,
Still bore the family arms, and had for his crest a cock argent
Combed and wattled gules, and all the rest of the blazon.
He was a man of honor, of noble and generous nature;
Though he was rough, he was kindly; she knew how during the winter
He had attended the sick, with a hand as gentle as woman's;
Somewhat hasty and hot, he could not deny it, and headstrong,
Stern as a soldier might be, but hearty, and placable always.
Not to be laughed at and scorned, because he was little of stature;
For he was great of heart, magnanimous, courtly, courageous;
Any woman in Plymouth, nay, any woman in England,
Might be happy and proud to be called the wife of Miles Standish!

But as he warmed and glowed, in his simple and eloquent language,
Quite forgetful of self, and full of the praise of his rival,
Archly the maiden smiled, and, with eyes overrunning with laughter,
Said, in a tremulous voice, " Why don't you speak for yourself, John?"

IV.

JOHN ALDEN.

Into the open air John Alden, perplexed and bewildered,
Rushed like a man insane, and wandered alone by the sea-side;
Paced up and down the sands, and bared his head to the east wind,
Cooling his heated brow, and the fire and fever within him.
Slowly as out of the heavens, with apocalyptical splendors,
Sank the City of God, in the vision of John the Apostle,
So, with its cloudy walls of chrysolite, jasper, and sapphire,
Sank the broad red sun, and over its turrets uplifted
Glimmered the golden reed of the angel who measured the city.

"Welcome, O wind of the East!" he exclaimed in his wild exultation,
"Welcome, O wind of the East, from the caves of the misty Atlantic!
Blowing o'er fields of dulse, and measureless meadows of sea-grass,
Blowing o'er rocky wastes, and the grottos and gardens of ocean!
Lay thy cold, moist hand on my burning forehead, and wrap me
Close in thy garments of mist, to allay the fever within me!"

Like an awakened conscience, the sea was moaning and tossing,
Beating remorseful and loud the mutable sands of the sea-shore.
Fierce in his soul was the struggle and tumult of passions contending;
Love triumphant and crowned, and friendship wounded and bleeding,
Passionate cries of desire, and importunate pleadings of duty!
"Is it my fault," he said, "that the maiden has chosen between us?
Is it my fault that he failed,—my fault that I am the victor?"
Then within him there thundered a voice, like the voice of the Prophet:
"It hath displeased the Lord!"—and he thought of David's transgression,
Bathsheba's beautiful face, and his friend in the front of the battle!
Shame and confusion of guilt, and abasement and self-condemnation,
Overwhelmed him at once; and he cried in the deepest contrition:
"It hath displeased the Lord! It is the temptation of Satan!"

Then, uplifting his head, he looked at the sea, and behold there
Dimly the shadowy form of the May Flower riding at anchor,

Rocked on the rising tide, and ready to sail on the morrow;
Heard the voices of men through the mist, the rattle of cordage
Thrown on the deck, the shouts of the mate, and the sailors' "Ay, ay, Sir!"
Clear and distinct, but not loud, in the dripping air of the twilight.
Still for a moment he stood, and listened, and stared at the vessel,
Then went hurriedly on, as one who, seeing a phantom,
Stops, then quickens his pace, and follows the beckoning shadow.
"Yes, it is plain to me now," he murmured; "the hand of the Lord is
Leading me out of the land of darkness, the bondage of error,
Through the sea, that shall lift the walls of its waters around me,
Hiding me, cutting me off from the cruel thoughts that pursue me.
Back will I go o'er the ocean, this dreary land will abandon,
Her whom I may not love, and him whom my heart has offended.
Better to be in my grave in the green old churchyard in England,
Close by my mother's side, and among the dust of my kindred;
Better be dead and forgotten, than living in shame and dishonor;
Sacred and safe and unseen, in the dark of the narrow chamber

With me my secret shall lie, like a buried jewel that glimmers
Bright on the hand that is dust, in the chambers of silence and darkness,—
Yes, as the marriage ring of the great espousal hereafter!"

Thus as he spake, he turned, in the strength of his strong resolution,
Leaving behind him the shore, and hurried along in the twilight,
Through the congenial gloom of the forest silent and sombre,
Till he beheld the lights in the seven houses of Plymouth,
Shining like seven stars in the dusk and mist of the evening.
Soon he entered his door, and found the redoubtable Captain
Sitting alone, and absorbed in the martial pages of Cæsar,
Fighting some great campaign in Hainault or Brabant or Flanders.
" Long have you been on your errand," he said with a cheery demeanor,
Even as one who is waiting an answer, and fears not the issue.
" Not far off is the house, although the woods are between us;
But you have lingered so long, that while you were going and coming
I have fought ten battles and sacked and demolished a city.
Come, sit down, and in order relate to me all that has happened."

Then John Alden spake, and related the wondrous adventure,
From beginning to end, minutely, just as it happened;
How he had seen Priscilla, and how he had sped in his courtship,
Only smoothing a little, and softening down her refusal.
But when he came at length to the words Priscilla had spoken,
Words so tender and cruel: " Why don't you speak for yourself, John?"
Up leaped the Captain of Plymouth, and stamped on the floor, till his armor
Clanged on the wall, where it hung, with a sound of sinister omen.
All his pent-up wrath burst forth in a sudden explosion,
Even as a hand-grenade, that scatters destruction around it.
Wildly he shouted, and loud: " John Alden! you have betrayed me!
Me, Miles Standish, your friend! have supplanted, defrauded, betrayed me!
One of my ancestors ran his sword through the heart of Wat Tyler;
Who shall prevent me from running my own through the heart of a traitor?
Yours is the greater treason, for yours is a treason to friendship!
You, who lived under my roof, whom I cherished and loved as a brother;
You, who have fed at my board, and drunk at my cup, to whose keeping
I have intrusted my honor, my thoughts the most sacred and secret,—
You too, Brutus! ah woe to the name of friendship hereafter!
Brutus was Cæsar's friend, and you were mine, but henceforward
Let there be nothing between us save war, and implacable hatred!"

So spake the Captain of Plymouth, and strode about in the chamber,
Chafing and choking with rage; like cords were the veins on his temples.
But in the midst of his anger a man appeared at the doorway,
Bringing in uttermost haste a message of urgent importance,
Rumors of danger and war and hostile incursions of Indians!
Straightway the Captain paused, and, without further question or parley,
Took from the nail on the wall his sword with its scabbard of iron,
Buckled the belt round his waist, and, frowning fiercely, departed.
Alden was left alone. He heard the clank of the scabbard
Growing fainter and fainter, and dying away in the distance.
Then he arose from his seat, and looked forth into the darkness,
Felt the cool air blow on his cheek, that was hot with the insult.
Lifted his eyes to the heavens, and, folding his hands as in childhood,
Prayed in the silence of night to the Father who seeth in secret.

Meanwhile the choleric Captain strode wrathful away to the council,
Found it already assembled, impatiently waiting his coming;
Men in the middle of life, austere and grave in deportment,
Only one of them old, the hill that was nearest to heaven,
Covered with snow, but erect, the excellent Elder of Plymouth.
God had sifted three kingdoms to find the wheat for this planting,
Then had sifted the wheat, as the living seed of a nation;
So say the chronicles old, and such is the faith of the people!
Near them was standing an Indian, in attitude stern and defiant,
Naked down to the waist, and grim and ferocious in aspect;
While on the table before them was lying unopened a Bible,
Ponderous, bound in leather, brass-studded, printed in Holland,
And beside it outstretched the skin of a rattlesnake glittered,
Filled, like a quiver, with arrows; a signal and challenge of warfare,
Brought by the Indian, and speaking with arrowy tongues of defiance.
This Miles Standish beheld, as he entered, and heard them debating
What were an answer befitting the hostile message and menace,
Talking of this and of that, contriving, suggesting, objecting;
One voice only for peace, and that the voice of the Elder,
Judging it wise and well that some at least were converted,
Rather than any were slain, for this was but Christian behavior!
Then outspake Miles Standish, the stalwart Captain of Plymouth,
Muttering deep in his throat, for his voice was husky with anger,
"What! do you mean to make war with milk and the water of roses?
Is it to shoot red squirrels you have your howitzer planted

There on the roof of the church, or is it to shoot red devils?
Truly the only tongue that is understood by a savage
Must be the tongue of fire that speaks from the mouth of the cannon!"
Thereupon answered and said the excellent Elder of Plymouth,
Somewhat amazed and alarmed at this irreverent language:
"Not so thought Saint Paul, nor yet the other Apostles:
Not from the cannon's mouth were the tongues of fire they spake with!"
But unheeded fell this mild rebuke on the Captain,
Who had advanced to the table, and thus continued discoursing:
"Leave this matter to me, for to me by right it pertaineth.
War is a terrible trade; but in the cause that is righteous,
Sweet is the smell of powder; and thus I answer the challenge!"

Then from the rattlesnake's skin, with a sudden, contemptuous gesture,
Jerking the Indian arrows, he filled it with powder and bullets
Full to the very jaws, and handed it back to the savage,
Saying, in thundering tones: "Here, take it! this is your answer!"
Silently out of the room then glided the glistening savage,
Bearing the serpent's skin, and seeming himself like a serpent,
Winding his sinuous way in the dark to the depths of the forest.

V.

THE SAILING OF THE MAY FLOWER.

Just in the gray of the dawn, as the mists uprose from the meadows,
There was a stir and a sound in the slumbering village of Plymouth;
Clanging and clicking of arms, and the order imperative, " Forward ! "
Given in tone suppressed, a tramp of feet, and then silence.
Figures ten, in the mist, marched slowly out of the village.
Standish the stalwart it was, with eight of his valorous army,
Led by their Indian guide, by Hobomok, friend of the white men,
Northward marching to quell the sudden revolt of the savage.
Giants they seemed in the mist, or the mighty men of King David;
Giants in heart they were, who believed in God and the Bible,—
Ay, who believed in the smiting of Midianites and Philistines.
Over them gleamed far off the crimson banners of morning;
Under them loud on the sands, the serried billows, advancing,
Fired along the line, and in regular order retreated.

Many a mile had they marched, when at length the village of Plymouth
Woke from its sleep, and arose, intent on its manifold labors.
Sweet was the air and soft; slowly the smoke from the chimneys
Rose over roofs of thatch, and pointed steadily eastward;
Men came forth from the doors, and paused and talked of the weather,
Said that the wind had changed, and was blowing fair for the May Flower;
Talked of their Captain's departure, and all the dangers that menaced,
He being gone, the town, and what should be done in his absence.
Merrily sang the birds, and the tender voices of women
Consecrated with hymns the common cares of the household.
Out of the sea rose the sun, and the billows rejoiced at his coming;
Beautiful were his feet on the purple tops of the mountains!
Beautiful on the sails of the May Flower riding at anchor,
Battered and blackened and worn by all the storms of the winter.
Loosely against her masts was hanging and flapping her canvas,
Rent by so many gales, and patched by the hands of the sailors.
Suddenly from her side, as the sun rose over the ocean,
Darted a puff of smoke, and floated seaward; anon rang
Loud over field and forest the cannon's roar, and the echoes
Heard and repeated the sound, the signal-gun of departure!
Ah! but with louder echoes replied the hearts of the people!
Meekly, in voices subdued, the chapter was read from the Bible,
Meekly the prayer was begun, but ended in fervent entreaty!
Then from their houses in haste came forth the Pilgrims of Plymouth,
Men and women and children, all hurrying down to the sea-shore,
Eager, with tearful eyes, to say farewell to the May Flower,
Homeward bound o'er the sea, and leaving them here in the desert.

Foremost among them was Alden. All night he had lain without slumber,
Turning and tossing about in the heat unrest of his fever.
He had beheld Miles Standish, who came back late from the council,
Stalking into the room, and heard him mutter and murmur,
Sometimes it seemed a prayer, and sometimes it sounded like swearing.
Once he had come to the bed, and stood there a moment in silence;
Then he had turned away, and said: "I will not awake him;
Let him sleep on, it is best; for what is the use of more talking!"
Then he extinguished the light, and threw himself down on his pallet,
Dressed as he was, and ready to start at the break of the morning,—
Covered himself with the cloak he had worn in his campaigns in Flanders,—
Slept as a soldier sleeps in his bivouac, ready for action.

But with the dawn he arose; in the twilight Alden beheld him
Put on his corslet of steel, and all the rest of his armor,
Buckle about his waist his trusty blade of Damascus,
Take from the corner his musket, and so stride out of the chamber.
Often the heart of the youth had burned and yearned to embrace him,
Often his lips had essayed to speak, imploring for pardon;
All the old friendship came back, with its tender and grateful emotions;
But his pride overmastered the nobler nature within him,—
Pride, and the sense of his wrong, and the burning fire of the insult.
So he beheld his friend departing in anger, but spake not,
Saw him go forth to danger, perhaps to death, and he spake not!
Then he arose from his bed, and heard what the people were saying,
Joined in the talk at the door, with Stephen and Richard and Gilbert,
Joined in the morning prayer, and in the reading of Scripture,
And, with the others, in haste went hurrying down to the sea-shore,
Down to the Plymouth Rock, that had been to their feet as a door-step
Into a world unknown,—the corner-stone of a nation!

    There with his boat was the Master, already a little impatient
Lest he should lose the tide, or the wind might shift to the eastward,
Square-built, hearty, and strong, with an odor of ocean about him,
Speaking with this one and that, and cramming letters and parcels
Into his pockets capacious, and messages mingled together
Into his narrow brain, till at last he was wholly bewildered.
Nearer the boat stood Alden, with one foot placed on the gunwale,
One still firm on the rock, and talking at times with the sailors,
Seated erect on the thwarts, all ready and eager for starting.
He too was eager to go, and thus put an end to his anguish,
Thinking to fly from despair, that swifter than keel is or canvas,
Thinking to drown in the sea the ghost that would rise and pursue him.
But as he gazed on the crowd, he beheld the form of Priscilla
Standing dejected among them, unconscious of all that was passing.
Fixed were her eyes upon his, as if she divined his intention,
Fixed with a look so sad, so reproachful, imploring, and patient,
That with a sudden revulsion his heart recoiled from its purpose,
As from a verge of a crag, where one step more is destruction.
Strange is the heart of man, with its quick mysterious instincts;
Strange is the life of man, and fatal or fated are moments,
Whereupon turn, as on hinges, the gates of the wall adamantine!
" Here I remain!" he exclaimed, as he looked at the heavens above him,

Thanking the Lord whose breath had scattered the mist and the madness,
Wherein, blind and lost, to death he was staggering headlong.
" Yonder snow-white cloud, that floats in the ether above me,
Seems like a hand that is pointing and beckoning over the ocean.
There is another land, that is not so spectral and ghost-like,
Holding me, drawing me back, and clasping mine for protection.
Float, O hand of cloud, and vanish away in the ether !
Roll thyself up like a fist, to threaten and daunt me ; I heed not
Either your warning or menace, or any omen of evil !
There is no land so sacred, no air so pure and so wholesome,
As is the air she breathes, and the soil that is pressed by her footsteps.
Here for her sake will I stay, and like an invisible presence
Hover around her for ever, protecting, supporting her weakness :

Yes! as my foot was the first that stepped on this rock at the landing,
So, with the blessing of God, shall it be the last at the leaving!"

    Meanwhile the Master alert, but with dignified air and important,
Scanning with watchful eye the tide and the wind and the weather,
Walked about on the sands; and the people crowded around him
Saying a few last words, and enforcing his careful remembrance.
Then, taking each by the hand, as if he were grasping a tiller,
Into the boat he sprang, and in haste shoved off to his vessel,
Glad in his heart to get rid of all this worry and flurry,
Glad to be gone from a land of sand and sickness and sorrow,
Short allowance of victual, and plenty of nothing but Gospel!
Lost in the sound of the oars was the last farewell of the Pilgrims.
O strong hearts and true! not one went back in the May Flower!
No, not one looked back, who had set his hand to this ploughing!

" Are you so much offended, you will not speak to me ? " said she.
" Am I so much to blame, that yesterday, when you were pleading
Warmly the cause of another, my heart, impulsive and wayward,
Pleaded your own, and spake out, forgetful perhaps of decorum ?
Certainly you can forgive me for speaking so frankly, for saying
What I ought not to have said, yet now I can never unsay it :
For there are moments in life, when the heart is so full of emotion,
That if by chance it be shaken, or into its depths like a pebble
Drops some careless word, it overflows, and its secret,
Spilt on the ground like water, can never be gathered together.
Yesterday I was shocked, when I heard you speak of Miles Standish,
Praising his virtues, transforming his very defects into virtues,

3 F

Praising his courage and strength, and even his fighting in Flanders,
As if by fighting alone you could win the heart of a woman.
Quite overlooking yourself and the rest, in exalting your hero.
Therefore I spake as I did, by an irresistible impulse.
You will forgive me, I hope, for the sake of the friendship between us,
Which is too true and too sacred to be so easily broken !"
Thereupon answered John Alden, the scholar, the friend of Miles Standish :
" I was not angry with you, with myself alone I was angry,
Seeing how badly I managed the matter I had in my keeping."
" No !" interrupted the maiden, with answer prompt and decisive ;
" No ; you were angry with me, for speaking so frankly and freely.
It was wrong, I acknowledge ; for it is the fate of a woman
Long to be patient and silent, to wait like a ghost that is speechless,
Till some questioning voice dissolves the spell of its silence.
Hence is the inner life of so many suffering women
Sunken and silent and deep, like subterranean rivers
Running through caverns of darkness, unheard, unseen, and unfruitful,
Chafing their channels of stone, with endless and profitless murmurs."
Thereupon answered John Alden, the young man, the lover of women :
" Heaven forbid it, Priscilla ; and truly they seem to me always
More like the beautiful rivers that watered the garden of Eden,
More like the river Euphrates, through deserts of Havilah flowing,
Filling the land with delight, and memories sweet of the garden !"
" Ah, by these words, I can see," again interrupted the maiden,
" How very little you prize me, or care for what I am saying.
When from the depths of my heart, in pain and with secret misgiving,
Frankly I speak to you, asking for sympathy only and kindness,
Straightway you take up my words, that are plain and direct in earnest,
Turn them away from their meaning, and answer with flattering phrases.
This is not right, is not just, is not true to the best that is in you ;
For I know and esteem you, and feel that your nature is noble,
Lifting mine up to a higher, a more ethereal level.
Therefore I value your friendship, and feel it perhaps the more keenly
If you say aught that implies I am only as one among many,
If you make use of those common and complimentary phrases
Most men think so fine, in dealing and speaking with women,
But which women reject as insipid, if not as insulting."

    Mute and amazed was Alden ; and listened and looked at Priscilla,
Thinking he never had seen her more fair, more divine in her beauty.

He who but yesterday pleaded so glibly the cause of another,
Stood there embarrassed and silent, and seeking in vain for an answer.
So the maiden went on, and little divined or imagined
What was at work in his heart, that made him so awkward and speechless.
" Let us, then, be what we are, and speak what we think, and in all things
Keep ourselves loyal to truth, and the sacred professions of friendship.
It is no secret I tell you, nor am I ashamed to declare it:
I have liked to be with you, to see you, to speak with you always.
So I was hurt at your words, and a little affronted to hear you
Urge me to marry your friend, though he were the Captain Miles Standish,
For I must tell you the truth: much more to me is your friendship
Than all the love he could give, were he twice the hero you think him."
Then she extended her hand, and Alden, who eagerly grasped it,
Felt all the wounds in his heart, that were aching and bleeding so sorely,
Healed by the touch of that hand, and he said, with a voice full of feeling:
" Yes, we must ever be friends; and of all who offer you friendship
Let me be ever the first, the truest, the nearest and dearest!"

Casting a farewell look at the glimmering sail of the May Flower,
Distant, but still in sight, and sinking below the horizon,
Homeward together they walked, with a strange, indefinite feeling,
That all the rest had departed and left them alone in the desert.
But, as they went through the fields in the blessing and smile of the sunshine,
Lighter grew their hearts, and Priscilla said very archly:
" Now that our terrible Captain has gone in pursuit of the Indians,
Where he is happier far than he would be commanding a household,
You may speak boldly, and tell me of all that happened between you,
When you returned last night, and said how ungrateful you found me."
Thereupon answered John Alden, and told her the whole of the story,—
Told her his own despair, and the direful wrath of Miles Standish.
Whereat the maiden smiled, and said between laughing and earnest,
" He is a little chimney, and heated hot in a moment!"
But as he gently rebuked her, and told her how much he had suffered,—
How he had even determined to sail that day in the May Flower,
And had remained for her sake, on hearing the dangers that threatened,—
All her manner was changed, and she said with a faltering accent,
" Truly I thank you for this: how good you have been to me always!"

Thus, as a pilgrim devout, who toward Jerusalem journeys,
Taking three steps in advance, and one reluctantly backward,

Urged by importunate zeal, and withheld by pangs of contrition;
Slowly but steadily onward, receding yet ever advancing,
Journeyed this Puritan youth to the Holy Land of his longings,
Urged by the fervor of love, and withheld by remorseful misgivings.

VII.

THE MARCH OF MILES STANDISH.

MEANWHILE the stalwart Miles Standish was marching steadily northward,
Winding through forest and swamp, and along the tread of the sea-shore.
All day long, with hardly a halt, the fire of his anger
Burning and crackling within, and the sulphurous odor of powder
Seeming more sweet to his nostrils than all the scents of the forest.
Silent and moody he went, and much he revolved his discomfort;
He who was used to success, and to easy victories always.
Thus to be flouted, rejected, and laughed to scorn by a maiden,
Thus to be mocked and betrayed by the friend whom most he had trusted!
Ah! 'twas too much to be borne, and he fretted and chafed in his armour!

  "I alone am to blame," he muttered, "for mine was the folly.
What was a rough old soldier, grown grim and gray in the harness,
Used to the camp and its ways, to do with the wooing of maidens?
'Twas but a dream,—let it pass,—let it vanish like so many others!
What I thought was a flower, is only a weed, and is worthless;
Out of my heart will I pluck it, and throw it away, and henceforward
Be but a fighter of battles, a lover and wooer of dangers!"
Thus he revolved in his mind his sorry defeat and discomfort,
While he was marching by day or lying at night in the forest,
Looking up at the trees, and the constellations beyond them.

  After a three days' march he came to an Indian encampment
Pitched on the edge of a meadow, between the sea and the forest;
Women at work by the tents, and the warriors, horrid with war-paint,
Seated about a fire, and smoking and talking together;
Who, when they saw from afar the sudden approach of the white men,

Saw the flash of the sun on breastplate and sabre and musket,
Straightway leaped to their feet, and two, from among them advancing,
Came to parley with Standish, and offer him furs as a present;
Friendship was in their looks, but in their hearts there was hatred.
Braves of the tribe were these, and brothers gigantic in stature,
Huge as Goliath of Gath, or the terrible Og, king of Bashan;
One was Pecksuot named, and the other was called Wattawamat.
Round their necks were suspended their knives in scabbards of wampum,
Two-edged, trenchant knives, with points as sharp as a needle.
Other arms had they none, for they were cunning and crafty.
"Welcome, English!" they said,—these words they had learned from the
     traders
Touching at times on the coast, to barter and chaffer for peltries.
Then in their native tongue they began to parley with Standish,
Through his guide and interpreter, Hobomok, friend of the white man,
Begging for blankets and knives, but mostly for muskets and powder,
Kept by the white man, they said, concealed, with the plague, in his cellars,
Ready to be let loose, and destroy his brother the red man!
But when Standish refused, and said he would give them the Bible,
Suddenly changing their tone, they began to boast and to bluster.
Then Wattawamat advanced with a stride in front of the other,
And, with a lofty demeanour, thus vauntingly spake to the Captain:
"Now Wattawamat can see, by the fiery eyes of the Captain,
Angry is he in his heart; but the heart of the brave Wattawamat
Is not afraid at the sight.   He was not born of a woman,
But on a mountain, at night, from an oak-tree riven by lightning,
Forth he sprang at a bound, with all his weapons about him,
Shouting, 'Who is there here to fight with the brave Wattawamat?'"
Then he unsheathed his knife, and, whetting the blade on his left hand,
Held it aloft, and displayed a woman's face on the handle,
Saying, with bitter expression and look of sinister meaning:
"I have another at home, with the face of a man on the handle;
By and by they shall marry; and there will be plenty of children!"

     Then stood Pecksuot forth, self-vaunting, insulting Miles Standish:
While with his fingers he patted the knife that hung at his bosom,
Drawing it half from its sheath, and plunging it back, as he muttered,
"By and by it shall see; it shall eat; ah, ah! but shall speak not!
This is the mighty Captain the white men have sent to destroy us!
He is a little man; let him go and work with the women!"

Meanwhile Standish had noted the faces and figures of Indians,
Peeping and creeping about from bush to tree in the forest,
Feigning to look for game, with arrows set on their bow-strings,
Drawing about him still closer and closer the net of their ambush.
But undaunted he stood, and dissembled and treated them smoothly;
So the old chronicles say, that were writ in the days of the fathers.
But when he heard their defiance, the boast, the taunt, and the insult,
All the hot blood of his race, of Sir Hugh and of Thurston de Standish,
Boiled and beat in his heart, and swelled in the veins of his temples.

Headlong he leapt on the boaster, and snatching his knife from its scabbard,
Plunged it into his heart, and, reeling backward, the savage
Fell with his face to the sky, and a fiendlike fierceness upon it.
Straight there arose from the forest the awful sound of the war-whoop.
And, like a flurry of snow on the whistling wind of December,
Swift and sudden and keen came a flight of feathery arrows.
Then came a cloud of smoke, and out of the cloud came the lightning,
Out of the lightning thunder; and death unseen ran before it.
Frightened the savages fled for shelter in swamp and in thicket,
Hotly pursued and beset; but their sachem, the brave Wattawamat,
Fled not; he was dead.   Unswerving and swift had a bullet
Passed through his brain, and he fell with both hands clutching the greensward,
Seeming in death to hold back from his foe the land of his fathers.

There on the flowers of the meadow the warriors lay, and above them,
Silent, with folded arms, stood Hobomok, friend of the white man.
Smiling at length he exclaimed to the stalwart Captain of Plymouth:
"Pecksuot bragged very loud, of his courage, his strength, and his stature,—
Mocked the great Captain, and called him a little man; but I see now
Big enough have you been to lay him speechless before you!"

Thus the first battle was fought and won by the stalwart Miles Standish.
When the tidings thereof were brought to the village of Plymouth,
And as a trophy of war the head of the brave Wattawamat
Scowled from the roof of the fort, which at once was a church and a fortress,
All who beheld it rejoiced, and praised the Lord, and took courage.
Only Priscilla averted her face from this spectre of terror,
Thanking God in her heart that she had not married Miles Standish;
Shrinking, fearing almost, lest, coming home from his battles,
He should lay claim to her hand, as the prize and reward of his valor.

VIII.

THE SPINNING-WHEEL.

MONTH after month passed away, and in Autumn the ships of the merchants
Came with kindred and friends, with cattle and corn for the Pilgrims.
All in the village was peace ; the men were intent on their labors,
Busy with hewing and building, with garden-plot and with homestead,
Busy with breaking the glebe, and mowing the grass in the meadows,
Searching the sea for its fish, and hunting the deer in the forest.
All in the village was peace ; but at times the rumour of warfare
Filled the air with alarm, and the apprehension of danger.
Bravely the stalwart Miles Standish was scouring the land with his forces,
Waxing valiant in fight and defeating the alien armies,
Till his name had become a sound of fear to the nations.
Anger was still in his heart, but at times remorse and contrition,
Which in all noble natures succeed the passionate outbreak,
Came like a rising tide, that encounters the rush of a river,
Staying its current awhile, but making it bitter and brackish.

Meanwhile Alden at home had built him a new habitation,
Solid, substantial, of timber rough-hewn from the firs of the forest.
Wooden-barred was the door, and the roof was covered with rushes ;
Latticed the windows were, and the window-panes were of paper,
Oiled to admit the light, while wind and rain were excluded.
There too he dug a well, and around it planted an orchard :
Still may be seen to this day, some trace of the well and the orchard.
Close to the house was the stall, where, safe and secure from annoyance,
Raghorn, the snow-white steer, that had fallen to Alden's allotment
In the division of cattle, might ruminate in the night-time
Over the pastures he cropped, made fragrant by sweet pennyroyal.

Oft when his labor was finished, with eager feet would the dreamer
Follow the pathway that ran through the woods to the house of Priscilla.
Led by allusions romantic and subtile deceptions of fancy,
Pleasure disguised as duty, and love in the semblance of friendship.

Ever of her he thought, when he fashioned the walls of his dwelling;
Ever of her he thought, when he delved in the soil of his garden;
Ever of her he thought, when he read in his Bible on Sunday
Praise of the virtuous woman, as she is described in the Proverbs,—
How the heart of her husband doth safely trust in her always,
How all the days of her life she will do him good, and not evil,
How she seeketh the wool and the flax and worketh with gladness,
How she layeth her hand to the spindle and holdeth the distaff,
How she is not afraid of the snow for herself or her household,
Knowing her household are clothed with the scarlet cloth of her weaving!

So as she sat at her wheel one afternoon in the Autumn,
Alden, who opposite sat, and was watching her dexterous fingers,
As if the thread she was spinning were that of his life and his fortune,
After a pause in their talk, thus spake to the sound of the spindle.
"Truly, Priscilla," he said, "when I see you spinning and spinning,
Never idle a moment, but thrifty and thoughtful of others,
Suddenly you are transformed, are visibly changed in a moment;
You are no longer Priscilla, but Bertha the Beautiful Spinner."
Here the light foot on the treadle grew swifter and swifter; the spindle
Uttered an angry snarl, and the thread snapped short in her fingers.
While the impetuous speaker, not heeding the mischief, continued:
"You are the beautiful Bertha, the spinner, the queen of Helvetia;
She whose story I read at a stall in the streets of Southampton,
Who, as she rode on her palfrey, o'er valley and meadow and mountain,
Ever was spinning her thread from a distaff fixed to her saddle.
She was so thrifty and good, that her name passed into a proverb.
So shall it be with your own, when the spinning-wheel shall no longer
Hum in the house of the farmer, and fill its chambers with music.
Then shall the mothers, reproving, relate how it was in their childhood,
Praising the good old times, and the days of Priscilla the spinner!"
Straight uprose from her wheel the beautiful Puritan maiden,
Pleased with the praise of her thrift from him whose praise was the sweetest,
Drew from the reel on the table a snowy skein of her spinning,
Thus making answer, meanwhile, to the flattering phrases of Alden:
"Come, you must not be idle; if I am a pattern for housewives,
Show yourself equally worthy of being the model of husbands.
Hold this skein on your hands, while I wind it, ready for knitting;
Then who knows but hereafter, when fashions have changed and the manners,
Fathers may talk to their sons of the good old times of John Alden!"

Thus, with a jest and a laugh, the skein on his hands she adjusted,
He sitting awkwardly there, with his arms extended before him,
She standing graceful, erect, and winding the thread from his fingers,
Sometimes chiding a little his clumsy manner of holding,
Sometimes touching his hands, as she disentangled expertly
Twist or knot in the yarn, unawares—for how could she help it?—
Sending electrical thrills through every nerve in his body.

Lo! in the midst of this scene, a breathless messenger entered,
Bringing in hurry and heat the terrible news from the village.
Yes; Miles Standish was dead!—an Indian had brought them the tidings,—
Slain by a poisoned arrow, shot down in the front of the battle,

Into an ambush beguiled, cut off with the whole of his forces;
All the town would be burned, and all the people be murdered!
Such were the tidings of evil that burst on the hearts of the hearers.
Silent and statue-like stood Priscilla, her face looking backward
Still at the face of the speaker, her arms uplifted in horror;
But John Alden, upstarting, as if the barb of the arrow
Piercing the heart of his friend had struck his own, and had sundered
Once and for ever the bonds that held him bound as a captive,
Wild with excess of sensation, the awful delight of his freedom
Mingled with pain and regret, unconscious of what he was doing,
Clasped, almost with a groan, the motionless form of Priscilla,
Pressing her close to his heart, as for ever his own, and exclaiming:
"Those whom the Lord hath united, let no man put them asunder!"

Even as rivulets twain, from distant and separate sources,
Seeing each other afar, as they leaped from the rocks, and pursuing
Each one its devious path, but drawing nearer and nearer,
Rush together at last, at their trysting-place in the forest;
So these lives that had run thus far in separate channels,
Coming in sight of each other, then swerving and flowing asunder,
Parted by barriers strong, but drawing nearer and nearer,
Rushed together at last, and one was lost in the other.

IX.

THE WEDDING-DAY.

FORTH from the curtain of clouds, from the tent of purple and scarlet,
Issued the sun, the great High-Priest, in his garments resplendent,
Holiness unto the Lord, in letters of light, on his forehead,
Round the hem of his robe the golden bells and pomegranates.
Blessing the world he came, and the bars of vapor beneath him
Gleamed like a grate of brass, and the sea at his feet was a laver!

This was the wedding morn of Priscilla the Puritan maiden.
Friends were assembled together; the Elder and Magistrate also
Graced the scene with their presence, and stood like the Law and the Gospel,

One with the sanction of earth and one with the blessing of heaven.
Simple and brief was the wedding, as that of Ruth and of Boaz.
Softly the youth and the maiden repeated the words of betrothal,
Taking each other for husband and wife in the Magistrate's presence,
After the Puritan way, and the laudable custom of Holland.
Fervently then, and devoutly, the excellent Elder of Plymouth
Prayed for the hearth and the home, that were founded that day in affection,
Speaking of life and of death, and imploring divine benedictions.

Lo! when the service was ended, a form appeared on the threshold,
Clad in armor of steel, a sombre and sorrowful figure!
Why does the bridegroom start and stare at the strange apparition?
Why does the bride turn pale, and hide her face on his shoulder?
Is it a phantom of air,—a bodiless, spectral illusion?
Is it a ghost from a grave, that has come to forbid the betrothal?
Long had it stood there unseen, a guest uninvited, unwelcomed;
Over its clouded eyes there had passed at times an expression
Softening the gloom and revealing the warm heart hidden beneath them,
As when across the sky the driving rack of the rain-cloud
Grows for a moment thin, and betrays the sun by its brightness.
Once it had lifted its hand, and moved its lips, but was silent,
As if an iron will had mastered the fleeting intention.
But when were ended the troth and the prayer and the last benediction,
Into the room it strode, and the people beheld with amazement
Bodily there in his armor Miles Standish, the Captain of Plymouth!
Grasping the bridegroom's hand, he said with emotion, "Forgive me!
I have been angry and hurt,—too long have I cherished the feeling;
I have been cruel and hard, but now, thank God! it is ended.
Mine is the same hot blood that leaped in the veins of Hugh Standish,
Sensitive, swift to resent, but as swift in atoning for error.
Never so much as now was Miles Standish the friend of John Alden."
Thereupon answered the bridegroom: "Let all be forgotten between us,—
All save the dear old friendship, and that shall grow older and dearer!"
Then the Captain advanced, and, bowing, saluted Priscilla,
Gravely, and after the manner of old-fashioned gentry in England,
Something of camp and of court, of town and of country, commingled,
Wishing her joy of her wedding, and loudly lauding her husband.
Then he said with a smile: "I should have remembered the adage,—
If you would be well served, you must serve yourself: and moreover,
No man can gather cherries in Kent at the season of Christmas!"

Great was the people's amazement, and greater yet their rejoicing,
Thus to behold once more the sun-burnt face of their Captain,
Whom they had mourned as dead; and they gathered and crowded about him,
Eager to see him and hear him, forgetful of bride and of bridegroom,
Questioning, answering, laughing, and each interrupting the other,
Till the good Captain declared, being quite overpowered and bewildered,
He had rather by far break into an Indian encampment,
Than come again to a wedding to which he had not been invited.

Meanwhile the bridegroom went forth and stood with the bride at the door-way
Breathing the perfumed air of that warm and beautiful morning.
Touched with autumnal tints, but lonely and sad in the sunshine,
Lay extended before them the land of toil and privation ;

There were the graves of the dead, and the barren waste of the sea-shore.
There the familiar fields, the groves of pine, and the meadows;
But to their eyes transfigured, it seemed as the Garden of Eden,
Filled with the presence of God, whose voice was the sound of the ocean.

Soon was their vision disturbed by the noise and stir of departure,
Friends coming forth from the house, and impatient of longer delaying,
Each with his plan for the day, and the work that was left uncompleted.
Then from a stall near at hand, amid exclamations of wonder,
Alden the thoughtful, the careful, so happy, so proud of Priscilla,
Brought out his snow-white steer, obeying the hand of its master,
Led by a cord that was tied to an iron ring in its nostrils,
Covered with crimson cloth, and a cushion placed for a saddle.
She should not walk, he said, through the dust and heat of the noonday;
Nay, she should ride like a queen, not plod along like a peasant.
Somewhat alarmed at first, but reassured by the others,
Placing her hand on the cushion, her foot in the hand of her husband,
Gaily, with joyous laugh, Priscilla mounted her palfrey.
"Nothing is wanting now," he said, with a smile, "but the distaff;
Then you would be in truth my queen, my beautiful Bertha!"

Onward the bridal procession now moved to their new habitation,
Happy husband and wife, and friends conversing together.
Pleasantly murmured the brook, as they crossed the ford in the forest,
Pleased with the image that passed, like a dream of love, through its bosom,
Tremulous, floating in air, o'er the depths of the azure abysses.
Down through the golden leaves the sun was pouring his splendors,
Gleaming on purple grapes, that, from branches above them suspended,
Mingled their odorous breath with the balm of the pine and the fir-tree,
Wild and sweet as the clusters that grew in the valley of Eshcol.
Like a picture it seemed of the primitive, pastoral ages,
Fresh with the youth of the world, and recalling Rebecca and Isaac,
Old and yet ever new, and simple and beautiful always,
Love immortal and young in the endless succession of lovers.
So through the Plymouth woods passed onward the bridal procession.

THE END.